THIS YEAR
IS DIFFERENT

HOW THE MAVS WON IT ALL:
THE OFFICIAL STORY

BY BOB STURM

Diversion Books
A Division of Diversion Publishing Corp.
443 Park Avenue South, Suite 1004
New York, New York 10016
www.DiversionBooks.com

For more information, email info@diversionbooks.com

First Diversion Books edition December 2011.

Print ISBN: 978-1-62681-141-6
eBook ISBN: 978-0-98398-858-8

ACKNOWLEDGMENTS

To my family —

My great and beautiful wife, Sally.
And my three children: Madeline, Brett and Justin.
They are what truly matter.
They always seem to understand that Dad has to work today. I will try
to adjust that perception.

CONTENTS

FOREWORD

Tremendous.

That's about the only word I can use to describe what the last 30 days have been like.

Professional sports is an incredibly humbling business. No team wins every year. Many teams have never won. Far more often than not, there is the game/series that got away from you that ended the season with a loss. Not this year.

Tremendous.

For me, the entire season came down to the last 90 seconds of Game 6 of the NBA Finals. Our clinching game. I can't even begin to tell you all the emotions I experienced in the course of those 90 seconds.

You see, I refused to let myself think we were going to win. I refused to get ahead of the game. Too many times, I had seen games get away from our team. Too many times, I had seen our team snatch away what the other side thought was a sure win. We had come from way behind to win games in every series in this playoff run. If we could do it to them, they could do it to us. In my mind, if I even began to think that a win was a certainty, I would jinx us.

It wasn't until there were about 90 seconds left in Game 6 that I let myself accept that we were going to be World Champs. I began screaming, letting out eight months of stress, releasing every doubt I had, every dumbass superstition. I was transitioning from "I know we can, I hope we can" to "We are the Champions." I was feeling joy for every guy wearing a Mavs uniform, and every Mavs fan around the world who had to be feeling just as happy as I was.

Thirty days later, it's still surreal. I'm still thrilled for every guy who put his blood, sweat and tears onto the court. I'm also happy for every player who was a positive part of the Mavs since I bought the team. We have a culture at the Mavs of which I'm very proud. It took a lot of experiences that taught our players, coaches, staff and even fans, and prepared us and motivated our guys.

In these last 30 days, there have been surprises as well.

The first is just how many people around the country were rooting for us. As I travel around the country, the response and support is far beyond anything I have experienced. People are genuinely pleased that the Mavs won. I got off a plane in New York a couple days after we won, and people at the terminal just stood up and started clapping. In New York!

The second, and still most amazing to me, is how Dallas-Fort Worth and all of North Texas is responding to the Mavs. I expect people to come up and congratulate me. But that isn't what is happening. Instead, people are thanking me. Thanking me for the unity and camaraderie everyone in the region felt as EVERYONE got behind the Mavs and cheered us on to a championship. Thanking me for the closeness people felt for each other as everyone cheered on the Mavs.

This wasn't my team. This wasn't the players' team. This was OUR team. Our family's. Our friends'. Our company's. Our city's. The Dallas Mavericks belonged to all of us and brought joy to all of us.

To be part of something so special is ... Tremendous.

– **Mark Cuban**
July 12, 2011

INTRODUCTION

I did not grow up a Mavericks fan. Instead, I was a Milwaukee Bucks fan as a boy growing up in Wisconsin, and the first coach of dominant influence on my life was Don Nelson. His tactics were always thought of as "outside the box" and a bit wacky. Milwaukee was the little kid on the block that had sand kicked in its face by Boston and Philadelphia, and Don Nelson was not going to go out without a fight. He had a style that was perfect for that setting, and dumped-on fans of Wisconsin found his abrasive style easy to rally behind.

I was just 11 when his team swept Boston in the 1983 playoffs, but he was clearly the first basketball coach to capture my imagination. When he left over a contract (as he is wont to do), the Bucks stayed strong for a few years, but soon dropped back to the obscurity that the basketball world believed Milwaukee deserved.

So, when I took my first big radio job in Dallas in June 1998, it certainly was noted that Don Nelson was running the show in my new home city. The week I was interviewed for the job was the same week that Dirk Nowitzki was acquired by the Mavericks in a draft-day trade with Milwaukee. During the time between my youth and 1998, Don Nelson certainly had moved perceptually from "wise tactician" to "mad scientist" in the minds of so many in the NBA. He had fallouts in Golden State and New York that did not reflect very well on him, and as the Mavericks continued floundering near the bottom of the NBA, Nelson was hired to try to fix it. And at first, it looked like he made it worse.

When I arrived in Dallas, the Stars had just signed Brett Hull as the final piece of the puzzle for the Stanley Cup they would win 12 months later. The Cowboys still had the legendary Triplets in place, and despite Troy Aikman, Emmitt Smith and Michael Irvin all getting to the point of their careers where another Super Bowl was appearing more remote, the city believed they could do it once more. The Rangers, a team that

3

had periods of futility rivaling the Mavericks', were on their way to another AL West crown. They would win three division titles in four seasons between 1996-99 and it would represent the most success the local baseball team would enjoy.

And then there were the Mavericks. It had been 10 years since their last real chance at taking down Pat Riley's Los Angeles Lakers in the playoffs in the halcyon days of the franchise, and the decade of decline since was nothing short of pathetic. By the time I moved into my tiny new apartment in Dallas, the Mavericks had completely disappeared into irrelevance on the local landscape. Things were so sad that the city actually turned out a rare capacity crowd when their 20-62 Mavericks had their one big smile of the season back in March 1998, defeating Michael Jordan and the Chicago Bulls at Reunion Arena for their 14th win. The home crowd, mostly present for a glimpse of the rock star roster of Chicago, didn't quite know how to react to the result. Most wore their Jordan and Pippen jerseys home. The majority of local basketball fans didn't feel they had a home team anymore.

Because of the third lockout in NBA history, the 1998-99 season was shortened to 50 games and didn't start until Feb. 5. Aside from catching a glimpse of the new German rookie Nowitzki, there was little reason to watch this team. Even the Nowitzki acquisition was thought of as the reach of a mad scientist. After all, Paul Pierce was available and everybody knew that he could play. But a 20-year-old from Germany? Be serious. Germany had never produced a player better than Detlef Schrempf, whom Dallas drafted in 1985. Schrempf was a nice enough player, but nowhere near worth a career of watching Paul Pierce or Robert Traylor. Or so the papers said.

My first trip to Reunion Arena was not until late March. My first job in Dallas was working nights on The Ticket (KTCK-1310 AM, America's Favorite Radio Station — just ask us), and therefore I was unable to attend most games. And, frankly, why would anyone want to hurry to an empty arena and watch bad basketball?

My first trip to see the Mavericks play in person in my new city was March 29, 1999. It was a Monday night and, ironically, Schrempf was starting for the visiting Seattle SuperSonics. On this night, the Mavericks were bringing the young Nowitzki off the bench as the ninth man. His 11 points were but a footnote to a thrashing administered by Gary Payton and the visiting Sonics. Dallas outscored Seattle in the fourth quarter by 12 points, and still lost by eight.

And my biggest memory? During a timeout in the second half, the Mavericks presented their mascot "Mavs Man," basically a guy in a spandex bodysuit that resembled Spider-Man but with the skin of a basketball. He was in one of those clichéd timeout routines where we are all supposed to be amazed that a human could dunk while launching off a trampoline, even though we were at a game where players (at least the visitors) were dunking without the aid of any launching apparatus.

But in a fashion that fit perfectly with the sparsely attended surroundings — thousands of empty seats, indifferent fans, poor basketball — Mavs Man launched into the air and immediately grabbed for his left knee. In what was poetry in motion, Mavs Man had blown out his ACL during a timeout. He was lost for the season. The Mavs were getting smashed and their mascot limped off into the tunnel and to the hospital.

As time went along, I found a fascination in Dirk and the Nelson plan to rebuild around him. Dirk Nowitzki was a rare talent and a person who was quite different from most stars in the world of sports. He was self-assured, but also quite friendly, cooperative and down-to-earth. He loved basketball, but it never seemed that he was part of the NBA cliché of power struggles, money grabs and overall survival of the fittest.

Each year, he worked harder to develop his game. At the same time, the team pushed a bit further forward. At first, the progress was amazing. But then, as they proceeded further up the NBA food chain, they quickly found out that the last final steps were going to be next to impossible. Time after time, season after season, Nowitzki and the crew would reload with renewed ideas and energy, only to run into a stronger wall the next year.

It was altogether fascinating and frustrating. As the years went along, Nowitzki was ridiculed in his own city for not being of championship quality. Doubters abounded. And the biggest loyalists may have survived past the 2006 debacle in the NBA Finals, but by 2007 or 2008, the resolve was weakening. By 2009 and 2010, the city had split over Nowitzki. There was the group that mocked Dirk's fate that would include no title, and the group that accepted their favorite player would never win a ring and didn't mind. He was that beloved.

Honestly, there may have been a third group — those who believed that he still could and would do it — but that group was very small. It appears Mark Cuban was in that group, but we will never know how many others truthfully never abandoned hope. I wrote this book because of this phenomenon and because, sadly, I was part of the second group of doubters who eventually conceded that the dream just wasn't going to happen to the player we so wanted to scale the highest peak. The greatest basketball player in his own city's history being almost unanimously doubted and dismissed despite the unquestioned greatness. Perhaps only John Elway has a comparable story where he played so well for so long and yet never won a title until the end of an amazingly long and painful odyssey. Elway was surely beloved in Denver, but even his strongest loyalists had to abandon hope about his happy ending with the Lombardi Trophy (or two) after playoff failures multiplied.

By the spring of 2011, I had finally given up hope. On our radio show, I promised I would not be Charlie Brown any longer as the Mavericks played the role of Lucy and pulled the ball away just when I ran to kick it again. I felt they were playing emotional games where they would play just well enough to get everyone to believe again, only to fail in the playoffs like always. It was so maddening.

As March grew into April, I felt like the team was headed down a familiar road. The team was wobbling down the stretch and forcing Rodrigue Beaubois into the lineup. The Mavs were smoked in Los Angeles and Jason Terry appeared to leave for Mars. I just didn't buy what they were trying to sell. This was going to be the same old Mavericks. Good, but nowhere near great enough to win a title. Dirk might have to go elsewhere to win a title with another cast — like Kevin Garnett, Pau Gasol or LeBron James would try to do with someone else's team, too.

The pairings came out in April and showed the Mavericks matched up with Portland. The winner would then move on to play the Lakers. I didn't think the Mavericks could beat Portland, because the Blazers appeared to be a poor matchup with multiple athletic big men who could hassle Nowitzki and then force the rest of the Mavericks to beat them. With Terry looking far from top form, that seemed to be death to Dallas. Also, add to that the Rose Garden and Dallas' putrid performance in playoff road games, and I had arrived at an alternate title for this book: "Portland in 6."

This book is my tribute to a championship that seemed impossible. I never thought it would actually happen to Dirk or the Mavericks. I had lost all hope. But I was reminded once again why I love sports so much. There is no explaining why something falls into place after years of failure. Those of us in the sports media business act as if everything is linear and explainable. But the truth is there is no formula or recipe for championships. Sometimes, they do seem to follow a schedule. But other times, such as with the 2011 Dallas Mavericks, they arrive just when the loyalists had given up their resolve.

I loved this title run as much as any that I can remember in my lifetime. I feel this way because of the pain and trials along the way. Many teams win titles without a whole lot of adversity, and while those accomplishments are not less significant, they are less theatrical. The long, strange trip of Dirk Nowitzki and his band of ever-changing cast members was a story that needed to be documented. I had never been so pleased to see someone accomplish their goal. We watched his every step from boy to man, it seemed. Now, I just hope I did it proper justice.

The idea to write the book arrived in my cluttered head on the way back from Miami after Game 6. I had spent so much time obsessing about the unthinkable coming true, that when it did come true after two months of intense basketball, I just had to put it on paper. Given that I really had never written anything longer than lengthy blog posts for the *Dallas Morning News* and *D Magazine*, a book was going to require plenty of help.

I have to thank many people for their contributions to this project. In particular, my editor, Ken Daley. Given that I am not a lifelong writer with extended schooling, but rather a self-taught blogger who has many unvarnished edges, he earned way more than he was given to edit this. He held my hand and offered incredibly valuable feedback and direction that I accepted with open arms. The man is incredibly talented as a writer himself, and surely can do anything he desires in the literary realm as far as I am concerned.

Beyond Ken, allow me to thank so many for their time in interviews specifically for this project. Rick Carlisle was incredibly thoughtful and generous with his responses. Dirk Nowitzki, Jason Kidd and Brian Cardinal all offered extended visits after the season. Many other players gave wonderful radio accounts of their experiences on the Bob and Dan Show during the season and playoffs, which were used for this project as well. Those players included Jason Terry, Tyson Chandler, Shawn Marion, J.J. Barea and Peja Stojakovic.

Others who helped out with interviews or clues to find the real stories behind the seasons include: longtime friend, GM and fellow Wisconsinite Donnie Nelson; assistant GM Keith Grant, statistician Roland Beech, trainer Casey Smith and equipment manager Al Whitley. Scott Tomlin and Sarah Melton of the Mavericks' Media Relations department really made a lot of things happen for this project. So did Mavericks Vice President of Marketing and Communications Paul

Monroe, broadcasters Mark Followill and Jeff "Skin" Wade, Cash Sirois, Dave Keeney, Tom Ward and Danny Bollinger.

Still, others contributed in ways from outside the organization, but are worthy of mention: Dan McDowell, Tom Gribble, Donovan Lewis, Michael Gruber, Sean Bass, Jeff Catlin and Dan Bennett put up with my A.D.D. on a regular basis so I can do side projects like this one while working at The Ticket. Also worthy of mention: Jordan Rodgers, Ben Rodgers and Tim Krajewski — a listener-turned-intern who did plenty of research projects on statistical findings for me. T.C. Fleming helped and compiled some of the audio for me to review from past radio appearances that would be relevant for the book. Thanks also to Mark Francescutti and the guys at the *Dallas Morning News* for employing me during this memorable year with the Mavericks to work on their blogs and develop whatever sort of writing skills I might possess.

All in all, I really appreciate those who helped me get to the bottom of everything. They are owed a large debt of gratitude. And thank you for giving this book your time. I hope you are happy with the decision.

- **Bob Sturm**

THE PARADE

(June 16, 2011)

June 16

Dallas Mavericks Championship Parade

Dallas, Texas

So this was what the view was like from the top.

Dirk Nowitzki towered jubilantly atop a parade float, a perch he heretofore only had imagined. Emblazoned on his shirt was the fantastic directive, "Raise the Banner."

His smile was broader than anyone had ever seen. He always had wondered what this might feel like. And whether he would ever make it here.

It had taken an untold number of shots and free throws over his 32 years, honed through hours in the practice gyms and executed under the bright lights of NBA arenas.

It had taken more than a thousand bruising professional games, including hundreds ending in defeat.

And it had taken the unshakable belief of a Bavarian teenager, tall for his age, that he could one day venture forth from Germany and succeed in the world's premier basketball league.

Looking out upon the frenzied fans, many wiping tears from their eyes, he struggled again with the emotions that so easily overtook him earlier in the week.

He still couldn't believe this was real.

But, as he rode down Young Street in downtown Dallas, he tried to soak it all in. This was the summit for which he had fought. This was what had pushed him when the doubters were mocking him. When season after season ended in disappointment and dejection, it could have been easy to accept defeat. Instead, Dirk kept fighting. That's what made it so sweet to stand here today, on top of the world.

The final float in the championship parade carried the veteran "Big 3" of the Mavericks. Riding together were Nowitzki, 33-year-old shooting guard Jason Terry, and the 38-year-old point guard Jason Kidd.

Four days earlier, they had done it. Against all odds as the playoffs began, and still against most experts' picks until the very end, the Dallas Mavericks had defeated the Miami Heat in the 2011 NBA Finals, 4 games to 2.

It was a triumph that capped a season of 111 games and, in some ways, a lifetime of effort.

The parade drew more than 300,000 to downtown Dallas to recognize the champions of the basketball world. Most of those in attendance honestly never thought they would see this procession — especially with those three players anchoring the final float.

Their window had closed, we were told time after time. We said it ourselves. The players heard it, and perhaps had come to believe it a bit, too. They would all have nice careers and make tons of money, but they would never be the principal characters in a dream season that ended with an adoring city lavishing them with love.

Yet here they were.

As the parade rolled on, the gleeful smiles in the crowd were matched by those atop the floats. This was a party to remember for anyone who had stuck with this team through all the tough nights.

First, the team's broadcasters drove past, followed by the support staff, assistant coaches, and various team officials. Next came Mavericks coach Rick Carlisle, seated with his family in the back of a convertible. Then, team owner and parade-funder Mark Cuban rolled through, joyously clutching the Larry O'Brien trophy in his arms. He looked like a guy who had chased something for so long, now that he had it, he wasn't quite sure what to do except laugh and smile.

Then came the players, rolling through in groups of two or three. Most were waving and chomping on victory cigars, huge smiles on every face. But, as the final float approached, it was apparent which player, by far, was the most animated. Without him, this victory would not have been won, nor would it have been as rich.

This day was about Dirk. And he was embracing the celebration with the untempered joy of a child on Christmas morning.

The entire basketball world, including those who confidently said he would never see this day, marveled at what Nowitzki accomplished on his way to becoming a champion in 2011. And now, he was thanking his adoring fans for sticking with him, even if they hadn't always done so.

His shirt sleeves were hiked to his shoulders on this gloriously sunny morning, and a scraggly beard darkened his face. His long blonde hair was casually unkempt as he enjoyed what he would call "the best day of my life."

He would soon lead the crowd in an unforgettable chorus of "We Are the Champions," from a balcony of the American Airlines Center. Nowitzki might not have made anyone forget Queen lead singer Freddie Mercury, but never has a version of that song been performed with more personal joy and passion. Dirk occasionally even hit a correct note along the way. And, as he sang, his adoring fans struggled to hold back tears.

An unthinkable victory had finally been achieved. And Dirk's career, his franchise and his city all were celebrating their redemption with this day of unified delirium. The Dallas Mavericks were world champions.

========

To fully understand the unique feeling of "Parade Day" in Dallas, a few things must be considered.

First, one must remember what this franchise looked like before Nowitzki arrived in Dallas. Of all of the characters in this story, only the man who targeted him, Donnie Nelson, has served more time with the Mavericks than the big man himself. When Nelson arrived in this city in January 1998, you could barely find 5,000 fans to attend a game.

Just making the playoffs seemed a fantasy to downtrodden fans. Mavs supporters had endured the frustration of star forward Roy Tarpley's drug problems; the ineffective coaching of Gar Heard, Quinn Buckner and Jim Cleamons; and the embarrassment of 10 consecutive losing seasons from 1990-2000. The low point was seeing the team win just 24 games over two seasons (11-71 in 1992-93, followed by 13-69 in 1993-94) to become the laughingstock of the league.

The franchise was near death, at a point where talk of relocation would not have sounded crazy. But fortunes began to change with the draft-day acquisition of Nowitzki in June 1998 and the arrival of a competitive, deep-pocketed young owner in Mark Cuban, who purchased a majority stake in the team in January 2000 for a reported $285 million.

Under Cuban, the Mavericks have enjoyed a fantastic renaissance, winning 69 percent of their regular-season games over the past 11 seasons and reaching the playoffs every year. Even so, there were four first-round playoff exits, four losses in the Western Conference semifinals, one ouster in the conference final and the most heartbreaking result of all: A come-from-ahead loss to Miami in the 2006 NBA Finals.

It was that postseason nightmare five years earlier that had made the word "parade" taboo in Dallas. With the Mavs up 2-0 in that championship series, city officials tempted (and incurred) the wrath of the sports gods by discussing plans and possible routes for a championship parade with newspaper reporters before the team had even landed in Miami for Game 3. That proved to be the first of four consecutive losses as the resurgent Heat stormed to their first NBA title.

How much inspiration the public parade plans gave Miami in 2006 can be debated (Dwyane Wade may have had more to do with it). But there had been no parade in Dallas, nor an NBA championship. And, for many, premature discussion of a parade was a convenient hot button when attempting to autopsy the Mavericks and their cratered dream season.

The 2006 Finals haunted the franchise. Those who were there — Nowitzki, Terry, Cuban and president of basketball operations Nelson — said all the right things but were asked about it constantly. What happened? How do you feel about it? Who do you blame? How can you sleep at night?

Not even those who joined the franchise after the 2006 Finals were excluded. They were asked to share their perception of what happened to the Mavericks, what the league thought of Dallas, and whether they thought the Mavs were haunted.

The questions never stopped. It was their identity. It shaped opinions of Dallas from sea to shining sea. And all roads led back to their German superstar, Dirk.

For that is how the NBA works. Each team that competes for the title does so as a team. But there are moments when *that* guy needs to make *that* shot. When your best player has to out-duel their best player. And despite enough heroic efforts through his long career to put Nowitzki on an elite level, those who did not wish to place him amongst the very best would always point to his track record in the postseason. Sure, he had big games and big nights. But did he ever put the franchise on his back and carry it all the way to an NBA title?

Until he did, the doubters would have their say on the Mavericks in general, and Nowitzki in particular. It didn't matter if it was fair. It was going to happen.

And that is why 2006 stung so badly. They were so close. They won the first two games in Dallas, and the planned parade route was being reported in *The Dallas Morning News.* A 13-point lead late in Game 3 disappeared in the fourth quarter, and Dallas ran into a freight train Miami team fortified by veterans who knew their role and were hungry for a ring.

Wade had some very heroic efforts in that series, but the Heat were able to slow down Nowitzki, double-teaming him effectively with Udonis Haslem tight and Shaquille O'Neal behind. O'Neal was not the force he once was, but was still a very capable defender and presence in the paint. Every time Dirk got around Haslem, Shaq was there waiting.

The younger Mavericks of 2006 either failed to comprehend how rare their opportunity was, or lacked the seasoning to properly seize it. As Game 3's slip was followed by Game 4's blowout, it seemed apparent the entire Mavericks organization was panicking. Attempts were made to save the ship, but the water was rushing in too fast. Referees were being blamed, the hotel was being changed, but ultimately the opportunity of a lifetime was being wasted.

Game 5 was decided through some questionable officiating (the call that made Bennett Salvatore even more famous), unforced errors by Dallas and a big dose of D-Wade. The Heat had assembled a roster of guys who knew what to do at big moments of big games. Gary Payton, in particular, made huge plays in Games 3 and 5 to help Miami sweep the three games in South Florida.

On the day between Games 5 and 6, Nowitzki tried to "celebrate" his 28th birthday. But the only thing he could think about was that NBA title slipping through his fingers, an opportunity he might never see again. His coach (Avery Johnson), team owner and many teammates had become distracted by the officiating of the series and were generating a fair amount of fines and consternation from the league office. The Mavericks were losing their composure, and the ability to focus on the true opponents wearing Miami uniforms. And, try as he might, Nowitzki was unable to pull his team out of its nosedive.

The series ended in Dallas the next day, with the Heat's fourth straight victory in The Finals. A season that had been considered the best in Mavericks history ended with a sour taste for all involved. It was that extremely rare confluence in which both the greatest and most disappointing year in the history of a franchise occurred in the same season.

The Mavericks had taken down the rival San Antonio Spurs and Phoenix Suns along the way in their longest-ever postseason march. But, in the end, nobody wanted to look back at a season that ended so painfully.

There are many examples in sports where swift revenge was attained by a team that had fallen just short of its goal. That certainly did not happen for Dallas.

Instead of punishing the NBA in 2007 for laughing at their misfortune, they supplied more grist for those insisting the Mavericks lacked championship quality. After dominating the regular season by winning a franchise-record 67 games (tied for sixth most in league history), the Mavericks became the first No. 1 seed to be eliminated by a No. 8 seed in a best-of-seven NBA playoff series, losing 4 games to 2.

That the eighth-seeded Golden State Warriors were coached by former Mavs coach Don Nelson enhanced the pain. Cuban and Nelson had not parted on the greatest of terms after the 2005 season, and it gave Nelson a fair amount of personal joy to take down his former employer with a far inferior squad.

Nowitzki had just been voted the league's MVP in 2007, receiving 83 of 129 first-place votes. But the first European-born winner suffered the indignity of being ousted from the playoffs before his trophy could be awarded.

Traditionally, the MVP award is given to the winner in front of his home crowd right before a playoff game begins. The arena goes bananas and the winner is properly recognized.

That opportunity went up in smoke when Nowitzki made just 2 of 13 shots and scored eight points in Game 6, a humiliating 111-86 loss that capped the biggest upset in league playoff history. It took until the final minute of the first half for Dirk to make his first field goal that night, and the Mavs trailed by 23 points by the time he made his second.

Did Nelson have the secret to defending Nowitzki? Based on much of the six-game series, it appeared so. Frustrated by double-teams and harassed incessantly by smaller defenders, Nowitzki averaged just 19.7

points per game and shot 38 percent in the series (he averaged 24.6 points on 50 percent shooting during the regular season). There were renewed questions about Nowitzki's mettle. And after the series-ending loss, Cuban was asked if he doubted Dirk as a leader.

"Not a little bit," the owner said defiantly. "Anyone who suggests otherwise is a moron."

When Nowitzki finally was presented his MVP award 13 days later in Dallas, the awkward ceremony took place at a news conference attended by Cuban, Johnson and NBA Commissioner David Stern. That trio tried to put the focus on Nowitzki's impressive regular season. But the dour German seemed preoccupied with knowing he was the first league MVP in 25 years (since Houston's Moses Malone in 1981-82) who had failed to win a single playoff series.

"Even when I heard I was the MVP, I was sad to watch all these playoff games and know that we're not a part of it," Nowitzki said that day. "It's heartbreaking, still, to me. I will think of this day for the rest of my life. But when I heard it, I was still a little sad because the playoff debacle was still fresh."

It was hardly a typical MVP acceptance speech. But, it was hardly a typical conclusion to a season for a MVP winner, either. Nowitzki had just finished 2006 by nearly leading his team to the NBA title. He came back the next year to lead a 67-15 team and was voted league MVP.

And yet, he seemed as wrung-out and disgusted by those two seasons as a player could be.

Dirk did not play for endorsements or recognition. He was paid handsomely, but it wasn't because his agent had leveraged his performances properly. He didn't have an agent. His deep loyalty to the Mavericks was a rare trait amongst the NBA star system.

He just wanted to be the best player he could be. He wanted to win a championship for the franchise that maneuvered a draft-day trade with Milwaukee to get him, and had stood by him. And yet, the closer he got to his goal, the further it seemed to be.

His critics called him soft. They said he didn't want it badly enough. They said he was not a warrior in the mold of past champions of the NBA. That explains how you can win in February, but not in June.

He also had the burden of representing the entire world outside the borders of the league. Aside from Hakeem Olajuwon's Houston Rockets, a team had never been led to the title by a prominent foreign-born player. And, as far as 90 percent of the NBA talking heads were concerned, that sure wasn't going to change with this German.

Dirk clearly didn't want it enough. How else would you explain David West disrespectfully patting Dirk's face in the '08 playoffs without retribution? Or letting Kenyon Martin body-check him out of bounds in the '09 playoffs? He won't even stick up for himself, they said. And his teammates wouldn't either.

Clearly, he just wasn't of championship quality.

Those who win — Kobe Bryant, Tim Duncan, Wade — were doing something he wasn't. They knew how to win in the playoffs. He didn't. He just wasn't tough enough. Wasn't enough of a leader. Wasn't cut from the right cloth. He was a Robin when the Mavericks needed a Batman. They should have traded him while they had the chance. These were the sentiments expressed through radio, newspapers and television in Dallas, even on the day Nowitzki received the award for being the MVP of the entire league.

It was madness. And yet, for Dirk, it was his reality. Until 2011, when all the work, determination and resolve to silence those critics finally bore its fairy tale ending. It was enough to make an entire city jubilant for one man.

A few days after the Dallas parade — the one that actually happened — a Dallas tourist saw a new Nike mural on the side of a five-story building in Munich, Germany. It was a photo from Game 6 of the 2011 Finals, featuring Nowitzki pumping his fist in triumph. The caption read, "ALLE TRAUME KLINGEN VERRUCKT. BIS SIE WAHR WERDEN."

Translation: "All dreams sound crazy. Until they become true."

2

THE TRADE FOR TYSON

(July 2010)

"This is the moment we have all been waiting for.
You are no longer merely spectators. You are gladiators.
Tonight, you take your place on the path to greatness.
I am proud to stand with you and fight; shoulder to shoulder;
shield to shield.
Players. Coaches. And Fans. We fight as 1.
This is our ground. Our time. Our destiny.
We attack in groups of 5, but in truth we are 20,000 strong.
We came for victory. We fight as Mavericks!"
– War Cry

The arena erupts as the video shown on the American Airlines Center big screen concludes. NBA teams try constantly to keep their fans engaged during timeouts, usually a losing battle in the era of addictive handheld devices.

This time, however, fans pay rapt attention. Because this 60-second video, shown during the third quarter of a March 12 game against the Los Angeles Lakers, is spot on pinpointing new center Tyson Chandler's role with the Mavericks.

Chandler is shown on horseback, urging on the "Mavericks Nation" to follow him into battle. Inspired by films such as *Braveheart* and *Gladiator*, it depicts Chandler as the spiritual and vocal leader of the franchise. And it nailed it.

Few could have imagined this eight months earlier, when the Mavericks acquired Chandler (then 27) from the Charlotte Bobcats in July 2010. The centerpiece of a five-player deal that sent Eduardo Najera and the disappointing Erick Dampier to the Bobcats, Chandler was considered by some as a nice player who may have already played his best basketball. Injuries had limited him to just 27 starts in his lone season for Charlotte.

In truth, Chandler was not the first option when the Mavericks became the sixth team in 10 years to acquire his rights. Cuban and Donnie Nelson first had joined most of the league in laying out welcome mats for marquee free agents LeBron James and Dwyane Wade.

Teams with foresight had been preparing for years for the mammoth opportunity the summer of 2010 would present. A high-stakes game of musical chairs was to unfold, with enough premier free-agent talent hitting the market to reshape standings for several seasons. General managers hoped to wield the proper combination of financial strength, salary cap room and attractive geography to not be left out of the mix.

The Mavericks' first priority was to secure their own franchise centerpiece, as Nowitzki opted out of the final year of his contract to become an unrestricted free agent for the first time in his career. The backbone to the Mavericks' decade of excellence, Nowitzki didn't seem the type to be whisked around the country in a private jet to be courted by other teams. But forfeiting a $21.5 million salary in the final year of his existing deal made Nowitzki eligible for a maximum four-year, $96 million deal if he stayed with Dallas and the rare chance to incorporate a no-trade provision into his new contract.

Dirk could have left Dallas — New York and New Jersey were among the first interested — but Nowitzki was a very content superstar. He did not aspire to a global brand, clothing line or record label. He cared about basketball, and little else.

The Mavericks had been loyal to him through the years, and he was not about to leave them, so long as he believed Cuban was still just as determined to reach the mountaintop as he was. And anyone who spent five minutes with Cuban since he bought the team knew that he didn't talk about profit-taking or keeping the team spreadsheets in the black.

Cuban cared about how to beat the Spurs and Lakers. Theirs was a marriage unlikely to fall apart.

But the Mavericks still had to respect the process and let Dirk know he was loved. The front office took nothing for granted. Nelson was poised to fly overseas if needed. But instead, Cuban met with Nowitzki in Dallas to discuss his plans to move the franchise forward, despite already exceeding the salary cap (and being taxed heavily by the league because of it).

Cuban was used to dealing directly with his superstar. And because Dirk has never had an agent (one of very few players in professional basketball who can say that), it was a conversation that spanned just 15 minutes in Cuban's living room.

"My son has to be able to watch you play," Cuban said as his infant son played nearby. It was a simple sales pitch and Dirk was sold.

"It was really emotional," Nowitzki recalled later. "He said to me, 'Hey, I love you. We've been through so much together and we are in the same boat.'

"He hit the nail on the head. And he has been so great to me, and he was there for me on and off the court. He had little tears in his eyes and I think I did, too. It wouldn't have felt right to leave this behind and go somewhere else."

They briefly talked strategy, and the plan moving forward. The plans were vague, because so many moving parts change by the minute in NBA free agency. One offer, trade or signing can send the dominoes tumbling, so teams must stay flexible and alert. Nelson has said on numerous occasions that for every completed transaction, there are maybe 100 that fall apart. It is not an exact science.

In the end, Dirk heard exactly what he wanted to hear. Mavericks basketball was all he really knew, or cared to know. He had spent most of his career with an owner who sat within arm's length of the Mavericks' bench on most nights. There has never been an owner closer to the action and more accessible and supportive than "Cubes." Dirk knew the city and knew the city loved him, and Cuban's personal loyalty was an enormous consideration.

Nowitzki chose to leave $16 million on the table, signing a new four-year deal (with a no-trade clause) worth $80 million, less than the league maximum he surely could have found elsewhere. It was his own way of investing in his team's future by leaving the organization a bit more cash (and lower salary-cap tax bill) with which to maneuver.

"Cuban always had my back," Nowitzki said. "And he was always saying that I was the guy he was building his team around and that he didn't want to start over with someone else."

Over the years, Nowitzki had heard the Kevin Garnett rumors, the Shaquille O'Neal rumors, the Kobe Bryant rumors. Some pundits and fans were eager to trade Dirk after the many playoff failures to get a guy who could win it all. The fact that Cuban never listened to or fed those rumors meant the world to Nowitzki. And now it was time to pay that loyalty back.

=========

With Nowitzki secured, attention quickly turned to how the Mavericks could improve their squad. In 2009-10, the Mavericks had another 55-win season and won their division. But for the third time in four years, they had lost in the first round of the playoffs, ousted this time by rival San Antonio in six games. It was the type of loss that again rocked the confidence of even the most loyal supporters, and the team's reputation grew as a strong regular-season squad that seemingly had no idea how to win when it mattered most.

It was like *Groundhog Day* for the Nowitzki-Cuban-Nelson-Terry quartet. The four were the only prominent holdovers from the 2006 Finals. Each year they fought to keep the dream of redemption alive, but the right combination proved elusive.

Such is life in professional sports. A fortunate few organizations figure out how to win titles, and the underwhelming rest must accept their role in the sporting universe. The NBA has crowned only nine different champions since 1980, far fewer than other major sports. But in the NBA, either you have one of the best players in the league and can assemble a competent supporting cast, or you don't. Dallas had a star player. The questions were whether he was "special enough" (especially in the playoffs), and whether there were proper pieces around him.

In July, the Mavericks would have to work many plans simultaneously. They would have to swing for the fences, just in case LeBron James would actually consider playing in Dallas. The departing Cleveland star had flirted with several clubs, but Miami soon emerged as the favorite. The Mavericks had hoped James might be enticed by his proclaimed love for the Dallas Cowboys, or the possibility of playing some games in Cowboys Stadium, where nearly 100,000 fans might see him perform. But chances were admittedly remote. The Mavericks couldn't clear massive amounts of cap space like so many other teams. Still, Cuban was never one to give up easily.

The Mavs' more realistic rebuilding plans mostly started with trades involving the "Damp chip." Veteran center Erick Dampier's contract amounted to a $13 million salary slot that was not guaranteed. Any team that traded for it could immediately release Dampier, getting salary (and perhaps also luxury tax) relief for their payroll.

The Mavericks were prepared to move on without Dampier after several lackluster seasons of service, but needed to mitigate the risk of being left without a center under contract.

"Let me tell you, that's not a good feeling," Nelson said. If things didn't break properly, the Mavericks could really be in a bind.

So, the search began in earnest.

First, they had to get Brendan Haywood locked in. Haywood was acquired in a February 2010 trade with Washington, and arrived to block shots, rebound and slam the ball down with authority. He wasn't Shaq in his prime, but he also wasn't Dampier or Shawn Bradley. For a franchise historically bereft of formidable big men, it wouldn't take much to exceed expectations at Dallas' center position.

There had been curious moments near the end of the 2010 season when Haywood and Carlisle seemed to have friction. But even if coach and player didn't always see eye to eye, they decided in the off-season they would like to remain together. This was best symbolized by Carlisle knocking on Haywood's door in Charlotte, NC, as the clock struck midnight to trigger the first moment of free agency.

The two discussed the plan for the future, which included Haywood being the new starting center. It was a decidedly easy pledge for Carlisle to make, given there were no other centers on the roster that the team planned to keep. Haywood signed a new deal for six years and $55 million, of which five years at $43 million was guaranteed. It was a huge commitment, but the price of big men in basketball has never been reasonable.

"When we did that, we felt we could go to war next year," Nelson said. "The position was not perfect, and we were still looking for versatility. But we could now put a team out there and feel good about ourselves."

From there, the media focused on the idea of Minnesota's Al Jefferson as a viable upgrade, after rumors surfaced that the 6-foot-10 forward was available. It was reported that Minnesota wanted too much in a trade. But in reality, it was the Mavericks' front office having second thoughts and internal discussions about whether Jefferson's game was too similar to Nowitzki's. Both players were far better on the offensive end of the floor, and both required the ball to be effective. If Jefferson was brought in, the Mavs' management team feared, defense would remain a liability and the team's offense would lose its focal point.

The conversations moved elsewhere. They started kicking the tires on Chandler, who with New Orleans in 2008 had tortured Dallas for an entire playoff series. Unlike the offense-minded Jefferson, Chandler didn't need the ball to impact a game. He concentrated on defense and, when healthy, played with remarkable energy. He seemed to play every night as if it was a game of extreme importance. And in the NBA, that is a special quality.

"It's important for Dirk to have energy around him," Nelson said. "And Tyson is such a positive, upbeat, never-say-die personality."

But Chandler already had failed one physical, forcing New Orleans to rescind a February 2009 trade with Oklahoma City. Word around the league was that Chandler just wasn't right. The failed physical with the Thunder was performed by Dr. Carlan Yates, the same doctor who had operated on Chandler's left big toe more than a year earlier. The doctor didn't like how the toe looked, and even though Chandler was only 26, Yates thought his career might not last much longer.

Five months after the Oklahoma City trade was rescinded, Charlotte agreed to take Chandler from New Orleans in exchange for Emeka Okafor, but squeezed only 27 starts from Chandler. He just wasn't the electric, high-flying big man that used to be on the end of Chris Paul's lob passes.

If Chandler was healthy, he would be exactly what the Mavericks needed and a perfect compliment to Nowitzki. But that seemed to be a big "if."

It would take Chandler's desire to play for Team USA in the 2010 FIBA World Championships that summer in Turkey to change perceptions. Casey Smith, the Mavericks' trainer since 2004, had also served as the head trainer for Coach Mike Krzyzewski's Team USA since 2005. If Chandler wasn't healthy, it wouldn't take anyone on the USA medical staff long to figure it out. But Smith told the Mavericks that, based on his observations, reports of Chandler being broken down at age 27 seemed unfounded.

Chandler had another prominent booster in Jason Kidd. The players share the same agent (Jeff Schwartz), so Kidd was familiar with Chandler's status and ambitions. If Chandler was healthy (and both Schwartz and Smith believed he was), then Kidd thought he could be the difference-maker the Mavs were seeking.

"I thought Tyson would be the 'athletic big' that Dirk had always needed but never had," Kidd said. "And I told Dirk it would change his game and make things so much easier for him."

If they had to cope with a center they must respect, Mavericks opponents would be far less able to use their big man to double-team Nowitzki when he posted up near the paint.

But the Mavericks would have to move fast. The Bobcats reportedly were on the verge of trading Chandler to the Toronto Raptors. Chandler already had begun telling those around him that he was going to Canada. But a fortuitous, last-minute breakdown in talks between Charlotte and Toronto allowed Cuban and Nelson to toss their hat into the ring. Dallas got Charlotte owner Michael Jordan to consider their offer of Dampier, Najera and Matt Carroll for Chandler and Alexis Ajinca. The payroll flexibility that accompanied Dampier's disposable contract was too good for the cash-strapped Bobcats to ignore, and the trade was made.

In less than a week, the Mavericks had gone from no centers on their roster to two. No matter who started, the Mavs knew they had to have size to compete with the massive front court of the two-time defending champion Los Angeles Lakers, who lined up the 6-foot-10 Lamar Odom alongside 7-footers Andrew Bynum and Pau Gasol. With those big men dominating the paint and complementing the dynamic Kobe Bryant outside, the Lakers had mowed through the NBA for two consecutive springs.

The Mavericks had Haywood to line up next to Dirk, and he was certainly considered an upgrade. But comparing Haywood to Dampier and comparing him to the Lakers' front line were two very different conversations.

Acquiring Chandler meant the Mavericks had two centers of NBA starting caliber. Two big men who could take turns battling inside and share 12 fouls in an effort to win the intense best-of-seven battles of late spring. It made sense from a basketball standpoint. Also, Chandler at his best specialized in two things of great importance to the Mavericks.

First was his ability to handle lob passes from the point guard, an athletic gift that opened a whole new dimension of attack possibilities for Kidd. Anyone remotely familiar with the Hornets' first-round victory over the Mavericks in the spring of 2008 remembered the many lobs Chandler slammed home against Dampier and the Mavericks' overmatched front line. Opponents had been cheating away from Dallas centers for years to double-team Nowitzki, but now the Mavs had an inside presence that would require defensive attention.

Secondly, Chandler can protect the rim. He may not be an extraordinary shot-blocker, but he battles hard and relentlessly to defend every inch of interior real estate. He would be a perfect player to funnel the ball toward if the Mavericks elected to run the zone defense they had employed for several years, and he would certainly hold his own as a rebounder. The Mavericks allegedly had defensive-minded centers for years in Dampier and Shawn Bradley, but few opponents held them in high regard. Chandler was cut from a different cloth. He could hold his own physically against just about any post player in the league, and he had the fierce will power to assure he would never be dominated.

Chandler had one more attribute that would prove critical — his booming voice.

On the court, the Mavs' best player was always going to be Dirk as long as he was anywhere near his prime. But he was not the type to imitate the rousing William Wallace depicted in *Braveheart*. Nowitzki will battle, but he is not one for regular inspirational speeches or primal screams after swatting away a shot.

Chandler isn't so bashful. He was naturally wired to become the confident voice of the franchise, almost from Day 1. He was equally comfortable when loudly protecting the rim, barking out defensive instructions from his command center in the paint, or saying what needed to be said in a huddle or within the privacy of the locker room.

"It's just such a good locker room and such a good group of guys that it's not hard to come in here and fit in," Chandler told ESPN's Dallas website. "They don't mind somebody getting in their face, and they don't mind somebody telling them when they're wrong. It says a lot about their character here that they are willing. And they just want to win.

"I'm an emotional guy. I play like it out there, and I voice my opinions sometimes in the locker room. Sometimes, people don't want to hear that. But this is a team that's all about winning, and it's been good."

Chandler preached defense at every turn and instilled a powerful heartbeat and pulse to a team that sometimes had lacked sufficient emotion. And all he cost was a few spare parts and an expiring deal? The Mavericks quietly hoped they were right.

Mavericks fans got their first taste of what was to come in the preseason opener against the Washington Wizards.

Early in the second half, Chandler was bumped on a post move and had his shot blocked by Wizards center JaVale McGee. Chandler turned, arms outstretched, pleading for a foul call that never came. But rather than whine, Chandler instead sprinted down the floor to catch up to the Wizards' Al Thornton.

"Give me that!" Chandler screamed as he authoritatively blocked the small forward's shot.

As the ball went the other way for a quick Mavericks dunk, Chandler marched down the court, beating his chest with his right fist and hollering like a man possessed.

Seeing such emotion from a Dallas center — in the first preseason game, no less — was both bewildering and exciting to the Mavericks' crowd and bench. The contrast in demeanor between Chandler and his predecessor Dampier could not have been greater. It wasn't long before Carlisle was gratefully acknowledging Chandler's role as "the spirit" of the team.

So months later, when that marketing department video showed an animated Chandler reining his horse, raising his sword and exhorting both his Mavericks' fans and teammates to follow him into postseason battle, it did not seem contrived. The big man had been in the middle of too many emotional moments, breathing life into his team whether on the court or waving his towel off it.

"The only question about Tyson had to do with his health," Carlisle said. "The signs were very good. We had watched and seen in the Team USA games that he had a charisma and a presence on that team. It was similar to what Kevin Garnett brought the Celtics. The enthusiasm, the infectious exuberance and the toughness were all components that fit in great with any team."

But on this team, with this superstar, Carlisle knew it was even more vital.

"It's really essential to surround Dirk with the right kind of athletes and toughness," Carlisle said. "Tyson is the best center that Dirk has played with, and he is also the best athlete that Dirk has played with. The combination of those two things was really major to us."

It was July 13 when the Mavericks usurped the Raptors to acquire Chandler from Charlotte. It just might have been the day that truly made this year different.

3

THE TATTOO

(October 2010)

On Oct. 19, the Mavericks were in Orlando, preparing for the seventh of their eight preseason games. The business of the regular season would commence in eight days.

Their preseason had taken them to such high-profile outposts as Grand Rapids, MI, and Palm Springs, CA. The veteran team was simply marching one day at a time through a series of rather uninspiring preseason dates.

There were a few storylines to keep track of, most notably the battle between Chandler and Haywood for the starting center job. But this was a team pretty well-settled, with players mostly comfortable in their roles.

Building camaraderie on a professional sports team is sometimes easier said than done, but this group of players seemed to genuinely enjoy spending time together. Such was not always the case for the Mavericks.

The Dallas teams of the mid-1990s, for instance, were famous for not getting along. The Mavericks established their highly touted "Three J's" era by selecting Jim Jackson, Jamal Mashburn and Jason Kidd with their first-round draft picks from 1992-94. But after various incidents and rumored incidents between them, the trio was disbanded by February 1997, scattered to the wind in three separate trades.

However, this version of the Mavericks had no such chemistry issues apparent. On this balmy Tuesday night in Florida, most of the team gathered happily for a backyard barbecue at the home of swingman DeShawn Stevenson in Windermere, a suburb of Orlando. Stevenson still has a house there from his days with the Orlando Magic (2004-06), and he invited teammates and a few friends, including his tattoo artist.

Stevenson is enamored with tattoos, which hardly makes him unique in the modern NBA. But Stevenson's body art is more eye-catching than most. Among the adornments on his skin, for instance, is the large image of Abraham Lincoln on his throat, framed by large numeral 5's on either side of his neck to simulate a $5 bill.

Stevenson can't say with certainty how many tattoos he now has, since so many of the ink designs have merged and blended up and down his arms, back and, yes, even face. His artist was invited to the barbecue just in case inspiration struck someone at the spur of the moment.

Conversation at the party, as so often was the case, was led by the gregarious shooting guard Jason Eugene Terry — "Jet" to his teammates.

Terry parlayed an accomplished tenure at the University of Arizona, which included winning the national championship with roommate Mike Bibby in 1997, into a solid NBA career. He was the 10th overall pick of the 1999 draft and spent five nondescript years with the Atlanta Hawks before being traded to Dallas before the 2004-05 season. Terry was brought in primarily to replace Steve Nash, signed by Phoenix as an unrestricted free agent.

Terry was not necessarily gifted in many facets of the game. But when it came to the all-important realm of scoring, Terry had a reputation for converting high degree-of-difficulty shots at the most crucial of times. Nash had been a fan favorite, frequent All-Star and Nowitzki's closest friend. But Terry wasn't intimidated by the big shoes he was trying to fill, so thankful was he to be escaping Atlanta, where he had peaked with 35 wins on a succession of bad teams.

"He was over the moon to be playing here," Mavericks public relations director Sarah Melton recalled.

But Terry's first year in Dallas was difficult. He proved to be merely adequate at point guard, while an inspired Nash was putting up an MVP season running the exciting show in Phoenix. After the Suns eliminated the Mavericks in the second round of the 2005 playoffs, fans were frustrated that Cuban had let Nash get away and bothered that Terry was not Nash.

But it was difficult to dislike Terry. A bubbly personality, Jet loves playing to a crowd and acknowledging the fans' presence. And as his high-flying nickname caught on, Terry began celebrating big shots by spreading his arms like airplane wings and flying down the court. He had become a fan favorite in his own right.

The media also loved Terry, one of the most talkative and cooperative players Dallas had seen in years. While some players tend to disappear when the locker room is opened to reporters, Terry always was at his locker, accountable. Big win? Terry is talking. Tough loss? Terry is talking. Big game? Terry is talking. Bad game? Yes, Terry is still talking.

Terry developed into the Mavericks' go-to guy when a team ambassador was needed off the court. Nowitzki was friendly and congenial, but still a bit shy. Terry could handle media or community relations speaking engagements with equal ease. Truth be told, his talking rarely stops on the court either.

For whatever reason, the Mavericks always had a hard time finding vocal players in the "Dirk era." It is assumed that all but the very strongest personalities defer to those above them in the pecking order, and the NBA is no different. If you have a quiet leader, those below him tend to be more quiet. If he is vocal and demonstrative, so are many of the foot soldiers. Nowitzki will definitely show emotion, but he picks his spots and they can be infrequent. He was not born to yell at teammates or command players. He was born to dominate the game with his unique skill set and amazing work ethic. Communication was not always high on his priority list.

It fell to others to fill that void. But, over the years, few players in Dallas seemed comfortable speaking out in front of one of the best players in the league. Michael Finley was generally quiet on the court. Josh Howard rarely spoke up and seldom seemed eager to touch the ball at moments of great importance. Dampier and Bradley? Not much was coming from there. Nash and Kidd could run a team, but neither wore war paint to the games.

That left veterans who were both amazingly confident and sometimes a little crazy. Nick Van Exel. Jerry Stackhouse. And, for the last several years, Terry. Playing to the crowd, defending a mate in a skirmish, or pushing the team out of a timeout, Terry's mouth was always flapping. He wasn't by any stretch the biggest player on the court, but he would never go down without a fight. He always was up for a battle.

On the court, his role was constantly being tinkered with. How do you best use him to take advantage of his strengths, while hiding his deficiencies? This was always the riddle for the Mavericks' staff, and the answer was a variety of changing positions and roles. Eventually, the Mavericks settled on Terry as a sixth man — an impact bench player who would play starters' minutes and always be on the floor at the end of the game. When Dirk and Jet were right and working the high pick-and-roll together, they could be virtually unstoppable.

Terry is one of the streakiest of shooters. When locked in and nailing his pull-up jumpers from either baseline, he is practically impossible to defend. At only 6-foot-2, he possess a rare ability to get his shot off and knock it down when you need him most.

Of course, streaky shooters sometimes find the barren side of that coin, as Terry did in Game 6 of the 2006 Finals. After making his first four shots in that game, Terry then missed 18 of his last 21 attempts, including a potential game-tying 3-pointer with one second left, enabling Miami to celebrate its NBA title in Dallas. It was a performance that had haunted Terry for five years.

Earlier in the 2006 playoffs, Terry had been involved in an another incident that was not his finest moment.

With the Mavs holding a 3-1 lead over San Antonio in the Western Conference semifinals, Dallas was trying to close out the Spurs on the road. Late in the game, Terry and the Spurs' Manu Ginobili dove for a loose ball. Terry collected the ball on his back as the former Maverick Finley reached in to wrestle it away. After referees blew the whistle, Terry was caught by television cameras punching Finley in the groin. For a split second, it seemed, Terry had lost his mind.

The Spurs hung on to win Game 5, submitted video tape of the incident to the league, and smiled as Terry was suspended for Game 6, which San Antonio also won in Dallas. Terry's momentary lapse in composure had helped turn a comfortable 3-1 series lead into a very uncomfortable 3-3 tie, with the decisive seventh game to be played back in San Antonio.

Terry faced enormous pressure for Game 7, but knew it was time to redeem himself. In a hostile environment where he always seems to do his best work, Terry was superb. He hit shot after shot and the Mavericks built a big lead early in front of rabid Spurs fans who had no patience for Jet and his open wings running back down the court.

Nowitzki will long be remembered for his heroic drive to the basket to tie the game near the end of the fourth quarter, and his gigantic 37-point, 15-rebound performance. But Terry pouring in 27 points was equally vital. He needed a big game to reconcile his suspension, and he stepped up and drained gigantic shots in the biggest of circumstances. From that point on, the Mavericks would go as far as Nos. 41 and 31 could take them in moments of truth.

Unfortunately, that has not always been a good thing. Since that sad ending to the 2006 Finals, Terry had played unevenly at playoff time. During the regular season, Dirk and Jet still had their magic. But in the playoff runs of 2009 and 2010, Terry's production fell off dramatically. A career 45 percent shooter, he dropped to 38 percent in the 2010 series loss to the Spurs and averaged 12.7 points per game, four under his season average.

The low point for Terry was the series-ending Game 6 loss to the Spurs, in which he made 1 of 7 shots and finished with just two points. In 62 career playoff contests, Terry had averaged 16.8 points per game and had been held to five points or fewer just twice. Both instances were in this series against the Spurs (five in Game 1, two in Game 6).

Terry was nearly 33. Kidd, who made 1 of 6 shots and managed just three points in the Game 6 loss, was 37. The performances from the aging backcourt seemed to reveal a sad truth nobody wanted to admit: The Mavericks' window of championship opportunity appeared to be closing, if not already shut.

For Terry, who shared the burden of the 2006 collapse with Nowitzki, there was no running from his performance against the Spurs. And though he intended to carry on, his organization was considering whether to replace him.

The leading in-house candidate was young Rodrigue Beaubois, the 22-year-old firecracker from the island nation of Guadeloupe. With amazing quickness and a 40-inch vertical leap, Beaubois was a raw but gifted prospect who occasionally flashed brilliance, such as his March 2010 game at Golden State when he dropped 40 points on the Warriors.

After Terry and Kidd disappointed, Beaubois was thrown into the Game 6 rout against the Spurs. He still looked raw and inexperienced, but there was no debating his explosiveness. "Roddy" replaced Terry with the Mavs trailing by 19 midway through the second quarter and began driving the lane with reckless abandon. He wound up scoring 16 points in 21 minutes and help Dallas claw back into a lead before succumbing to their hated rival yet again. Fans and critics spent the summer wondering why the Mavericks had not used him sooner. What did Carlisle have against him? Why were they forcing the creaky old men, Kidd and Terry, to play so many minutes when youth was available?

And that was what Terry had to take with him into the summer of 2010. His days appeared numbered. Fans and media spent the off-season projecting Beaubois' impact on the upcoming season. Nowitzki needed a dangerous secondary scoring threat with whom to share the offensive load, and it no longer looked as if Terry could be relied upon as that guy. This young, dynamic kid from Guadeloupe, perhaps, could. Maybe this would be the secret formula for success and Terry wouldn't even have a significant role anymore. All this, based on 21 minutes of basketball in a Game 6 blowout.

The rhetoric came not exclusively from fans and media. During a summer league interview in July, Carlisle admitted Beaubois could possibly be a starter. The belief was that, with a proper amount of summer league seasoning and his planned stint with the French national team, Beaubois could ready himself for a significant role in the coming season. It seemed extremely optimistic that all the game instincts Beaubois lacked could suddenly bloom over one summer of non-NBA competition. But sometimes 16 points in 21 minutes can send hopes soaring.

Those hopes came crashing down on Aug. 8, when Beaubois cracked a bone in his foot during training in France. The initial diagnosis was that Beaubois would be sidelined at least three months, ruling him out of the Mavericks' training camp and likely the first month of the season. There would be no challenge to Terry's minutes just yet, but the talkative veteran was still ready to push himself. And when Terry met the tattoo artist at Stevenson's barbecue, he thought of a way to prove it.

"As many tattoos as (Stevenson) has, I don't even know why the guy was there," Terry recalled later. "But, he was, so I got my mother's name tattooed. And we had been talking all night about winning the championship this year. And I said, 'I'm serious. I don't know about you guys, but I am serious.'"

Terry found a picture of the NBA's championship trophy and gave it to the artist.

"Hey buddy, why don't you just tattoo that trophy right here on my arm?" Terry said. "I'm going to show these guys just how serious I am. And everyone looked at me like I was crazy."

That's right. Terry had a new tattoo of the NBA championship trophy permanently inked onto his right biceps.

Since 2006, Terry had made sure each player in the Dallas locker room had a picture of the Larry O'Brien trophy posted in their locker, a reminder about why each practice and game was so important. The trophy had slipped from their grasp in that painful 2006 collapse, but the Mavs had never given up pursuit. And now, one of their most vocal leaders was willing to put his biceps where his mouth was.

A little crazy? Sure, but that was Jet. As the artist's needle buzzed, etching that trophy before nodding teammates, a message of intent spread through the room. The season was nigh upon them, and their goal was clear. While the rest of the NBA pondered whether the Lakers could three-peat again or whether the star-studded Miami Heat would cruise to their expected title, the Mavericks had quietly assembled a determined team that appeared as deep and talented as any they had ever put together.

If only they could figure out how the pieces fit together.

=========

Some general managers envy Donnie Nelson, the Mavericks' President of Basketball Operations/General Manager, because he works for a deep-pocketed owner unafraid to devote resources toward winning.

Others shudder at the thought of working for Cuban, who has had his long, mostly unhelpful history of run-ins with the commissioner, league officials, referees and opponents. And who is generally believed to be as hands-on (i.e., meddlesome) as any owner in the league.

Nelson has worked for the Mavericks since 1998, predating Cuban, but is he truly the architect of the team? Or has Cuban emulated Jerry Jones, the NFL celebrity seemingly so taken with the glamor of owning the Dallas Cowboys that he named himself GM as well?

"Ultimately, it is the same as every other franchise," Nelson explained. "The owner makes the final decision because there is a price tag attached to it. What is different (in Dallas) is that because Mark is involved in everything in the day-to-day operation. And because he is ever-present, in a lot of respects it makes my job easier. I don't have to educate him on everything. Mark knows the issues. He is here."

Cuban and Nelson insist theirs is a joint cooperative, with Nelson focusing on the basketball aspects of a given deal while Cuban weighs the business ramifications. What happens when they disagree? Well, they have been emphatic that disagreements mean no deal will be consummated. It has worked that way for more than a decade now.

"Not a decision happens without it making basketball sense and financial sense," Nelson said. "There have only been a couple of occasions where we didn't fully see eye to eye. Mark always says, 'You are the basketball guy. What do you think?' He knows I am not perfect, and nobody bats 1.000 in this business."

It is a unique arrangement, to be sure. But since Cuban bought the franchise in 2000, traditional organizational flow charts of authority were replaced with a more team-oriented mentality.

Donn Nelson (Donnie), along with his father Don Nelson (Nellie, now the winningest coach in NBA history), were in place when Cuban bought the Mavericks. And though there were early signs that the Nelsons had hit on a budding star with their draft-day deal for Nowitzki in 1998, he was hardly a superstar yet when Cuban came aboard in Dirk's second full season.

The prevailing opinion in Dallas when Cuban took over was that the new owner should perhaps clean house, starting with the powerful Nelsons. Instead, Cuban's only move was to add a chair for himself in their meeting rooms. He was not interested in being an absentee owner, or in allowing the "basketball people" to handle his franchise with impunity. Cuban wanted to learn everything there was to learn, and he recognized the Nelsons were fantastic resources.

Donnie Nelson had something on his resume that no GM in basketball history can match. On June 24, 1998, Donnie acquired two future league MVPs in one rather complex transaction.

Donnie had just joined his father in Dallas after three seasons as an assistant coach in Phoenix, where he had gotten to know an unheralded backup point guard out of Santa Clara (by way of Canada) named Steve Nash. The elder Nelson had taken over as coach and GM in Dallas just weeks after Kidd had been moved to Phoenix in a controversial trade. Nash now was buried deeper on the Suns' depth chart behind Kidd and veteran All-Star Kevin Johnson.

Donnie had designs on bringing Nash to Dallas. He also got his father intrigued by a 7-foot German prospect named Dirk, whom they could take with an audacious gamble using the sixth overall pick in the 1998 draft.

Depending on who you ask, it is suggested that previous owner Ross Perot Jr. encouraged a trade down to save money (about $100,000) on Nowitzki's contract, assuming the Mavs were correct in their belief few other teams were targeting Nowitzki high in the first round.

Milwaukee agreed to give the Mavericks the 9th and 19th overall picks in exchange for Dallas' No. 6 pick, which the Bucks used on Michigan's Robert "Tractor" Traylor. Nowitzki went to Dallas at No. 9, and Donnie packaged the Bucks' 19th pick along with Bubba Wells,

Martin Müürsepp and Dallas' first-rounder in 1999 to get Nash from Phoenix.

In one evening, Nelson had traded for Nowitzki (the 2007 NBA MVP) and Nash (the 2005 and 2006 league MVP) — a singular accomplishment in the annals of NBA history. Of course, when you are trading futures, you must endure ridicule before the dividends mature. But, with each passing year of the two friends' All-Star careers, Donnie has appeared ever wiser. No one spoke of nepotism anymore.

But even as Nash & Nowitzki matured, it seemed that, year after year, very good Dallas teams either would run into a hot team or an unfortunate break and end their season in disappointment. Regular-season success, though nice to have once again, ultimately meant little when the Mavericks remained unable to break through to the other side.

This burden was carried by the players, but also by Cuban and the Nelsons. The two had tried bold annual strokes to find the right combination of players to complement their stars. A major trade for Juwan Howard in 2001 helped push the Mavs into the playoffs for the first time in more than a decade. In 2002, it was another major deal for Nick Van Exel and Raef LaFrentz. In 2003-04, two major swaps brought Antoine Walker and Antawn Jamison. In 2004-05, more deals landed Dampier, Terry and point guard Devin Harris. Those last few deals boosted the Mavs into the 2006 NBA Finals under Avery Johnson and to the brink of a title.

That 2006 team, despite having the most successful year in franchise history, crashed and burned in the NBA Finals after taking a rather commanding lead. They had been so close to the prize, but seemed still so far away. Never had a Mavericks team performed so valiantly at the right time of year, nor had one broken its city's heart so painfully. But Donnie Nelson and Cuban kept scheming, alchemists who wouldn't rest before discovering the correct formula.

A complicated 10-player deal brought Kidd back from New Jersey in February 2008. Johnson was fired as coach later that spring, replaced by Carlisle after another damaging playoff defeat to New Orleans. Shawn Marion was acquired in 2009, and 2010 brought a deal for Haywood, Stevenson and the dynamic Caron Butler. Now, in the summer before the 2010-11 season, the Mavs beat Toronto to the punch in the trade for Chandler.

"Every year, we have developed a team that we felt had a real shot," Donnie Nelson said. "I compare it to the Indianapolis 500. You have all of these teams. But it's not just about the best crew and best engine. You have to stay off the walls and things have to break right for you, too.

"We have always rolled out a car — every year a different one — but a car that we believed had the chance to be there at the end. It just hadn't worked out. It could have worked in 2006, but it didn't."

This year, they had built what they believed to be their deepest and most fortified roster yet. Could this year possibly be different?

4

THE START OF THE MARCH

(Oct. 31-Nov. 8, 2010)

The Mavericks opened their 31st season in Dallas with a home game against Charlotte on Oct. 27. But it was hardly the biggest game of the night to local sports fans.

The Texas Rangers were opening their first-ever trip to the World Series the same night in San Francisco. Dallas-Fort Worth always loves a winner, and the Rangers had put together an October that was off the charts.

The scrappy Rangers were dominating local headlines, and everyone wanted to see if they could finish the impossible dream. They beat Tampa Bay in the American League Division Series, ousted the hated New York Yankees in the AL Championship Series, and now were just four wins from their first World Series crown.

Many of the Mavericks found themselves caught up in the excitement. Television cameras caught Nowitzki and his new buddy, backup power forward Brian Cardinal, watching playoff baseball at Rangers Ballpark, clad in new Texas jerseys. Not only was it great fun, but it demonstrated again how transformative a deep playoff run can be to an entire city or region.

On this night, however, the Mavericks were competing with Rangers Fever. The Cliff Lee-Tim Lincecum matchup from AT&T Park was overshadowing their scheduled tipoff against the Bobcats. And while opening night is still a big occasion for NBA diehards, this particular opening night slipped under the radar of many local fans.

The past decade had conditioned Mavericks fans to enjoy their successful regular seasons, but to wait until the playoffs before judging the true quality of their team. Forgetting the futility of the 1990s, the city had become spoiled by the tremendous regular-season records of the Cuban Era.

From the start of the 1990-91 season until the day Cuban purchased the team (Jan. 4, 2000), the Mavericks had missed the playoffs every year. During that decade of futility, the team won 210 games and lost 531, a dismal .283 winning percentage that left plenty of good seats empty. But things changed the day Cuban took the keys from Ross Perot Jr. From that day through the start of the 2010 season, the Mavs went 594-278 (.681).

Changes in coaches, players and Nowitzki blossoming into one of the game's greatest performers had a great deal to do with the reversal of fortunes. But when one considers that after the 1990 playoffs the Mavs did not play a postseason game again until after Cuban's first full season as owner in 2001 — and that the Mavs haven't missed a postseason since — the impact of committed ownership seems apparent.

Under Cuban's tenure, the Mavericks resuscitated their dormant fan base. In fact, on this night in October, the team was starting what would become its 11th consecutive 50-win season, and extending what would be an NBA-record streak of 399 consecutive home sellouts by season's end.

Only the Los Angeles Lakers (12 seasons from 1980-91) and the San Antonio Spurs (12 seasons from 1999-2011) have exceeded Dallas' streak of consecutive 50-win seasons. But the Lakers also hung five championship banners during their stretch, the Spurs three. The Mavericks' barren rafters served as a grim reminder that they had been really, really good without ever becoming great enough to win it all.

The Rangers owned the spotlight as they battled to win their own first world championship. So it was that the Mavericks embarked on another 50-win season, amid relative peace and quiet.

=========

Rick Carlisle and his staff started the season grappling with what most coaches would consider a "good problem." His roster overflowed with established NBA players capable of handling more minutes than he could give them.

Nowitzki and Kidd were unquestioned starters. But then there were Caron Butler, Shawn Marion, DeShawn Stevenson and Jason Terry, all in the mix for two starting spots at either shooting guard or small forward. The logjam would likely get worse in a month, when Roddy Beaubois was expected back from his foot injury.

Carlisle had two capable starting centers in Tyson Chandler and Brendan Haywood, and had to disappoint one of them with his decision.

None of the Mavs' top eight healthy players were accustomed to playing reduced minutes, or perhaps being forced to watch from the bench at crunch time. But the reality of this dawning season was that some sacrifice, patience and understanding would be required.

"It was clear that we had great depth on our roster," Carlisle said. "It was also clear to me that we were a strength-in-numbers team that had a collection with 14 or 15 guys that could each do something unique. And everybody would always have to be ready for when they would be needed to perform.

"The night before training camp in our meeting, I talked briefly about that. But I never thought it would be an issue for us. Our experience level was too high and we had too good of guys who were really invested in winning. But, we were going to have some guys coming off the bench that were not accustomed to doing that."

Backing up Nowitzki would be Cardinal, a veteran forward known for hard fouls, hard picks, a surprisingly deft shot and improv-caliber comedy skills. Behind Kidd at the point was the quick but undersized J.J. Barea. Neither Cardinal nor Barea had any illusions that they should unseat the future Hall of Famer starting in front of them, but they also knew there was a plan with their name on it.

"I remember that meeting and Rick said this is not a one-man show," Cardinal recalled. "It is not just Dirk's team. When we get in the playoffs, it will not be 'Throw it to Dirk and hope he makes a great shot while we all watch.' He said that from Day 1. We are all going to play a role. If you have a question about your role, please come talk to me. But we are going to use everybody. He felt that from Day 1."

But for others, the loss of a starting job and/or a reduction in expected minutes could feel like an insult. Carlisle had made it clear on the first day of camp that he expected everyone to handle their shifting roles with professionalism.

"Anybody that presents themselves with that kind of selfishness isn't deserving of being in a Maverick uniform," Carlisle told reporters during training camp. "That's my feeling about it. I know it's Mark's feeling about it. This ain't going to be about role definition. It's going to be about role acceptance. We'll see the character of our team ... and that's what is going to define us as a special team, as opposed to a good team."

Some NBA coaches don't see all the way down their bench on game nights, but Carlisle wants all his players to be prepared for his call, whenever it might come. It would be a theme of the season that the coach might spot a matchup that could tip in his team's favor, and suddenly a player deep on the bench would find himself on the floor for a period of big responsibility. It was up to them to be ready if the moment came.

Carlisle keenly understood the value of this to a team, not only because he had majored in psychology at the University of Virginia, but also because he had played the part himself.

His five-season NBA playing career began when he was the lone rookie to make the roster of the 1984-85 Boston Celtics. The most action he saw was the next season, when he averaged 9.9 minutes for a Celtics' world championship team that boasted four future Hall of Famers. In nearly 200 career games for the Celtics, Knicks and Nets, Carlisle started a game only once.

Now, more than 20 years later, Carlisle told his Mavericks team that his biggest fear as a player was not about his minutes or salary, but about letting Larry Bird or Kevin McHale down when he was needed. That, he explained, was role acceptance.

Instilling that attitude was as important to the Mavericks' preseason as figuring out who went where. Even if this was the best, most complete team in franchise history, until there was a different outcome in the spring, nobody wanted to hear it. There surely wasn't much appreciation from the public about the process of building the team.

Carlisle's staff was one of the biggest in the NBA. Cuban believed one way to maximize his assets in a salary-capped league was to spend where he could unfettered, such as on a customized plane and creature comforts for his players, and on an unrivaled support staff for his coach.

Terry Stotts and Dwane Casey were Carlisle's chief assistants. Stotts would coordinate and focus on offense, Casey handled the defense. Assistants Monte Mathis and Darrell Armstrong completed the coaching staff from a traditional standpoint.

But Cuban also employed a sports psychologist (Don Kalkstein), a free-throw coach (Gary Boren), and a statistics nerd (Roland Beech) plucked from an internet website that focused on basketball metrics (www.82games.com). It sounded very *Moneyball*, but Beech was hired before the 2009 season and given the innovative title Director of Basketball Analytics.

The entire staff travels with the team, at the disposal of players and fellow coaches, to fulfill the main mission of everyone on board: Win more basketball games.

Beech's hiring, in particular, speaks to Cuban's belief that no stone be left unturned in a sport often resistant to creative thinking. Beech was simply a guy studying statistical trends in the NBA. Cuban saw him as a 21st Century resource, whose findings should be brought to bear exclusively for the Mavericks' advantage. Would any other owner even think of hiring a statistical guru and giving him coaching staff-level security clearance?

"As far as a stats guy, I believe I am the only one (employed by an NBA team's coaching staff)," Beech said. "My coaching background was non-existent before joining the Mavericks."

Anyone with a calculator and a DVR can compile shooting percentages, rebound totals and turnover counts. Beech operates on a different plane, running elaborate programs that analyze player combinations, scenario matchups, even practice routines. Virtually anything that can be measured and evaluated is, all in the hopes of discovering any possible edge to exploit.

Cuban became a rich man because of forward thinking that was often mocked. But he never stopped believing the old poker adage, "If you can't spot the sucker at the table, then it's probably you."

========

Chandler and Haywood, both starting centers throughout their careers, knew training camp was their time to go *Highlander* on each other. There could be only one.

Haywood had been told he was the starter when Carlisle visited his home July 1. But that was before the Mavericks acquired Chandler, a rather important caveat.

"When we signed Brendan, we intended he would be the starter," Donnie Nelson recalled, "but it wasn't unconditionally promised."

Nor, Nelson says, did the Chandler trade seal any decision about who would start.

"Coming into camp, you have your ideas," Nelson said. "But training camp is for these things to sort themselves out. You cannot get into promising anything to anyone because you have to have the competition in camp. We didn't lock into a starter-backup feeling until the start of the season."

When Opening Night arrived, it was Chandler who got the nod. He would not relinquish the position, starting every game of the season for which he was physically available, 74 times in all. Only once in his 10-season career had Chandler made more starts.

"They battled in practice and they really got after each other," Mavericks communications manager Scott Tomlin recalled. "But when it came time to call on Tyson to be the starter, it didn't seem there was any doubt about it. … I'm guessing even Brendan knew that, too."

It was also decided the team would be best served with Terry starting at shooting guard, at least until Beaubois was back from his broken foot. Caron Butler would start at small forward. This meant that, for the first time in his career, Shawn Marion would come off the bench.

Marion entered the league in 1999 and had been named an All-Star four times. Of his 820 career games over 11 seasons, he had started 805 of them. Clearly, many assumed, this would strain the bounds of Carlisle's "role acceptance" demands.

However, after being traded three times in 18 months and with a 33rd birthday looming in the Spring, Marion was ready to reevaluate his place in the league. Bouncing from his longtime home in Phoenix to Miami, Toronto and finally Dallas had been eye-opening for a player who had garnered a bit of reputation for sometimes being "high maintenance." Marion disliked that perception. He just wanted to know what was expected of him, so that he could be prepared.

"Maybe as big a key to our season as anything was Marion's acceptance of coming off the bench and how he embraced it," Carlisle recalled. "I thought that was a very important aspect of the good vibe we had coming out of training camp."

Once Marion was settled, so was the Mavericks' rotation. Nowitzki, Kidd, Terry, Butler and Chandler would start. Off the bench, every night, would be Barea, Haywood and Marion. Stevenson and Cardinal would be used as needed. Learning on the job would be youngsters Ian Mahinmi (a French big man who had been cut loose by San Antonio) and rookie shooting guard Dominique Jones (Dallas' first-round pick from South Florida).

Those 12 were the Mavericks in uniform for Opening Night. The three additional roster spots were held by the injured Beaubois, the 7-foot project center Alexis Ajinca, and journeyman forward Steve Novak. The Mavericks had their roster set for the 2010-11 campaign.

Another training camp decision was to employ zone defense with greater regularity. The zone has never been fully embraced in the NBA, but more teams have turned to it as a change-up since the league rewrote its defensive statutes in 2002. Defensive creativity was rarely a strong suit in the NBA, where the machismo of man-to-man matchups had served for generations.

"I'd say the majority of teams have some kind of zone, but we took a different tact this year," Carlisle explained. "We decided to make it a conscious goal to be the best zone team in the league. And to make every effort to make it a tangible part of our identity and to really be the best at it. Before I got to Dallas, I had played little bits of zone, but was never really a believer in it. Like most coaches, I thought it compromised your toughness."

The Mavericks, however, were willing to consider anything. Defense had been their undoing in many crucial situations over the past decade, so why keep exposing the same Achilles' heel? With Chandler now patrolling the paint, the Mavs finally had a center who could handle having players funneled toward him, making everyone's job a bit easier. A zone defense works best when you have a center who can truly protect the rim.

"But what we found here was that it was a valuable weapon and that our veteran experience and our basketball IQ led to being a very good zone team," Carlisle said. "And, going into this year, we wanted to change our identity. We have always been viewed as a team that can score. And, when Dallas shoots well, they win. But what else were they really great at? There were some things we wanted to become great at, and I believe zone was one of them.

"I felt that we needed to get there defensively. I told the team in camp that the great teams in the NBA are in the Top 10 defensively, and we were 11th entering the year. We knew we had to get higher."

Casey, the coaching staff's "defensive coordinator," worked with Carlisle to devise the Mavs' zone scheme. If playing man-to-man in a tight game, opponents routinely sought to attack against Nowitzki, Terry or Barea. Throwing a fourth-quarter zone change-up at the enemy could negate some of that, perhaps at a crucial possession. And, depending on their division, there were some teams that simply didn't face a zone very often, and would be forced to cope while trying to keep up with Dallas' high-octane offense. But they needed the players to buy in.

"Over all of training camp, we talked about getting into the Top 10 in both categories — offense and defense. And, if we are, we can play for a championship," Kidd recalled. "Historically, that is where the great teams have been to win a championship. We already believed that we had the offense to do it. And when we had Tyson come on board, we had the defense to do it, too."

The zone went from a novelty to a full-fledged option during the Oct. 15 preseason game in Chicago. There, the Mavericks played zone for the entire four-point victory (a rare exhibition overtime game) to try working out the bugs of different situations. It was an unconventional tactic that drove Bulls bloggers crazy but had Cuban's full support.

"It was probably the only time ever (to play zone exclusively) in a NBA game of any kind," Cuban said. "The goal in the preseason was to play zone better than any team ever had, as a way of playing to our team-defense strength."

And Beech knew the Mavericks would find a statistical benefit if they could master zone play.

"We certainly play the most zone of any team, and I am sure we practice more zone than any team, which has a double effect," Beech explained. "Because not only are we good at it on defense, but we also actually are a very good zone team on offense against it, because we see it so much."

How much would zone defense be emphasized in Dallas?

"Most teams won't play five possessions a game and some won't play 50 possessions of zone a year," Beech estimated. "We might play 25 possessions in a game."

It was evolving from a change-up to a full-fledged strategy.

========

The Mavericks had their sellout for Opening Night against the Bobcats, though many of those sold seats at the American Airlines Center sat unused.

Those less interested in the World Series saw a largely forgettable start to the Mavs' season. Nowitzki, sporting the longest hair of his career (held in place with an NBA headband), led the way through an easy 101-86 victory with 28 points and 13 rebounds.

Was Dallas ready? The Mavs jumped to a 16-0 lead from the opening tipoff. They forced 21 turnovers and held Charlotte to 39.7 percent shooting from the field. Kidd dished out 18 assists, including his first official lob to Chandler, who threw down a resounding dunk over former teammate Stephen Jackson. The feral scream that accompanied it had fans murmuring. This new guy wasn't like any Dallas Mavericks center they remembered.

"Our center combo will be great all year," Nowitzki predicted after the Opening Night victory. "Tyson's all over the place."

Splitting the next four games, however, demonstrated the Mavs still had some early kinks to work out. They lost a tight game at home against Memphis (a team that would pose difficulty all season), on a night when Nowitzki's streak of consecutive free throws ended at 82. They trounced the Clippers by 16 points in Los Angeles on Halloween Night, a game in which Kidd scored with a heave from the opposite free-throw line just before the halftime buzzer. Then the Mavs split a home-and-home series with Denver, the road team winning each time.

Carlisle was relatively pleased with the play from his first unit, but the lack of scoring punch from his bench was a concern. With Terry in the starting lineup, it seemed only the diminutive Barea was willing to create shots among the reserves. The coach already was pondering his first lineup change of the season, and his roster was about to see his "stay ready" mantra put into effect.

"I met with Kidd, Dirk and Terry after our game with Denver when we lost at home," Carlisle recalled. "Both of the first two years, we all felt collectively that Jet coming off the bench was best for our team. We had made him a starter because of our slow starts, but we just didn't have the right answer at that point. Inevitably, when Terry starts, his minutes get run up into the high 30s and we have to keep his minutes reasonable so he can maintain his high level of energy throughout the year."

The decision was made to return Terry to his sixth man role, and elevate someone else into the starting lineup. The schedule showed Boston next, so the Mavs would need a capable backcourt defender to hound Celtics sharpshooting guard Ray Allen. DeShawn Stevenson, who had played only two minutes over the first five games of the season, would be given the first chance to join Kidd in the starting backcourt.

"We talked about all sorts of names: Jones, Barea and Stevenson," Carlisle said. "Stevenson's name didn't come up until the end of the meeting. The main reason his name popped up was because we had Ray Allen next, and then maybe we might go with Barea after that. But Stevenson played a great game against Boston, and we stuck with him and rolled with it. That allowed us to bring Jet, Barea, Marion and that group off the bench and that turned out to be a real positive thing for us."

Despite his heavily tattooed appearance, traumatic childhood and scrapes with the law off the court, Stevenson had built a reputation over his 10 NBA seasons for being professional and prepared. He had entered the league straight out of high school in 2000, joining Utah as the 23rd overall pick, and had to grow up fast. By most accounts, he had managed.

"He's a warrior, man, a true warrior," said former Wizards coach Eddie Jordan, who had Stevenson for two seasons in Washington. "He's just a true pro. This is a man's league and he is a man. In the dictionary next to that word, there is a picture of DeShawn Stevenson."

In the opening minutes of his first start, Stevenson made his presence felt by hitting a 3-pointer and then drawing a charging foul against Allen. But this 89-87 home victory over the Celtics proved more of a coming-out party for Chandler.

Facing a marquee opponent known for bruising, physical play would have been enough to whet Chandler's appetite. But this Monday night game also drew a big crowd and held the full attention of a city left disappointed by the Rangers' final loss one week earlier in Game 5 of the World Series. Chandler, it appeared, wanted to put on an extra-impressive show against Kevin Garnett and company.

And so he did. Chandler was a dominant force on both ends of the floor, grabbing rebounds and blocking shots on defense, assaulting the rim on offense, including three dunks in the second period. By halftime, he had 10 points, nine rebounds, two blocks and a devoted new fan base.

Mavericks television announcer Mark Followill spoke for many when he said, "What I love about Chandler is that there is so much emotion and fire and passion after plays like that from him. Nice to see that from the center position."

The Celtics would not go quietly, of course. One of the league's elite teams, Boston knew how to drag an opponent into deep water and see just how badly they would battle for a win. Behind Paul Pierce, Allen and Garnett, what had been a 10-point deficit for the Celtics at halftime had become a six-point lead with six minutes to play. Nowitzki could see clearly what needed to be done, in part because he had finally trimmed his long hair earlier in the day, administering a self-performed buzz cut.

"The girl who cuts my hair was on her honeymoon," Nowitzki explained, "so I just decided to take matters into my own hands."

He handled the closing moments of the game much the same way. Garnett is one of the better defenders in the league, but Nowitzki drove right past him for layups on consecutive possessions, once to his right, once to his left. When Terry chipped in by burying an open 3-pointer, the game was tied 87-87 with 1:13 to play.

Dallas' defense, fortified by Chandler and Marion, made another big stop and got the ball back in Dirk's hands. This time he was guarded by Glen Davis, who backed off a bit, wary of seeing the same drives to the rim that had scorched Garnett. Nowitzki simply pulled up and stuck a 21-foot jumper in Big Baby's eye for the game-winning shot. The Mavericks had scored the final seven points in their 89-87 victory.

"I think what won us this game was our defense," Nowitzki said. "We showed a lot of will. And we collectively came together and said, 'This is *our* game.'"

It was only the sixth game of 82, but it was the type of victory that set imaginations free. It was a playoff-type game against a championship-worthy opponent. It confirmed to the Mavericks that they had both the defensive fortitude and the roster depth to compete against any opponent they would see this season.

"That win was all about will and all about toughness," Carlisle concluded.

It was a heck of a win. Now the Mavericks just needed to find consistency.

5

THE OLD KIDD

(November 2010)

Two weeks into the season, only Boston's Rajon Rondo was averaging more assists per game than Jason Kidd. Just four months shy of his 38th birthday, the Mavericks' point guard clearly was enjoying the addition of Tyson Chandler to his list of passing targets.

Each night, the Mavs burned opponents by running an offensive set in which Chandler would appear to be setting a pick near the free-throw line. Instead, the big man would make an athletic launch toward the basket, with Kidd tossing a lob toward his destination. Chandler could leap like no Dallas center before him, and his merciless assaults on the rim had fans roaring with approval.

Kidd was starting his 17th pro season with great energy and enthusiasm. But surely most fans would need a longer sample before becoming convinced he could be the oldest starting point guard to win an NBA title. Ron Harper had started at point for the 2000 Lakers at age 36. But alongside Shaq and Kobe, Harper wasn't asked to do the same heavy lifting as the Mavericks' owner, GM and coach were asking of Kidd.

With each postseason disappointment, public discontent with the Mavericks' personnel decisions grew. Donnie Nelson may have been the genius to predict greatness from Nowitzki and Nash, but he still wasn't a GM with a championship ring.

Nelson is a basketball lifer. A man whose career door had been opened by his legendary father, Donnie disparagingly says of himself, "I'd be a high school coach somewhere if it wasn't for Dad." Don't believe that for a second. Donnie started as a Milwaukee scout in 1984 while his dad coached the Bucks. He followed his father to Golden State, where he was his father's assistant for eight seasons. He then struck out on his own, serving as an assistant coach with the Phoenix Suns for three seasons.

When Don Nelson took the GM job in Dallas in early 1997, he called his son to help with the massive Mavericks rebuilding project. "When a guy who has helped you have a career says he needs you," Donnie said, "you come."

The Nelsons became the faces of the franchise, partly because Dallas had few players that captured anyone's imagination. They survived the ownership transfer to Cuban in January 2000, and before long were building competitive and winning teams. But Don Nelson, a man who never had much use for authority, began developing friction with Cuban as the years went on.

It started to become problematic in 2003, when during the Western Conference finals against San Antonio, Nowitzki suffered a knee injury early in the series and the franchise chiefs disagreed on whether their star player should try to play through it. Cuban, after hearing from team doctors, thought that if Dirk felt ok, he could try to play. Nelson didn't want Nowitzki playing hurt, arguing it was too big a gamble with the star's future.

To Nelson, the doctors' opinions were just that — opinions. As a player himself in this league, he knew there were times when medical staff members advocated for the desires of the team (their employers), not necessarily for the player to enjoy a longer and healthier career. Nelson and Cuban both felt they were in the right, and disagreed sharply with the other.

Nelson won the battle (Dirk did not play again that postseason), but lost the series. The dispute also seemed to fracture Nellie's relationship with his boss. It would take nearly two more full seasons before the actual divorce (this split was far more complicated than over just a single incident). But when Don Nelson left the Mavs, Donnie had a difficult decision to make. He decided to remain the team's general manager.

Donnie had become one of the most well-respected personnel minds in basketball. Many credit him with spearheading the NBA's recent push into the worldwide talent pool. His passport certainly could rival the stamp count of any seasoned world traveler. He is credited with finding hidden gems around the globe, and he parted long ago from his father's shadow. If the Mavericks ever decided to cut ties with Donnie (and it is believed that he has always worked without a contract), it would take roughly five minutes for another franchise to snap him up.

Still, the inability to bring home a title hung over Cuban, Donnie and the entire Mavericks franchise like a dark cloud. More than one newspaper columnist sought to put Donnie on the hot seat in the summer of 2010. Some second-guessing of decisions dated all the way back to the draft night in 1998, when the Nelsons rolled the dice on Nowitzki even though Kansas star Paul Pierce was still on the board. Once Pierce won a ring with the 2008 Celtics, those comparisons were revived. That Pierce had a ring and Nowitzki didn't seemed to have more to do with Allen and Garnett joining Boston than anything Dirk was doing wrong. But logic doesn't always apply in sports debates.

One of Donnie's other critical decisions, however, wasn't considered controversial so much as simply branded a failure: The February 2008 deal that brought Kidd back to Dallas.

Kidd's epic tale in Dallas began when the Mavs made the Cal point guard the second overall pick of the 1994 draft, after Purdue's Glenn Robinson (No. 1 to Milwaukee) and ahead of Duke's Grant Hill (No. 3 to Detroit). Kidd essentially was asked at age 21 to save a franchise in desperate need of saving.

The next 2½ years were full of both promise and headaches. Kidd shared NBA Rookie of the Year honors with Hill in 1995, and the following season became the first Mavericks player to start an All-Star Game. But he (and his mostly young teammates) lacked the maturity to handle everything coming his way as an instant NBA celebrity with a $54 million contract. There were off-court transgressions, a missed practice, personality and ego-driven clashes with teammate Jim Jackson and then-coach Jim Cleamons. The "Three J's" began to unravel, and in December 1996, the club decided Kidd needed to go. He was exiled to Phoenix as the stunned centerpiece of a seven-player trade on the day after Christmas.

Ross Perot Jr. had bought the team from longtime owner Don Carter in May 1996, and quickly appointed one of his trusted business assistants, Frank Zaccanelli, to run basketball operations until they got around to hiring a full-time general manager. Don Nelson wasn't hired until February 1997, two months after Kidd was jettisoned. It was Zaccanelli who declared on the day of the trade, "Jason isn't the guy who could take us to the next level. Management wasn't comfortable putting the franchise in his hands."

Eyebrows were raised around the league at the deal, and the perceived lack of experienced basketball brainpower behind it. But once the deal is done, there is no going back.

Kidd spent 4½ years in Phoenix, then nearly seven seasons in New Jersey, where he played point guard at an elite level. During that stretch, he went to eight of 11 All-Star Games and was voted to the All-NBA first team five times. He led the Nets to back-to-back NBA Finals appearances in 2002 and 2003, but his team was beaten handily by the Lakers and Spurs, respectively.

Kidd had matured, improved the jump shot that so often had been ridiculed earlier in his career, and from about 1999-2005 set the industry standard for point guard play. By that time, though, he was 32, an age when most point guards in league history begin their inevitable decline.

In Dallas, after the heartbreak of the 2006 Finals and the sickening upset loss to Golden State a year later, there was plenty of internal belief that the team was just not getting strong enough play when it mattered from its young backcourt. Josh Howard and Devin Harris were considered bright talents, but were struggling with the NBA growth curve. Neither could be categorized as a failure, but both were being asked to step into gigantic situations and deliver on the same level as Nowitzki and Terry. The Mavericks lacked an experienced field general, and the former point guard coaching the team (Avery Johnson) was running out of patience.

"We didn't have leadership from the point in 2006," Donnie admitted. "In 2006, we had two scoring guards (Terry and Harris) who were doing their best at taking a crack at the point guard position. But it was, 'Get the ball over half-court and get the ball to Dirk.'"

Miami caught on quickly during the 2006 Finals. The Heat could marshall all defensive resources against Nowitzki and Terry in closely contested games (Games 3, 5, and 6), because Howard, Harris and centers Dampier or DeSagana Diop tended to disappear at crunch time. Before long, the reliable Dallas offense had been choked into submission.

In fairness, Harris was just a pup and Howard had many big moments earlier in games. But late in the fourth period, when postseason games are usually won, Nowitzki and Terry were "playing offense two-on-five," according to one senior team official.

The Mavericks' internal discussions eventually led to trade talks during the 2008 All-Star break. Dallas wanted a veteran point guard who could remain composed late in key games. Kidd was targeted, both for his high basketball I.Q. at the position and for the elite-level defense he could still flash, even at 35. Kidd's stay in New Jersey was rumored to be ending soon, as he didn't seem to care for the team's direction. Kidd had nearly been dealt to the Lakers in the summer of 2007, but L.A. refused to include Andrew Bynum in a deal. The Mavs and Nets couldn't seem to settle on a deal, but Dallas was determined to bring Kidd home to help Nowitzki, before either of their windows closed for good.

The first attempt was quashed when Dallas' Devean George refused to waive his no-trade clause. A second attempt was rejected by the league after Jerry Stackhouse said publicly that he planned to return to Dallas after New Jersey bought him out of his deal (a violation of league policy). Finally, six days after the first attempted trade was reported, the Mavericks and Nets completed a mammoth 10-player deal. For Kidd, Malik Allen and Antoine Wright, the Mavs gave up Harris, Diop, Trenton Hassell, Maurice Ager, the retired Keith Van Horn (for salary cap purposes, a move that netted Van Horn a nice payday), their first-round picks in the 2008 and 2010 drafts and $3 million.

The staggering price was compared locally (and not favorably) to the Dallas Cowboys' 1989 trade of running back Herschel Walker to Minnesota. Involving 18 players and draft picks, that transaction (still the biggest in NFL history) supplemented the Cowboys' franchise for years in exchange for one aging player whom the Vikings had deluded themselves into thinking was the final piece of their Super Bowl puzzle.

Those who had been criticizing the play of Harris now howled that he was only 24 and seemed to have a tremendous future ahead. And to include two first-round picks for a point guard in his mid-30s? Donnie Nelson and Cuban must have lost their minds.

Opinions of the trade went from bad to worse in the 2008 playoffs a couple months later. The Mavericks drew the up-and-coming New Orleans Hornets, pitting Kidd against Chris Paul, one of the brightest young point guards in the league. New Orleans took the series in five games, with Paul badly outplaying Kidd. CP3, as Paul was known (initials and his uniform number), blew past Kidd to average 25 points and 12 assists during the series.

There were enough humiliations taking place on the court, but the Mavs faced them off the court as well.

On the morning of Game 3 (the only game Dallas would win), Josh Howard created a stir by admitting on a radio show that he smoked marijuana in the offseason. Two days later, after a crushing Game 4 loss at home, Howard went through with his birthday party plans at a Dallas nightclub, oblivious to how that might appear.

Johnson was furious The coach kicked the entire team out of their practice before Game 5 in an effort to send a clear message how angry he was at their apparent lack of judgment and accountability to and for each other. The team responded by staging a "players only" practice later in the day. But the damage was done and the season ended the next night in New Orleans. It was second consecutive first-round exit since the collapse in the 2006 Final, and for Cuban it signaled the end of the "Avery Era." Kidd's effectiveness, it seemed, had been hampered by Johnson's tight reins and insistence on calling plays from the sideline each possession, rather placing more of the responsibility on Kidd. Communication problems between the coach and point guard weren't the only reasons for the postseason flameout, but made the decision to fire Johnson easier.

Still, it appeared the Mavericks had rolled the dice and lost big, getting soundly beaten in a trade involving Kidd for the second time. Meanwhile, Nash had won two league MVP awards since the Mavs' decision to let him return to Phoenix as a free agent after the 2004 season. The team seemed to be getting worse, not better, and hopes of redemption for the 2006 title that got away seemed to be vanishing.

Sometimes, things can go from bad to worse.

The Mavericks made their first post-trade visit to New Jersey the next season, on Dec. 19, 2008. Kidd, now closing in on his 36th birthday, received an appreciative ovation before the game. But the real cheering from Nets fans started as Harris torched his former team for 41 points to lead a 121-97 rout of Dallas.

It was already the eighth time in the young season that Harris had scored at least 30 points, and by the fourth quarter, fans were serenading the visitors with a chant of, "Thank You, Cuban!"

A few months later, in April 2009, Dallas did finally win another playoff series. The arch-nemesis San Antonio Spurs were without injured scorer Manu Ginobili for the first-round series, and the Mavericks prevailed in five games. Kidd ran the offense well, but his inability to contain Spurs point guard Tony Parker made it appear his days as an elite defender were over. It was becoming clear that Kidd was not able to keep up with the water bug-type point guards anymore.

However, we would learn later that Kidd could still defend quite well against elite scorers at the shooting guard and small forward spots.

A five-game loss to Denver in the second round ended another Mavs season, and Kidd entered the summer of 2009 needing a new contract. The Mavs had gone 6-9 in postseason games and won one playoff series in the 15 months since reacquiring Kidd. Now they had to decide whether to sign him for three more years (through nearly his 40th birthday) at $25 million, or gamble on finding another point guard before the 2009-10 season.

"Once both sides thought the numbers were fair, I don't think there was any question we would bring him back," said Mavericks assistant GM Keith Grant. "He is still going to play significant minutes. Players love playing with him. And he still delivers the ball right on the spot, and there is a lot to be said for that. I don't think it was that hard of a decision. We were comfortable with him. Very comfortable."

However they reconciled the deal, the Mavericks were setting sail bravely ahead with Kidd still running the team. He was exceptionally conditioned and committed to staying at the top of his game, but the way Paul and Parker had exposed him in the playoffs was not fueling much championship optimism amongst fans. And when the Spurs again eliminated the Mavericks in the first round of the 2010 playoffs, 4-2, the frustration level reached a boil. They were just too old and incomplete. And if the Mavericks couldn't win in the playoffs when Kidd was 35, 36, or 37, how would things improve when he turns 38 or 39?

From 2008-10, Kidd played in 21 playoff games for the Mavericks. In those games, the man who had made playoff triple-doubles a regular feat (he had 11, second-most in history to Magic Johnson's 30) only eclipsed 10 assists once and only grabbed 10 rebounds twice. Forget triple-doubles; Kidd managed only two *double*-doubles in those three playoff runs. And, most damning of all, the Mavs went 8-13 in those 21 playoff games with Kidd at the helm.

Kidd seemed determined to prove he wasn't done as the 2010-11 season began. He set a torrid tone on Opening Night when he dished 18 assists against the Bobcats. Less than three weeks later, Kidd had eight assists in a 99-90 victory over Philadelphia, joining John Stockton as the only players in history with at least 11,000 career assists. Fittingly, Kidd reached the milestone on a back-door lob to his new buddy Chandler.

Coming on the heels of a road win in Memphis, the victory over the Sixers improved the Mavericks to 6-2. The team was starting to find its stride, but the schedule was about to get tougher.

New Orleans was the last unbeaten team in the league, but Dallas ended that distinction by winning the first of a home-and-home set with the Hornets. A home loss to Chicago and a win at Atlanta left the Mavs at 8-4, and staring down the barrel of four games in five nights during Thanksgiving Week. Included in that gantlet were "showdown" games Wednesday in Oklahoma City and Friday in San Antonio (the division-leading Spurs had started 13-1). Then, a visit from the league's marquee team, the Miami Heat, Saturday night in Dallas.

Nowitzki had added even more moves to his arsenal during the off-season, and was being increasingly described as "unguardable." The Pistons would not argue, as Dirk hung 42 on them to start the week with an 88-84 victory over Detroit. He was second in the league in scoring, exciting a national television audience that would tune in to watch him the next night battling the league's top scorer, Kevin Durant, in Oklahoma City.

This game on Thanksgiving Eve proved to be a preview of the Western Conference finals in more ways than one. The Thunder are loaded with young talent, but still must learn the maturity and poise needed to execute efficiently at crunch time. Oklahoma City led 80-73 with seven minutes left when Nowitzki took over, scoring seven points in two possessions. In just 28 seconds, Dirk erased the entire deficit himself, burying two 3-point shots and a free throw after being fouled on the second deep strike.

The Mavs wound up amassing a 36-point fourth quarter to score a big road win, 111-103. Nowitzki outscored Durant, 34-32. And Chandler particularly enjoyed torturing the team that had doubted his health and rejected his trade two years earlier, finishing with 17 points and 18 boards.

With that victory, the Mavs seemed to first find their real groove, and the belief that they now had an elite-level defense to go with their long-elite offense. They had an effective zone defense, a dynamic new center, more depth than they had ever enjoyed, and they were starting to raise eyebrows around the league. The statistic that pleased Carlisle the most was that the Mavericks ranked first in the league in fourth-quarter defense, limiting opponents to just 21.6 points per game in the final period.

"We really believe in each other as a team," Carlisle said after the Oklahoma City game. "There is nothing so far this year that has gotten us down."

But that belief was about to be sorely tested before week's end.

6

THE ROLL THROUGH
THE HOLIDAYS

(Nov. 26-Dec. 26, 2010)

The day after Thanksgiving, the Mavericks generated headlines for all the wrong reasons. During the morning shootaround in San Antonio, Coach Rick Carlisle ordered Brendan Haywood off the court, out of the team hotel and to catch a flight back to Dallas. The Mavs would face the rival Spurs that night without him.

Witnesses to the incident said Carlisle was rankled by Haywood's poor body language that morning, and admonished the center to show more effort. Haywood's reply sent Carlisle through the roof.

To suggest their shouting match sprung from nowhere would be to ignore the simmering resentment Haywood felt. Serving as a backup to another center, even one so clearly effective as Chandler, was not what Haywood felt he had been promised in July. The expectations Haywood had when he signed his new deal had disappeared with surprising suddenness. But while the team might appreciate a competitive nature and each individual's desire to play, there are boundaries that cannot be crossed. Carlisle demanded effort from everyone, and felt Haywood's insubordination deserved a one-day suspension. Cuban and Donnie Nelson backed his decision.

The swift and severe punishment harkened back to Carlisle's message on the first day of training camp: There would be no bickering or complaining about roles, only role acceptance. No one's personal agenda would come before the team's ultimate goal.

Haywood wasn't the only veteran player with cause to complain or feel slighted by reduced minutes. But he made the mistake of being the first to flaunt his discontent. Carlisle was not about to let such conflicts become typical and disrupt the team chemistry being developed, so Haywood was made a bit of a public example. It may not have been a big deal by some standards, as tempers flare every season, but Carlisle's response set the tone for the squad. Carlisle, Cuban and Donnie Nelson would determine roles; the players needed to simply play.

In Haywood's absence, the Mavericks closed ranks and turned their attention to ending the first-place Spurs' 12-game winning streak.

Dallas' rivalry with San Antonio cannot be overstated. The Spurs' franchise has roots in Dallas, starting there as the Dallas Chaparrals of the old American Basketball Association. The ABA team moved to San Antonio as the Spurs in 1974, then merged into the NBA in 1976-77. After 34 seasons, the Spurs could boast of 30 playoff appearances, 16 division titles (a 17th was on the way), and an impressive 4-0 record when reaching the NBA Finals.

That San Antonio's four world championships were won over the past 12 years, when Nowitzki was leading the Mavericks and Tim Duncan the Spurs, was lost on no one. Meetings between the rivals are always heated and intense, and the disdain the opposing players and fan bases have for each other is genuine. The teams already had collided in the playoffs five times since 2001, with the Spurs winning three of those series.

On this night, the teams squared off and battled in classic form. Nowitzki continued his week of spectacular play, hitting 12 of 14 shots en route to 26 points. Chandler served notice with a 19-point, eight-rebound effort against the Spurs' big men. Seldom-used Ian Mahinmi and Alexis Ajinca combined for 17 serviceable minutes backing up Chandler in Haywood's absence. And on the strength of a 14-2 run in the game's final five minutes, the visiting Mavericks snapped the Spurs' 12-game winning streak, 103-94.

Haywood's one-game suspension for a "violation of team rules" was announced by the Mavericks about an hour before tipoff. After the game, Carlisle remained mum on the situation, other than to say, "Everyone is held to a high level of accountability." He did, however, insist by the next day that Haywood's punishment was over and dealt with. Despite the morning drama, the 11-4 Mavericks returned home officially on a roll.

========

There never has been an owner in professional sports quite like Mark Cuban. More than a decade after purchasing the Mavericks, he has mellowed on several fronts, but is still a man who wears his heart on his sleeve.

He is hard-driving and obsessed with beating his competition. He is willing to speak his mind regardless of whether that makes things easier or more difficult for himself or his team. He seems never to sleep, and rarely misses anything said or written about him or his team. And occasionally, it seems he says things just to make everyone's day a little more interesting.

It was only a matter of time before Cuban would say something about the Miami Heat.

The Heat became the most polarizing team in the NBA in the summer of 2010, maneuvering (or being maneuvered toward) a free-agent talent haul never before seen. When the dust settled and LeBron James had finished announcing "The Decision" of where he would play on live television, Miami had assembled a Super Friends trio of James, Dwyane Wade and Chris Bosh to start what surely would be a cascade of championships.

The Mavericks had courted James and the others, but lacked the cap space to truly contend for big signatures, despite the hometown discount they received in re-signing Nowitzki. It seemed James, Wade and the Dallas-born Bosh were doing their own team engineering, whether the idea came to them that week or while winning a gold medal for Team USA at the 2008 Olympics in Beijing (along with Kidd). In the end, all that mattered was that James had traded Cleveland for South Beach to attempt a player-controlled, ready-made dynasty.

No one begrudged the players their collectively bargained free agent right to sign where they chose, but many resented the manner in which they did it. The Heat adhered to league rules in assembling their team, but that didn't mean other teams or fans had to like it.

The last straw was probably the over-the-top rally the Heat staged in July after the trio signed. It was the kind of celebration normally reserved for after a title was won. James, Wade and Bosh danced inside American Airlines Arena under falling confetti and a sign that boldly proclaimed "Yes We Did," before even running through their first practice as Miami teammates. James played to the South Florida crowd by saying they had come to win "not one, not two, not three, not four, not five, not six, not seven" championships. The entire production was televised live, and the rest of the NBA was watching and taking mental notes.

Like others, Cuban seemed bothered by James leaving a Cavaliers franchise that had shown him so much love. He felt for Cleveland's fans, city and owner. Perhaps he imagined how gutting it would be for a franchise to lose its face, for instance if Dirk had taken the money and run off to Los Angeles or New York. It would take years for an organization to recover. And while a free agent is, by definition, "free," what happened to Cleveland just didn't seem right. And while much of the NBA would be rooting for Miami to fail, few would say so in front of open microphones.

Cuban, however, wasn't bashful when asked about Miami's 8-7 start in a November interview with ESPN Radio's Ben and Skin:

"Hallelujah, boys, is that great or what?" Cuban cackled. "How cool is that? Now, they could still turn it around and win out for all that matters, but you're starting to see some of the problems. Any team with a strong big guy that can score, they're getting abused by. They just don't have size to battle. They have the fewest points in the paint of any team.

"My buddy (Cavaliers owner) Dan Gilbert is smiling all the way, too. Again, it's early in the season and you never quite know how it's going to play out. But, how glorious."

The Heat's Nov. 27 visit to Dallas came at a time when the Mavericks were mowing down everyone in their path. Miami, on the other hand, was playing like a team that never had played together — for obvious reasons. There were new faces up and down Heat coach Eric Spoelstra's roster, yet only three players seemed worthy of much salary and notoriety. But while the growing pains lingered, the league was not showing mercy. The Heat had lost seven of 16 games as they arrived in Dallas.

The arena was buzzing for what seemed a special game among the scheduled 82. Dallas strained to a 51-49 lead at the half but then stepped up the pressure. The Heat missed their first 10 shots of the second half as Kidd pushed the Mavs on a 13-0 scoring blitz. Kidd was dominating the game while hardly scoring, controlling the ball and distributing it where needed to guide his team to a steady stream of easy baskets. The third-quarter play-by-play sheet had the 37-year-old point guard's fingerprints all over it:

• Chandler dunk (Assist to Kidd), 53-49

- Nowitzki layup (Assist to Kidd), 57-49
- Butler layup (Assist to Kidd), 61-49
- Butler 3-PT shot (Assist to Kidd), 64-49

In just four minutes, a two-point halftime lead had swollen to 15 and the game was won. Kidd had 13 assists and eight defensive rebounds, only one field goal. At 6-foot-4, Kidd could take defensive rebounds as well as any point guard in history, then dart the other direction to carve opponents up with his superior court vision and passing ability. Miami's three point guards (Carlos Arroyo, Mario Chalmers and Eddie House) combined for three assists in their 52 aggregate minutes on the floor.

After the final whistle blew on the Mavs' 106-95 victory, the Heat closed their locker room for a players-only meeting. They were 9-8, including just 2-7 against opponents with winning records. The Mavs were 12-4, off to the second-best start in Dallas history. In 108 instances of being scheduled to play four games in five nights, this was only the third time the Mavericks had swept all four games. And this time, the dance card included league heavyweights Oklahoma City, San Antonio and Miami.

Cuban again was asked about the team Miami had assembled.

"If Miami had Jason Kidd, there would be no problems whatsoever," Cuban said. "Because you'd have somebody who'd make sure everybody got the ball where and when and how they wanted it, and would do the math in his head to make sure they got the ball enough and could deal with any criticisms directly from the guys and could be a liaison for the coach. That just shows you the power of a veteran, Hall of Fame player who is still in his prime like Jason Kidd."

Also significant in the Miami game was the play of Mavs forward Caron Butler, who scored a team-high 23 points against the Heat. Butler had been one of the slower projects to come around in the first month finding his role in the team. He had averaged at least 19 points a game for three of his 4½ seasons in Washington. Now, sharing minutes with Shawn Marion, it was not always easy for either to feel comfortable.

Butler and Marion had spent much of the summer together, working out in Chicago with the same trainer and participating in each other's charity functions. At this point of their careers, each wanted to be part of something special and make a run for the title. It became almost comical how often Marion would work the phrases "I am here to win" and "I just want a ring" into his interviews. He certainly was saying all the right things. Was this their best chance at winning a title? If the first chunk of the season was any indication, the answer was pretty clear as they combined for nearly 30 points and eight rebounds a game sharing the forward position opposite Nowitzki.

As the winning streak continued, reaching seven through home wins over Houston and Minnesota, a regular rotation began to crystallize. The Mavericks' starting unit of Nowitzki, Chandler, Butler, Stevenson and Kidd would play together for about seven minutes. At the 5:00 mark in the first and third quarters, Nowitzki and Stevenson would be replaced by Marion and Terry. A few minutes later, Haywood would replace Chandler at center. Shortly before the quarters ended, Nowitzki would return with J.J. Barea (replacing Butler and Kidd), and Marion would slide from power forward to small forward.

Carlisle would almost always stick with Nowitzki, Chandler, Terry and Kidd in the final minutes of each half, and decide by feel whether to come back with Butler at that point or stay with Marion.

Giving Nowitzki the earliest rest among the starters and then having him enter in tandem with Barea was a big discovery for the coaching staff. The statistical analysis compiled by Roland Beech had shown that combination to be far more effective than Barea entering games by himself. When Nowitzki and Barea teamed to run a simple high pick-and-roll, defenders were usually reluctant to leave the 7-footer, providing Barea quick entry points to the basket. This jump-started the little guard's season.

Barea is a rare type of backup player in that he needs to be carefully placed to be effective. When he is, he can single-handedly win a game or (as Lakers coach Phil Jackson would find out) perhaps turn an entire series. But if not used judiciously, Barea can be exposed by the league's bigger guards. Because he is barely 5-foot-10, it is not uncommon for opponents to go out of their way to attack Barea. But the Puerto Rican guard is skilled at getting under an opponent's skin and then baiting them into a charge. In the entire NBA, only one player (Phoenix's Grant Hill) drew more offensive fouls last season than Barea.

Here in early December, however, Barea was suffering through one of the worst shooting slumps of his career. In fact, for the first two months of the season, Barea ranked as the second-worst 3-point shooter in the NBA, and this certainly had the coaches concerned. Some believed he was placing excessive pressure on himself due to his upcoming free agency. But Barea would have the chance to play his way out of the slump, in part because Beaubois had suffered a setback in his rehabilitation and remained out indefinitely with his broken foot.

Since replacing Terry with Stevenson in the starting lineup, the Mavs had won 11 of 13 when they arrived in Utah for a Dec. 3 game.

Longtime Jazz coach Jerry Sloan told the Salt Lake Tribune that morning what many were noticing about Dallas' squad:

"They have all veteran players on their team," Sloan said. "They've got guys who know what they are doing. They just don't make many mistakes. You look at their team — the whole team, the whole picture, the starters and the guys off the bench — and they have two teams that are very good. That is probably about as good as you will see in this league."

Sloan's team had won seven in a row, but was held to 38 percent shooting that night and lost, 93-81. Dallas was making a habit of slamming the brakes on hot teams and their streaks. Already, the Mavs had stopped the winning streaks of Boston (five games), New Orleans (eight games), Oklahoma City (five games), San Antonio (12 games) and now Utah.

"We feel we can beat anybody, anywhere," Butler said after the game.

And after Dallas erased a five-point deficit in the final two minutes to win the next night in Sacramento (105-103), Butler's team had improved to 16-4. The Mavs' winning streak was up to nine, and counting.

========

Equipment manager Al Whitley was in the Mavericks' locker room, readying gear for the morning practice, when reserve forward Brian Cardinal approached, smiling broadly.

"We won our 16th game, right?" Cardinal asked.

Whitley, confused a bit by the purpose of the question, answered, "Yes."

Cardinal smiled, pumped his fist, and went on his way.

It took Whitley a few moments to realize the significance of the Mavs' Dec. 4 victory total to Cardinal. But 16 wins had eclipsed the 15 games won the entire previous season by Minnesota, where Cardinal had played the past two seasons. The kid was just giddy to be playing on a winner.

Cardinal also felt his role on the team entailed more than just playing.

"It's such a long season and an emotional grind, that if you can't laugh at yourself or each other, it is going to be painful," Cardinal said. "I took it upon myself to not be guarded and to lighten up the room. Whether it was Dirk's hoop earring (seen in pictures from his rookie season) or Tyson's tight pants or someone getting dunked on, nothing was off-limits. My wife tells me I have a gift for delivering lines where others would get punched in the mouth. It was one of my roles on the team — to have fun and bring light to the room."

The comedy inside the Mavericks' locker room helped this team of professional basketball players grow into a group of guys who genuinely enjoyed spending time together. Those who dished out the good-natured barbs would receive plenty of return fire.

"We all had our flaws," Cardinal said. "I am bald. We made fun of J.J. because he is little. He knows he is little, but we still all had fun with it. Caron bought him a "Little People" truck and put it over his locker. And I went and got J.J.'s bobble-head doll and put him behind the wheel in the truck and everyone enjoyed that quite a bit. We just had a great time in there."

The giddiness continued as the Mavs' winning streak grew from nine consecutive games to 12 over the next four days. During another successful homestand, Dallas took down Golden State (despite Chandler out with a stomach illness), New Jersey and Utah.

"I don't think the team really cares about the win streak," Carlisle said after the 103-97 victory over the Jazz. "Our core guys that have been here a long time, they've been on streaks a lot longer than this. These guys won 17 in a row one year (2007). That part of it isn't a novelty to our team. We're a veteran team and we're trying to become a great team."

A 13th consecutive win seemed nearly in the bag on Dec. 13, when Milwaukee came to town and fell 20 points behind in the second quarter. The Mavs had let a 25-point lead slip away in the previous game before rallying to beat Utah. This time, they let the Bucks erase a big deficit but couldn't get the lead back, losing a 103-99 stunner at home. It was only the third road win of the season for the mediocre Bucks.

There was one interesting footnote, however. This marked the fifth time in Bucks history the team had ended an opponent's winning streak of 12 games or more. It had happened previously against the 1972 Lakers, the 1974 Celtics, the 1983 Philadelphia 76ers and the 2007 Spurs. Each of those teams went on to win the NBA championship that year.

========

At 19-5 on Dec. 14, the Mavericks just wanted to get to Christmas on another tear. They had lost once since Nov. 19, and were as confident and as deep as any Dallas team in memory. Experienced, too, of course. But despite a roster with more than 100 combined seasons of

NBA experience, there wasn't a single Mavericks player who had ever won an NBA championship ring.

Funny thing about age on sports teams. If the team is winning, it's the "veteran experience" that often is lauded. If the team is losing, the criticism is that the same players have gotten too old. The Mavericks had not mounted a serious title challenge since 2006. Despite this season's promising start, the notion this team could actually get better as it grew from old to older wouldn't have great support.

But the Mavericks kept going about their business. They closed out their homestand with relatively routine victories over Portland and Phoenix, the latter game made easier when Nash collided with Chandler chasing a loose ball in the first quarter. Nash temporarily lost feeling in his extremities because of a neck injury and could not continue.

All that remained between the Mavericks and their Christmas break was a two-game road trip to Florida, where they would face the Miami Heat and Orlando Magic on back-to-back nights.

The Heat were a different team than the disorganized unit Dallas had beaten two days after Thanksgiving. Since that loss to the Mavericks, and the players-only meeting that followed, Miami had reeled off 12 consecutive victories. The Heat (21-8) weren't just beating opponents, they were embarrassing them. Only two of their victories during the streak were by fewer than 10 points, and five times they had won by at least 20.

As the Mavericks disembarked from their team bus within the bowels of Miami's American Airlines Arena, most of the traveling party went down a hallway to the visitors' locker room. Terry went in a different direction. He had his video camera rolling and marched right out to the court, revisiting the crime scene like a CSI investigator.

It had been five years since the humiliating collapse here in the 2006 Finals, but to Terry the wound was still just as deep and fresh. He felt compelled to record another walk out to the empty arena floor and panned his lens up, zooming in on the Heat's 2006 world championship banner. It featured the Larry O'Brien trophy, just like Jet's right bicep.

A couple of hours later, the game was a brutal street fight. Each team went on several double-digit scoring runs, only to get counterpunched by the other. With 2:45 left in the first half, however, came a sequence that would make Carlisle nauseous.

It began with Miami's Chris Bosh missing a 20-foot shot. The rebound was grabbed by Mike Miller, who passed to Mario Chalmers for a 3-point attempt. Chalmers missed, but another long rebound caromed out to Miller. He found Dwyane Wade, who missed a 3-point try from the top of the arc. That rebound was grabbed by Bosh at the free-throw line. The ball was kicked back out to Miller, but his 3-point attempt glanced off the front of the rim and was rebounded by Chalmers. He found Wade slashing to the basket, but Wade's reverse layup missed and bounced right back into his hands. Bosh took a pass, missed a 10-footer, and Heat center Joel Anthony rebounded. Anthony found Miller, who missed his second 3-pointer of the possession, but Chalmers rebounded.

Chalmers finally buried a three, ending a 52-second possession that included eight shots and seven offensive rebounds. Talk about demoralizing. Most teams are annoyed by surrendering more than 10 offensive rebounds in a game, never mind seven in a single possession. The long fight for points gave Miami a 42-39 lead with 1:53 left, and the Heat took a one-point lead into halftime.

Miami had gotten little from LeBron James in the first half. The two-time league MVP had picked up three early fouls, played just 12 minutes and had not scored. However, despite his inspirational pregame filmmaking, Terry also failed to contribute. He was 0 for 5 from the floor and scoreless through the first three periods. Speaking to the team at halftime, Carlisle noted acidly that the Mavs were only down one point, even though Terry was "still at the hotel."

But shooting at the East end of the floor — under that 2006 championship banner — jarred Terry back to life in the final period. He scored all 19 of his points in the final 11 minutes, erasing a five-point Miami lead. Terry took over the game, hitting 6 of 10 shots in the final period while the rest of the Mavs went 3 of 10 (including Nowitzki's 0 for 5). Miami cut the Dallas lead to one point four times in the final 6:27, but the Mavs never relinquished it, winning 98-96.

Statistics showed NBA teams trailing at the end of three quarters were coming back to win only 19 percent of the time. Pulling games out of the fire late, especially against elite teams on the road, was something this Mavericks unit was doing better than any Dallas team before it. They had now trailed after three quarters eight times, but were 6-2 in those games.

The next night brought another impressive road win, a 105-99 triumph in Orlando. Nowitzki scored 17, notable because that ran his career scoring total to 21,798 points, moving him past Hall of Famer Larry Bird into 25th place on the all-time list.

That accomplishment seemed to resonate with Nowitzki, a longtime admirer of Bird. Carlisle, a teammate of Bird's in Boston and the first head coach hired by Bird in Indiana, had presented Nowitzki with a signed jersey from "Larry Legend" in June 2008, when as the newly hired Mavs coach he visited his star player in Germany. Bird wrote, "To Dirk, Best Wishes to a Great Player," then signed his autograph. This was not just any jersey, either. It was Bird's actual practice jersey from the 1986 season that Carlisle had kept for himself for years. The gesture was treasured by Nowitzki, and was one of the few sports artifacts Dirk displays at his Dallas home. This scoring milestone meant a bit more than the dozens of others Nowitzki had passed.

The Mavs celebrated Christmas with records of 23-5 overall and 10-1 on the road. The only teams with better overall records were San Antonio and Boston, teams Dallas already had defeated. Optimism and holiday spirited abounded on the flight back to Love Field.

But when the season resumed after the holiday, many of the Mavericks' smiles would quickly disappear.

7

THE INJURIES

(Dec. 27, 2010-Jan. 17, 2011)

Two days after Christmas, the Mavericks headed back to Oklahoma City, without their head coach.

Carlisle underwent arthroscopic knee surgery three days before Christmas, and would require a little more time to mend before joining the team. Assistant Dwane Casey, himself a head coach of 122 games in Minnesota before joining Carlisle's staff, took the reins for this trip against the young and talented Thunder.

Things were going along nicely, the Mavs leading 39-36 with 9:10 left in the second quarter, when the team was forced to collectively hold its breath.

Nowitzki worked one of his familiar post moves from the left side, hitting a 13-foot jumper after his pump fake drew a flying foul from Serge Ibaka. As Nowitzki landed, his right foot was caught awkwardly beneath him, and the torque of the landing sprained the capsule behind his right knee. Nowitzki limped to the line to make his awarded free throw, then exited the game for good.

Nowitzki's fans and teammates had become accustomed over the years to seeing the big German go down with myriad ankle and leg injuries that usually appeared worse than they proved to be. With the help of trainer Casey Smith, Nowitzki almost always recovered quickly.

In fact, since the 2001-02 season, nine ankle sprains of various degrees had forced Nowitzki to miss just 16 games. So it wasn't completely surprising that concerned teammates found him smiling on the trainer's table at halftime.

"He told us, 'No problem. You guys got this,'" Terry said.

Dirk was partly right. Butler scored 21 points and Marion stepped up with 20 points and nine rebounds off the bench as the Mavs rolled to a 103-93 victory in Nowitzki's absence. But there was a problem. Though X-rays revealed no fracture, the MRI exam of Dirk's knee the next morning showed a sprain severe enough to sideline him indefinitely. It was then that Nowitzki admitted the knee had already been bothering him for about two weeks.

"So maybe that's why it gave in a little bit," he told reporters. "Hopefully, I'll be back in action soon."

Until then, it would be up to Marion to prove the Mavericks' depth was the strength they thought it was.

Marion had completely reworked his game since averaging nearly 20 points a night and 270 3-point attempts per season as part of coach Mike D'Antoni's running-and-gunning Phoenix Suns squads from 2003-08. He had become a defensive stalwart who, during this season, would join Julius Erving, Hakeem Olajuwon, Karl Malone and Kevin Garnett as the only five players in NBA history to amass at least 1,500 steals and 1,000 or more blocked shots in their careers.

In Dallas, Marion's role was to defend the best scorer the opposition could offer, and to take about 80 percent of his own shots from inside the paint. "The Matrix" deserved great credit for transforming and tailoring his game to the Mavericks' needs, and for accepting a more workmanlike role that lacked the glory of his previous seasons.

Behind another fourth-quarter eruption by Terry, and with Marion and Kidd smothering the Thunder's Kevin Durant and Russell Westbrook, the Mavericks had limited Oklahoma City to just 12 points in the fourth quarter. It was becoming clear that during "winning time" — the final five minutes of a close game — the Dallas defense was capable of turning the opposition's offense off like a faucet. Even without Nowitzki and Carlisle, the Mavs had improved to 11-1 on the road.

The next night brought an unexpected bump in the road. The Mavs were home to face Toronto, a team that had not won in Dallas since a 1999 game at Reunion Arena in the heyday of Vince Carter and Tracy McGrady. On this night, it was lesser-known rookie Ed Davis doing the damage for the Raptors (11-20), with a career-high 17 points and 12 rebounds. The Mavericks struggled to score without Nowitzki. Dallas starters combined for just 39 points in an 84-76 loss to one of the league's worst teams.

Unable to play, Nowitzki sat in with Mavericks television announcers Mark Followill and Bob Ortegal. Followill was thrilled to have Dirk on the air because, as he explained, "When Dirk's on the broadcast, I think the fans and viewers get exposed to Dirk in a way they don't typically. He just really seems to shine in those situations." Followill was just about to hit Dirk with some viewer questions that had been e-mailed in, when a huge dunk by Chandler created TV gold:

Followill: "They asked some questions that we want to pose to you, so this is the first one from the legion of Dirk fans out there."

(Dunk by Chandler)

Nowitzki: "OOOOOOOH! TAKE THAT WITH YOU!!!"

Ortegal: "Maybe that is the turn-around basket, huh? What do you think? One hell of a play, that was."

Nowitzki: "UHHHH!"

It was hardly the most descriptive broadcasting, but Dirk had created a new catch-phrase that swept Dallas. Radio shows delighted in the new sound effect. T-shirt designers and DJs ran to their laptops to start their designs and remixes. Eventually, phonetic spelling adjusted the phrase to "Take Dat Wit Chew," and it caught fire for the rest of the season. It was a new way to punctuate great moments in the office or on the playground. Tell someone to "take dat wit chew," and any local knew exactly what it meant.

"It was obvious what gold we had on our hands," Followill said. "And, between The Ticket (Dallas' top-rated sports radio station), YouTube, I started using it as a call on Chandler alley-oop dunks, DJ Steve Porter, etc. ... it caught on with the whole organization and fan base.

"To me, it was the Mavs' equivalent of the 'Claw and Antlers' for the Rangers. It started with a player, it was organic in how it caught on, and it was unique to our fans."

But Nowitzki remained unavailable to play two nights later, when division-leading San Antonio came to town. Kidd produced a triple-double (12 points, 10 rebounds, 13 assists) and Butler scored 30, but the Mavs still didn't have enough against the team with the league's best record. The Spurs (28-4) enjoyed a 21-2 run early in the game and held on to win, 99-93.

Haywood, suspended for the first meeting with the Spurs, never played a minute this night, either. He was dressed and on the bench, but Carlisle gave Alexis Ajinca all 11 minutes at backup center, preferring this matchup against the Spurs' front line. Cardinal scored nine as the power forward starting in place of Nowitzki, with Marion coming off the bench to tally 10.

Spurs coach Gregg Popovich told reporters he would not put much stock in the victory with Nowitzki absent.

"Because Dirk's not there, you win ... fine. You lose, you feel like (expletive)," Popovich said. "It's like a win-win (for Dallas). If we win, in a way, we won't give a crap. If you think about it, what exactly does it mean? If you lose, you really feel like crap because they don't have all their guys. It's a lousy situation. I hate it."

Cuban had watched the Toronto loss from his vacation home in the Cayman Islands, seething from afar over the home loss to an inferior team. He had flown in to witness in person the loss to the Spurs, which left the Mavericks with a record of 24-7. After the game, the owner called out his team for being "too cocky."

"We can't be that way," Cuban told ESPN.com. "We've got to learn to compete against ourselves to be the best that we can be. If we do that, then I'm going to be singing our praises every which way. We've bought in for the big game. Now we've got to buy in for every game. When we learn that's what we have to do to win a championship, at least in my opinion, I think we are going to be unstoppable. But we're not there yet."

It was a public challenge to his team, all the more daring because the Mavericks' front office knew Nowitzki was going to be sidelined longer than had been divulged publicly.

"Could he technically play this week? Maybe," trainer Casey Smith said. "But if we wait four more games — which to the outside world seems like an eternity, but to us we are only 30 games into the season — he will be much better in nine days."

If the team could handle a two-game trip to Milwaukee and Cleveland, then Nowitzki should be nearly ready and all would be well again soon. Or so it seemed. Things changed significantly on New Year's Day at the Bradley Center, home of the Bucks.

Marion was ruled out before the game because of a bruised thigh suffered against the Spurs. Without Nowitzki and Marion, the Mavericks needed plenty from Caron Butler.

This was a homecoming game for Butler, who was raised in Racine, Wis., about 30 miles from Milwaukee. Butler had overcome tremendous odds as a teenager, including 15 arrests by age 15 for drug possession and other offenses. While incarcerated, Butler took up basketball and eventually used it to build a better life. His story read like a movie script for a boy from the wrong side of the tracks working his way to a life of fame and fortune in the NBA.

Butler had been in terrific form, providing a strong offensive counterweight to Nowitzki in the starting lineup, an important role especially when Terry wasn't on the floor. No one could have predicted this game would be his last of the season.

"It happened right in front our bench," Smith remembered. "As soon as Caron went up, he grabs his knee in the air and goes right down. Now, knowing Caron, I know it is serious. Little things don't bother him, and I rush out there to see how bad he is."

It was very bad. Butler had ruptured his patellar tendon, which essentially holds the kneecap in place. When the tendon below the kneecap snaps, tension from the quadriceps muscle often yanks the kneecap up the front of the thigh. In this case, Butler's kneecap was several inches north of where it belonged, protruding gruesomely from the under the skin.

"I see what it is, and I start looking for help to carry him off," Smith said. "I motion for Al (equipment manager Al Whitley). Butler starts asking me what's going on. He then takes his right hand and pushes his kneecap back down to where it belongs and says, 'Let's get the (expletive) out of here.'"

Smith marveled at Butler's determination not to be carried off on a stretcher in front of so many family members there to see him play. With Smith's assistance, Butler walked off the court, almost as if nothing was wrong. Only that he shook his head slowly while biting the collar of his jersey betrayed that he knew his season was finished.

Back in the training room, Butler told Smith about his terrible string of luck playing in Milwaukee. In other "hometown" games over his career, Butler had injured a shoulder and broken a wrist playing the Bucks.

"You aren't playing in Milwaukee anymore," Smith warned Butler before they flew him back to Dallas for surgery to repair the torn tendon.

Assistant GM Keith Grant said, "When it first happened, it didn't look that bad, because he got up and walked off the floor. So we hoped it wasn't super serious. And then when you found out what happened and you realize that just him being able to walk off the floor might have been one of the greatest sports achievements I had ever seen in my life

... That just shows his grit. But that is what he has been since he got with us. Huge loss. Huge loss."

The Mavericks battled with their remaining crew, but the Bucks swept the season series with a 99-87 triumph. The Mavericks were 0-3 with Nowitzki in street clothes, and now had lost Marion for a game and Butler (who had averaged 17 points per game in December) for the rest of the season.

The mood was somber as the Mavericks arrived in Cleveland the next day. An injury such as Butler's forces athletes to reassess their sense of invulnerability, a most unwelcome process. Marion insisted he could play, and returned to score a season-high 22 points. Stevenson also stepped up, contributing a season-best 21 points, and the Mavs ended their three-game skid with a 104-95 victory over the Cavs.

Stevenson had hit five 3-pointers in Cleveland, and kept firing from long distance two nights later in an 84-81 home victory over Portland. He was 4 of 9 from behind the arc for part of his team-leading 18 points against the Trail Blazers, and by now was celebrating with his "3-monocle."

The referee hand signal for a 3-point shot is to pinch the thumb and forefinger together in a circle and extend the three remaining fingers. Stevenson would hit a shot, mimic that signal and put the circle around his right eye as he retreated down the floor. The "3-monocle" excited fans and annoyed opponents. Both were reactions Stevenson very much enjoyed.

Nowitzki, meanwhile, sat out his fifth game in a row. The Mavs were 2-3 without him, and there was no telling when he might return.

"When Dirk's ready to play, we'll let everybody know," Carlisle snapped to reporters. "He's making gradual progress, but that's going to be it. We're not going to have a daily Dirk Update or Dirk Watch."

=========

With Oklahoma City coming to town for the 35th game of the season, the Mavs were entering what would be their toughest stretch of the season. The three players many had predicted would be the season's top three scorers (Nowitzki, Butler and Beaubois) all were sidelined with injuries. Butler was done for the year, Beaubois had now been idled five months with no return in sight, and no one knew when Nowitzki would play next.

The scoring burden fell to Terry, Marion and Kidd. But as the Mavs wrapped up their three-game homestand with losses to the Thunder (99-95) and Orlando Magic (117-107), it was apparent Dallas no longer had enough firepower to stay with healthy, talented teams for 48 minutes. Chandler averaged 14 points and 15 rebounds during the homestand, but even that couldn't outweigh the loss of two starting forwards.

The Orlando game was particularly disturbing. Seven Magic players scored in double figures, and the Mavs gave up 66 points in the second half. Carlisle was ejected in the fourth quarter, his team lost for the fifth time in seven games, and a difficult four-game road trip loomed ahead. Worse, Nowitzki (now out a career-long seven consecutive games) tried to run at the morning practice but experienced more knee pain and was ordered to shut it down again.

"I don't believe in the excuse game," Carlisle said after the game. "We've got to get it done with the people available."

The Mavericks, understandably, looked somewhat lost offensively without their 7-foot German superstar to work around. Nowitzki had played at least 76 games per season since his rookie year, and was on the floor at least 36 minutes in each of those nearly 1,000 games. He was always there.

Others might pick up some slack of his scoring output, but no one could replace the threat and effect Nowitzki's presence has on opponents' defenses. Teams have to try double-teaming Nowitzki, which inevitably opens the floor (and scoring opportunities) for Dirk's teammates. Without him, there was no need to double-team, no open man for the Mavs to find. The players they had left were opportunistic scorers, not primary scorers. There is a big difference.

The Mavs' turnover rate soared without Nowitzki, as the offense went from relying on precise spacing to often-chaotic improvisation. Carlisle was not pleased.

"What we need to do is stay aggressive and avoid situations where we're giving the other team an opportunity to score when we can't get back because we've made an unforced error of some sort," Carlisle said. "We're going to keep studying it, we're going to keep working to get better. We're two weeks into this now, and the guys that we have, I have a lot of confidence in. So, we're just going to keep pressing forward."

The front office tried to help. On Jan. 10, Donnie Nelson waived forward Steve Novak (who had played just 18 minutes all season) and signed free-agent small forward Sasha Pavlovic to a 10-day contract, hoping he could provide some perimeter shooting and defense. With their new teammate in tow, the Mavericks embarked on a circuitous trip that would have them visit Indianapolis, San Antonio, Memphis and Detroit. And things went from bad to worse.

Carlisle, who had been fired as the Pacers' coach after the 2006-07 season, could only grit his teeth and bear it as Indiana maintained at least a six-point lead for the final 10 minutes of a 102-89 victory. The Mavs had been accused by Cuban of being too cocky two weeks earlier, and now they couldn't stay on the court with the Indiana Pacers? They were miles from cocky. Their confidence was shot.

Next was another trip to the Alamo City, where the Spurs awaited with the league's best record (33-6). For the second consecutive game, Carlisle tried a two-center starting lineup. And both times, he went with the young and raw Alexis Ajinca next to Chandler in the post, with Haywood on the bench. This time Chandler got into early foul trouble and the Mavs' three centers combined for only 16 points and six rebounds in 49 minutes. The Spurs outrebounded Dallas 52-39 en route to an easy 101-89 victory. The Mavs were now 2-7 without Nowitzki.

The next night, Jan. 15, Dirk was back in the starting lineup in Memphis. The Mavs were hardly at full strength, however, as Chandler was out with flu symptoms and Nowitzki looked tentative and concerned on his balky knee. He would score just seven points and play only 15 minutes before being ejected by second-year referee Eric Dalen.

With 8:08 remaining in the third quarter, Nowitzki was whistled for pushing off against Zach Randolph while playing defense in the low post. He protested the call, and was hit with a quick technical foul by Dalen. Players of Nowitzki's stature generally are afforded a bit more leeway than others when speaking to officials, but not this time. Dalen slapped Nowitzki with a quick second technical (and automatic ejection) as the dissent continued.

"I guess I didn't think it was a foul," Nowitzki told reporters. "We talked about it, and I got tossed."

Some in the Dallas organization believed the ejection to be almost premeditated. Dalen and Nowitzki crossed paths in the Dec. 9 home game against New Jersey, and it was suggested the referee thought he had been "shown up" by Nowitzki after a call in that game. The young referee, it was believed, had been looking for a chance to teach Nowitzki a lesson and seized the slightest opportunity in Memphis' eventual 89-70 victory. It was the Mavs' fifth consecutive loss, and fourth in a row by 10 points or more.

His team was officially reeling, but Cuban chose to voice his support via his popular Twitter account. He tweeted:

"hang in there Mavs fans, we WILL get it back on track. A lot of time to go…"

On Jan. 17, exactly three weeks from when the Mavericks were 24-5 and sitting atop the NBA world, they arrived in Detroit having lost eight of 10, along with their swagger. Butler was through, Nowitzki still hobbling, and Chandler still unavailable because of his illness. But the Pistons were only 14-26.

Didn't look like it on this day. Even with Nowitzki regaining his form (32 points in 31 minutes), the game was another disaster for the Mavs. The new guy, Pavlovic, suffered a busted nose in a second-quarter collision. The Pistons, playing without Richard (Rip) Hamilton and Ben Wallace, shot a scorching 65 percent from the floor in the second half. They outscored Dallas every quarter en route to an easy 103-89 victory, the Mavs' sixth straight loss. This, it appeared, was what rock bottom looked like.

Carlisle had seen enough and seemed eager to send a clear message through the media.

"Our competitive level has got to come up, it's as simple as that," he said. "What happened in the second half is not acceptable.

"In these situations, you never get out of it just because it's time to get out of it. You must fight out of it, and we've got to fight harder. That's really the beginning and end of it. We didn't have enough fight to get us over the hump, or even near the hump, and that's disappointing."

No one could doubt the difference Chandler seemed to make in the fighting spirit of this team. In the previous two games without him, the Mavs played without conviction or purpose.

The seething coach summed it up in three words: "Unfortunately, we caved."

8

THE RESPONSE

(Jan. 19-Feb. 5, 2011)

"You know, if we win this game tonight, then everything is going to be fine around here again."

Donnie Nelson was speaking within earshot of several people during the Jan. 19 morning shootaround at the American Airlines Center. The Mavericks had just returned from their worst road trip since 2000 (0-4), and any swagger developed before Christmas was long gone. But, with the Los Angeles Lakers in town this evening, Nelson understood how quickly the weather could change in the NBA.

The Mavericks had lost nine of 11 games over their miserable last three weeks. Among the things being questioned publicly was their effort, their dedication, even their professional pride. They had made basketball appear so easy and then, facing the adversity of injuries, had just stopped competing. Players and management seemed to know they weren't this bad, that the tide would turn soon. But players were keeping their composure so well, Carlisle was getting annoyed. He wanted the team to find a balance between composure and urgency to end the slump. He needed it over, now.

"I am still very optimistic," Carlisle told ESPN's Dallas web site, "but I know that optimism alone isn't going to pull you through this kind of a hard time. You've got to really fight as a group. You've got to have a strong collective will. You've got to rebuild your spirit, and the time for talk is over. We're going to have to play."

Meanwhile, the front office was pondering its own response. Was a bold strike needed to replace Butler via trade? With a new collective-bargaining agreement coming down the pike in the summer, most teams were exercising caution. Acquiring a genuine impact player likely would mean taking on another big contract. And with uncertainty over what the next salary cap restrictions would be, that wasn't necessarily good or smart business.

There was also hope that, perhaps within the next two weeks, things could look much rosier if Nowitzki was fit, Chandler was well, and young scorer Roddy Beaubois finally was ready to play. Carlisle even speculated that Beaubois might be able to replace most or all of Butler's 17-point nightly scoring average. It seemed a lofty goal for an unproven player who had been sidelined since August, but such was the optimism Beaubois had inspired.

Other teams liked Beaubois' promise, too. Players such as Charlotte's Gerald Wallace, Denver's J.R. Smith or Detroit's Tayshaun Prince could be had, but the asking price always included Beaubois. Cuban and Nelson preferred to keep searching for a cheaper scoring option.

An old Mavericks nemesis came to mind. At 33, Peja Stojakovic no longer was the young sharpshooter who often had wounded Dallas and other teams a decade earlier for the Sacramento Kings. But he was an experienced veteran with a reliable shot, who currently was serving little purpose at the end of Toronto's bench. Carlisle had seen Stojakovic average 19.5 points per game for him during their one half-season together in Indiana (2006) and both indicated they had enjoyed working together.

Perimeter shooting was a key to making the Mavericks' offense improve from good to great. When Dallas is hitting open 3-pointers, opponents cannot collapse on Nowitzki the same way. But with Butler finished, Terry streaky and both Kidd and Barea inconsistent, that 3-ball threat just wasn't up to par. The league averaged about 35 percent shooting behind the arc, but Barea was making only 15 percent (second-worst in the NBA) and Kidd 25 percent over the past month.

Stojakovic was a 40-percent shooter from 3-point range over the course of his career. But his acquisition was not simple and, in fact, was put on hold for a few days of league examination after other contending teams protested.

Cuban and Nelson had received permission from Toronto to speak with Stojakovic's agent and see whether the veteran small forward would have interest in joining a playoff run in Dallas. The Serbian agreed that, if a buyout from Toronto set him free, he would sign with the Mavericks.

Without cap room, the Mavericks would have to bring Stojakovic in at the pro-rated league minimum salary, which meant the Raptors would have to buy out the remainder of his $15 million contract and waive Stojakovic. After that was done, the Mavs and Raptors negotiated a deal to send backup center Alexis Ajinca, a draft pick and cash to the Raptors in exchange for the rights to 2007 second-round pick Georgios Printezis (who was playing in Spain), which just happened to open a roster spot for Stojakovic. The league ruled these were two separate transactions, though opponents argued the Mavs were circumventing salary cap rules by essentially trading a player for another who had been bought out and waived to become a free agent.

It would be five more days before Stojakovic was permitted to sign with Dallas, and two more weeks before the gimpy-kneed forward was in sufficient shape to play. Meanwhile, the Mavericks signed Pavlovic to a second 10-day contract and prepared to face the Lakers.

========

The Mavericks have had an unpleasant history with the Lakers, dating to their playoff runs in the 1980s. Since the Nowitzki Era began, the teams had not yet met in the postseason. But overall, the Lakers held a 31-14 edge in the all-time series since Dirk's arrival.

Los Angeles came in having won 10 of 12, while the Mavericks were hoping to end a six-game losing streak, their longest skid in 12 years. Chandler was back in the starting lineup, though he spent much of the first half vomiting in the locker room and could play only 28 minutes. Pavlovic, who started at small forward, appeared to re-break his nose on the first play of the game and could play only 24 minutes.

The Mavericks trailed by 11 at halftime and were still down eight points midway through the third period when they finally dug their heels in. The defense produced stop after stop, and hot shooting from Terry (22 points), Marion (22 points) and Kidd (season-high 21 points) turned the tide. Dallas roared back to take a nine-point lead at the end of three and led by at least seven points for the entire fourth quarter in winning, 109-100.

Even though far from full strength, the Mavericks learned that Chandler (10 points, six rebounds, outstanding interior defense) could make life very difficult for the Lakers' Pau Gasol and Andrew Bynum. And they learned that when the Lakers swarmed against Nowitzki, the open shots to beat them would be there. Dallas drilled 12 of 26 3-point attempts to make Los Angeles pay.

Nowitzki made only 5 of 15 shots against the Lakers, and when he hit just 6 of 16 the next night in an 82-77 loss in Chicago, even TNT analyst Charles Barkley was saying Dirk's knee still didn't look right.

"It's probably gonna take a few more games," Nowitzki admitted to reporters, "but it's improving."

The Mavericks' training staff was confident that Nowitzki had not come back too soon. The current problem, they believed, was not with Dirk's knee but with his conditioning.

While sidelined, Nowitzki had tried to maintain fitness through swimming and other aerobic work. But 19 days off the court is tough to overcome. Starting players might average about six miles of running during a game, and the challenge is not in the distance. It is the constant starting, stopping, jumping, leaning, pushing and sprinting that NBA play demands. No treadmill or swimming pool can replicate NBA basketball.

Two nights later in New Jersey, Nowitzki was having another poor shooting night (6 of 23). But with his team trailing by a point with 20 seconds left, Carlisle still ordered the ball into Dirk's hands. Nowitzki backed 6-6 small forward Stephen Graham down from the free-throw line, spun right, pump-faked once and hit a 12-foot jumper from the lane for the winning basket with six seconds left in an 87-86 victory.

"When it comes down to it, there is really only one place to go in that situation," Carlisle said.

A four-game homestand was next, and the prospect of facing the Los Angeles Clippers and high-flying rookie Blake Griffin seemed to bring out the best in Haywood.

Chandler attacked the rim on offense, scoring 21 for his first 20-point game in three years. But it was Haywood attacking on defense that probably made the difference in this 112-105 victory.

The Mavericks had just gone on a 23-6 spurt to overcome a 15-point deficit and take their first lead of the game late in the third quarter. Griffin drove past Haywood on the baseline and tried to rise for another monster dunk that would invigorate his team. Haywood would have none of it, reaching up with both hands, grabbing Griffin's dangling left arm and jerking him hard to the floor.

Haywood received a technical for what was ruled a flagrant foul, but the message was clear. The rim would be protected by the Dallas big men.

"Every play can't be a dunk-contest dunk," Haywood shrugged after the game.

Griffin missed the start of the fourth quarter getting a protective sleeve on his arm, and after the game had a huge ice pack around the elbow he landed on.

That wasn't the only bit of feistiness. Nowitzki was cut on the face in the first quarter. And in the fourth, Carlisle and Clippers guard Baron Davis exchanged heated words and received technicals after Davis had knocked down Barea with two forearm shoves. Barea could well have deserved an Emmy nomination for his foul-drawing flop, but it was the Carlisle-Davis argument that got truly heated. It ended with Davis telling Carlisle to "go have some lunch," a comment that, to this day, no one but Davis appeared to understand.

========

Keeping such a veteran team motivated during the "Dog Days" of the season was perhaps Carlisle's most difficult task. The coach (along with players, fans, media and the owner) knew the Mavericks would only be judged on their performance in the playoffs, which still were 11 weeks away. Playoff seeding and homecourt advantage could be important, but ultimately any measure of success would be decided against the Spurs, Lakers or perhaps both sometime in May.

The Jan. 27 victory over the Houston Rockets illustrated Carlisle's frustration. His Mavericks roared to an early 25-point lead in the first half, then seemed to check out mentally and move on to the next opponent. The Rockets clawed back to take a one-point lead inside the final minute. It took a clutch jumper by Barea and late free throws from Nowitzki and Terry to win what should have been a laugher, 111-106.

Nowitzki, shooting just 39 percent since his return, found more of his groove with an 8-for-11 shooting night in a 102-91 victory over Atlanta in which the overall team focus seemed better. But next came a Washington squad that was 0-23 on the road. When the Wizards ran up a nine-point lead in the second quarter, Carlisle had seen all the lackadaisical play he could take. He called timeout, slammed his clipboard to the floor and gave his stunned players a loud lecture that was noticed from every corner of the arena.

"I was pissed, really as pissed as I've been all year," Carlisle said later. "The reason I was pissed is because I care about these guys. I believe in what we can be. I'm going to tell them what's on my mind. I'm going to tell them what's right and they can disagree if they want to, but I'm all about trying to help them win. Right now, that's all this is about."

The wake-up call was heard. The saucer-eyed Mavericks came out of that huddle and outscored the Wizards by 19 points the rest of the way, storming to their fifth straight victory, 102-92. Chandler (18 points, 18 rebounds) was again lauded by his coach, who hoped the center's intensity would rub off on some of his more seasoned veteran teammates.

January was over, and it was time for the Mavericks to pack up and head East. With Dallas-Fort Worth about to host Super Bowl XLV in six days, and a crippling snow and ice storm on the way, it was as good a time as any to be playing six of the next seven on the road.

========

Stojakovic had joined the Mavericks six days earlier (Jan. 25), but still had not appeared in a game since Nov. 26. The knee tendinitis that had sidelined him in Toronto had subsided, but he would stay behind as the Mavericks visited New York, Boston and Charlotte to continue working on his conditioning and fitness.

Meanwhile, Beaubois also was approaching launch time. The Mavericks left both players behind in Dallas for what amounted to a two-week minicamp, with twice-daily workouts under the direction of longtime collegiate coach and NBA assistant Tim Grgurich.

"We wanted (Stojakovic) in as good of shape as he would have been coming out of training camp," Mavericks trainer Casey Smith explained. "He did everything we asked. He didn't necessarily love it at the beginning, but he did everything we asked and got ready."

Pavlovic, who had played relatively well, faced a decision after the Atlanta game of Jan. 29. His second (and final allowable) 10-day contract had expired, and the Mavs had to sign him for the rest of the season or cut him loose. Even though Stojakovic was not yet ready as his replacement, the decision was made to maintain some roster flexibility, set Pavlovic adrift, and hope the reinforcements would arrive soon.

The trip began in New York, with new Knicks star Amar'e Stoudemire keen for the game. Stoudemire scored 21 first-half points but his team trailed by four at the break. The Mavs ramped up their defense, holding Stoudemire scoreless on 0-for-5 shooting in the second half. Nowitzki, meanwhile, flashed his MVP form with 29 points and 11 rebounds to key a 113-97 laugher.

The winning streak reached seven two nights later in a nationally televised game in Boston. Nowitzki again poured in 29 and the Mavs scored the final 10 points of the game to beat the powerful Celtics on their own floor, 101-97. Dallas was now 24-1 when scoring at least 100 points.

Big games in Boston were nothing new for Nowitzki. In fact, only three visiting players in history have averaged more than Dirk's 27.7 points per game in at least 10 visits to Boston. You might have heard of them: Kareem Abdul-Jabbar, Wilt Chamberlain and Michael Jordan. Whether it was his career-long comparisons to Larry Bird and Paul Pierce, or his personal rivalry with Kevin Garnett, Dirk loved playing the Celtics.

Garnett generally is considered one of the best defenders of his generation. But Nowitzki lit him up for 100 points during the Mavs' three-game sweep of Minnesota in the 2002 playoffs, and hasn't let up. Since that series, Nowitzki had averaged 25 points a game vs. Minnesota Garnett (winning 10 of 16 head-to-head matchups) and 28 per game against Boston Garnett (winning 3 of 7 head-to-head battles). It clearly made Garnett crazy.

The book on the Mavericks used to be that if you played them physical, they would lose composure and get off their game. But the 2011 Mavericks were cut from a different cloth. Chandler and other veterans reveled in games where the referees would swallow their whistles and "let them play." This team might not always take Washington and Houston as seriously as it should, but it was always up for a good street fight against the Spurs, Celtics, Lakers or Heat.

This game in Boston was officiated more like "playoff rules" than strictly by the book, meaning Chandler and Marion were allowed to play physical without falling into early foul trouble. They stood tall on both ends of the floor, combining for 27 points and 24 rebounds while contesting everything inside from Pierce, Garnett and Kendrick Perkins.

But the Celtics were ranked No. 1 in the league on defense, and when they led 97-91 with 2:30 to play at home, it looked as if they would secure their split of the season series. Instead, just as in November, Dirk started taking Garnett to the rim.

His first drive resulted in a three-point play as Garnett's foul sent Nowitzki to the line, cutting the lead in half. The teams traded missed shots (Chandler pulling down two big defensive rebounds), and another Garnett foul put Terry on the line for two free throws. The Celtics' lead was down to 97-96 with 56 seconds left. After a Ray Allen miss and a Dallas turnover, Garnett had a chance for glory but missed a 20-foot jumper. Nowitzki grabbed the rebound with 15 seconds to play and called timeout.

In the huddle, Carlisle drew up a play to seek Terry coming off a double screen. If Boston closed it down, he would have Dirk in the post and various safety valves elsewhere.

On the inbound, things turned chaotic quickly. Terry was swarmed and flung a pass near Dirk's ankles. Nowitzki recovered the ball but was surrounded with few options. Garnett was poised to intercept a return pass to Terry, but Nowitzki spotted Kidd at the top of the 3-point arc.

Kidd received the ball with six seconds left and saw Allen flying toward him. Kidd pump-faked, let Allen leap past, then drilled the 3-ball with :02 on the clock. Dallas had scored eight straight points and led, 99-97.

Boston's last chance failed when Rajon Rondo overshot his pass to Garnett on a backdoor cut. Garnett had to foul Nowitzki, whose two free throws provided the final margin.

The Mavericks had regained their swagger. Inside a festive locker room, Carlisle's players once again believed they could go toe-to-toe anywhere, with any heavyweight in the league, and win a playoff-style street fight.

The trip ended the next night with an easy 101-92 victory in Charlotte. After slipping to fifth in the Western Conference, the Mavs were back up to second with a 35-15 record after 50 games. They landed in Dallas in the wee hours of Super Bowl Sunday, Feb. 5. Nowitzki, Kidd, Terry and Marion would be among those who went to Cowboys Stadium later that day to witness in person the Green Bay Packers climbing the mountain to win a world championship.

And they were starting to dream of their own championship possibilities.

9

THE HOLGER ROUTINE

(Feb. 7-March 4, 2011)

On Feb. 3, Dirk Nowitzki was named to his 10th consecutive All-Star team as a reserve on the Western Conference squad. He long ago had joined that exclusive group of players for whom All-Star selections were routine and congratulations almost seemed unnecessary.

A superstar in his sport, Nowitzki lacked only the championship to feel truly in place among the game's legends. Notification of another All-Star honor caused perhaps a flicker of a smile for Dirk, and then a return to work.

Nowitzki's training routine had become the stuff of legend — often referenced but seldom explained. But to understand how Dirk became Dirk, it is imperative to know that this player in his 13th professional season still followed the same regimen he learned as a skinny German teenager. That his personal coach, Holger Geschwindner, has been there every step of the way since Nowitzki was 16 only adds to the mystery and intrigue.

A 2008 *Time* magazine story said of Geschwindner: "A former captain of the German national team and a physicist, he has developed a series of formulas that may reveal the optimum arc for jump shots, using a combination of player height, arm length and release point. 'Take differential and integral calculus. Make some derivations and create a curve,' he recently said. 'Everybody can do it.'"

Clearly, not everyone can do it. Through thousands of practice hours, Nowitzki has become one of the most amazing shooters in history. Before he was thought of as a complete player, he was regarded as an elite sniper. A decade later, as he has continued to hone his craft, even the game's greats marvel at Nowitzki's skills.

It all stems from Nowitzki's daily grinds in the gym. Not the mandatory team practices, but the voluntary, individual workouts he demands of himself. Despite having earned a fortune of $140 million and counting, Nowitzki's hunger to improve, sharpen and add to his skills has not diminished.

"It's hard to explain his routine, but it is the same thing every single time," said Mavericks equipment manager Al Whitley, one of Nowitzki's closest friends in the organization. "When Holger is in town, it's just those two in the gym and Holger rebounds the shots. Starting close, and working out further. The weirdest shots you have ever seen, (which) Holger incorporated to improve balance and footwork. One-footed shots. Left-footed shots. Left-handed shots. Left-handed foul- and 3-point shots. You have to see it to understand what is going on.

"It is so different than a North American workout. It is the same routine every time. It doesn't alter. It is keeping the fingers wide. It is all about how the ball comes off his fingers."

Over and over. Shot after shot. Swish after swish. Just watching the routine makes you tired.

"About 45 minutes to an hour, to where (Nowitzki) is dripping in sweat," Whitley said. "It just works on his footwork. And all of those shots you see, he has been practicing — hard. Holger comes three or four times a year. And when he comes, he is here for a couple weeks to a month. And every day he is here, they come back at night and do the shooting routine in the gym. Holger was here every night in the playoffs, so they would come back every single night. It keeps (Nowitzki) sharp and he is more than locked in."

The methods might seem unorthodox, but Nowitzki has adhered to Geschwindner's plan even as each of his seasons ended in disappointment. Nowitzki has a deep faith in what got him here, and he would not abandon it. And while he has earned the respect and sometimes friendship of other NBA stars, Dirk isn't so immersed in their fraternity that he shares agents and summer vacations as some players do. Nowitzki is both a superstar and an iconoclast.

After the playoff loss to Golden State in 2007, Nowitzki and Geschwindner went on a five-week trek through the Australian outback, New Zealand and Tahiti to help clear the player's head. They slept in hostels, camped in the brush, dozed on the beach, enjoyed fine hotels, even slept in a car for a week. That was the only time in Nowitzki's career that he didn't spend the entire summer developing a new aspect of his game. But actually he did. The time for reflection gave Nowitzki a new skill: The mental ability to not beat himself up over what he couldn't control and to focus only on what he could. He couldn't control people's perceptions of him. He could only control his own effort, decisions and determination to climb that title mountain.

The summer of 2010, after the playoff loss to the Spurs, was spent honing a new weapon. Before starting his 13th season, Nowitzki and Geschwindner perfected what would become the go-to move in the forward's already loaded arsenal. It was a step-back, fall-away, left-footed shot that uses his right knee to ward off defenders. And, for a 7-footer with Nowitzki's high-arcing shooting touch, it makes guarding him virtually impossible.

"They work on things years in advance, to bring them out down the road," Whitley explained. "That one-foot, off-balance shot, it is an unguardable move. It is something he worked on for a long time that he has finally utilized this year more and more. It is just unguardable and it's something he finally feels really comfortable with now. You are just at his mercy.

"Holger is so calculated and his thought process is so advanced that he puts Dirk in isolation in every situation that he is going to see and puts him in a place to be successful. Because Dirk is so tall and his release is so high, he can get his shot off anytime he wants. And on one foot, leaning back, fadeaway for someone that big?"

The new move also came with a counterweight to keep defenders honest.

"We really saw that this year he is also taking his 'attacking the basket' to the next level," Whitley said. "When he is hitting his jump shot, he can then drive and there is just nothing you can do."

Nowitzki idolized other NBA greats who were never content with their skill set, players such as Magic Johnson, Larry Bird and Michael Jordan. Their examples, coupled with the lingering disappointment of 2006, stoked Nowitzki's determination to expand his game each summer.

"I learned a lot from (2006), and I wanted to become a better player and a better closer," Nowitzki said. "That made me continue to want to be better, and every summer I kept working. It all stemmed from '06 and from that Final that just stung so deep. It was a valuable experience to go through."

Whitley marvels at the work ethic shown by a player who could easily be content with his accolades and just enjoy spending his money. Instead, Nowitzki continues honing new weapons.

"He has been working on a sky hook for two or three years and it isn't part of the arsenal yet," Whitley said. "Look for that coming soon. Where he really kills it is in the summertime. He takes off three or four weeks to start the summer now that he is older, but he never used to do that. Then he is back with Holger, doing two-a-days, and that is where really he molds his craft and puts up numbers.

"You would be hard-pressed to find too many guys who put up the same number of shots as he does. He is similar to Kobe Bryant, because they are in the same mold. Those guys live, breathe and die basketball. The greats do. They have to. That is why they are so good. To do what he does, day in and day out, to the normal person seems crazy. But it is just what he does. The only thing he wants to do is win, and he is willing to do whatever it takes."

=========

After the Eastern road trip, the Mavericks had 12 more days before the All-Star break, and 18 until the trade deadline. Things were going to start happening fast, and with just 32 games left until the playoffs, it was time to find some rhythm.

That would start with Stojakovic, who finally was in playing shape and ready to make his Dallas debut on Feb. 7. Carlisle started him at small forward, and he produced eight points and five rebounds in a 99-96 victory over Cleveland.

Carlisle doesn't comprise his starting lineup under the old-school thinking of choosing the five best players on the team and grouping them together. The Mavericks' coach wants to set a rotation, and bring in reserves with no detectable drop in team performance. He felt it particularly important to have Terry and Marion open on the bench and bridge gaps when Nowitzki and Kidd needed a rest. The goal was to spread out the Mavericks' quality so that all 48 (or more) minutes were adequately covered. Now Stojakovic would get a chance to show whether he belonged in the mix.

Once again, the Mavericks apparently were having trouble staying motivated against one of the league's bottom-feeders. The Cavs came in having lost 24 consecutive games, one shy of the NBA record. But Dallas let a 15-point lead melt away and gave Cleveland two potential game-tying possessions in the final 15 seconds. They were fortunate the sad-sack Cavs missed one shot, then overpassed to let time run out before taking a second attempt.

The Mavs had extended their winning streak to nine, but in such unimpressive fashion their coach was hardly pleased.

"I'm glad we won," Carlisle said, "but we took steps back."

With Nowitzki nursing a sore wrist, the Mavericks won a close and exciting game in Sacramento (102-100) as Barea scored 15 of his 20 points in the fourth quarter. But the winning streak was snapped at 10 the next night in Denver, when Arron Afflalo hit a dramatic 20-foot buzzer-beater over Marion for a 121-120 upset. The Nuggets had overcome a nine-point deficit in the last 2:51 to win.

"This is the NBA," Kidd said philosophically. "You win games sometimes when you're not supposed to, and you lose games when you're not supposed to."

Through his first three games, Stojakovic was 5 for 20 from the field, including a dreadful 1 for 11 from 3-point range. But two nights later in Houston, he finally found his touch, scoring 22 points on 8-of-12 shooting (4 for 6 from behind the arc). The Mavs won, 106-102, and were about to add another intriguing player to the mix.

Mavericks fans had been waiting since the previous May to see Rodrigue Beaubois back on the floor. And in the Feb. 16 home game against the Kings, they finally got their wish.

Still barely 6-foot-1 and 170 pounds, Roddy B's expected potential and impact had somehow only grown in the minds of fans during his seven-month recovery from the broken foot. He didn't start this game — Carlisle still had DeShawn Stevenson in the lineup, perhaps out of respect for the job he had been doing — but it took only 2:07 into the game before Carlisle had Beaubois strip off his warmups and check in.

The Mavs' video board played a clip resurrected from the previous season. Cribbed from the movie *Rudy*, it features Beaubois' grimacing face superimposed over the film version of Notre Dame's famed undersized walk-on "Rudy" Ruettiger, as he charged to make a tackle. As the clip played, the AAC crowd stood and chanted, "Roddy! Roddy! Roddy!"

Who, exactly, was this savior?

Beaubois was born Feb. 24, 1988, in Pointe-a-Pitre, Guadeloupe. He hadn't started playing the sport until he was 17, but immediately gained notice at an open tryout camp on his native island. By 19, he was already playing professionally in the French A League, and by 21 was in his first NBA camp. In a prearranged deal, Oklahoma City had selected him with the 25th overall pick in 2009, but sent him and a second-round pick to Dallas in exchange for Byron Mullens, whom the Mavs had taken at No. 24.

The Mavs were intrigued by Beaubois' physical gifts and athleticism. The lanky guard had a wingspan of nearly 7 feet, a 39-inch vertical leap and quickness that was off the charts. The raw talent was there in abundance, but the Mavs found Beaubois still lacking the basic basketball instincts and acumen needed to compete in the most elite league in the world.

So, in his rookie season, Carlisle tried to find places to play him. And when Beaubois did play, the resulting highlights could be jaw-dropping. By March 2010, he was starting to see semi-regular minutes and demonstrated a natural scoring flair. In three consecutive games, he scored 17 points against Minnesota, 22 against Sacramento and 24 against Chicago. His game was still spotted with defensive lapses and untimely turnovers, but given his upside, the Mavs were willing to accept some growing pains.

On March 27, 2010, the Mavericks played at Golden State. Beaubois entered a rather nondescript contest against the Warriors and unloaded 26 points in the first half (his career high for a game had been 24). He finished with a 40-point night in just 30 minutes of action, hitting 9 of 11 3-point attempts, grabbing eight rebounds and even blocking three shots. This, thought Mavericks fans, was a kid who needed to play.

The Dallas coaching staff did not yet agree. Beaubois was still a project, the fifth guard on the depth chart behind Kidd, Stevenson, Terry and Barea. And while the YouTube highlights that had fans drooling were impressive, Carlisle and his assistants were still finding fault and lessons to be learned in Beaubois' overall game. Defense, spacing, positioning, understanding where to switch and when. All were things Beaubois still needed to learn. Within five games of his legendary 40-point night, Beaubois was back to having "DNP-CD" on his scoresheet (Did Not Play - Coach's Decision).

Fans demanded to know why and the "Free Roddy B" movement was launched. Carlisle saw no benefit to outlining the young player's faults and weaknesses in the newspaper. He was trying to set a rotation for the playoffs, and frankly a rookie fifth guard wasn't a priority. The Mavs had again drawn San Antonio, and it didn't seem a good idea to throw Beaubois up against Tony Parker just yet.

But that series did not go well, especially for Dallas' veteran guards. Three times in the six-game series, Kidd scored only one basket from the floor. He shot 30 percent in the series (26 percent over the final five games) and looked every bit of 37 years old. Terry, arguably the streakiest shooter in club history, had games ranging from two points to 27 points, but only eclipsed 13 points twice in the six-game series.

They looked like an old guard(s) that needed to be changed, and Beaubois was the handsome young prince waiting in the wings. He had played only 10 minutes in the first five games of the series, but when Carlisle finally let him off the leash with the Mavs trailing by 19 in Game 6, Beaubois responded with 16 points and five rebounds in 21 minutes.

"Game 6 against San Antonio last year, to me, was the ultimate 'Hail Mary,'" Mavs TV announcer Mark Followill said. "We are getting our butts kicked by 20 in an elimination game on the road. We could crumble and easily lose by 50. So Carlisle is thinking, 'I am going to throw a Hail Mary pass,' and he completed it. Roddy came in with no pressure on and played great for a couple quarters and they actually took the lead."

The Mavericks ended up losing, but the media focus turned to how the series might have been different if Beaubois had been used more.

Followill continued, "Everyone, to a man, felt like Roddy had to be the No. 2 scorer on the team (entering the 2010-11 season). The thought was that you can't win a championship if you don't have a sidekick scorer for Dirk, and Jason Terry had perhaps proven in recent years that he might not still be able to do that. ... And the bang-to-hype ratio (for Beaubois) just got way out of whack."

The Mavericks' management triad (Cuban, Donnie Nelson and Carlisle) added fuel to the fire when discussing Beaubois in the summer. Carlisle told a local radio station in July that, "There's a very realistic chance that he could be one of our starters. I don't think there's any question about that."

Again, fans and media put more weight into a "starting" role than does Carlisle, who thinks in terms of a full-game rotation, each player's minutes meshing with others' like the moving gears of a machine. But to the public, it seemed Beaubois had pushed past Terry in the team's pecking order to see who would help Nowitzki win his title.

All that changed when Beaubois broke his foot while practicing with the French national team for last summer's world championships. In August, the prognosis was for Beaubois to be sidelined 2-3 months. He suffered a setback in October and was put back in a walking boot. The expected November return turned to December, then January.

After Butler was lost New Year's Day, the hope for Beaubois was to be back by February. He was the constant source of hope on the horizon.

One member of the franchise felt Carlisle wasn't doing Beaubois any favors.

"When he was in his media scrums, he would talk about the absence of another scorer and the loss of Caron," the source said. "His security blanket was to say, 'We have that scorer, and when he gets healthy we will see him.'"

It was hard to tell whether Carlisle was sincere in joining others in high expectations of Beaubois' impact, or preparing him for a reality check if he ever got back on the court. After all, how had Beaubois improved the decision-making and instinctual deficiencies shown last spring when all he'd done for months was hobble around in a walking boot? This is the same coach who had hesitated to use him against "elite" competition last season. While recovering from an injury, it is difficult to see how much progress could have been made. As Beaubois trotted onto the court to a standing ovation on Feb. 16, it was time to find out.

His first scoring opportunity summed up the state of his game perfectly. Beaubois was at the top of the circle and decided to try an ill-advised pass to Chandler under the hoop that would have to elude three Sacramento players. The pass was swatted right back out to him, so Beaubois drove the lane and brought the crowd to its feet again with a twisting layup. His improvisational skill was sensational, but the entire play started with a poor decision. Such decisions weren't likely to be carefully debated on the radio or television. But, behind closed doors, coaches still felt Beaubois' instincts were betraying him. One of his favorite moves was to try to split a double-team with a risky dribble in traffic, the kind of move that certainly had worked numerous times for him on his way to the NBA. Carlisle and his staff were going to change such low-percentage instincts, or pull their hair out trying.

The Mavericks cruised to a 116-100 victory, with Beaubois providing 13 points, six assists and three steals in 21 minutes of action. Eight Mavs scored in double figures that night, but the spotlight seemed reserved solely for Beaubois. Many thought the savior had arrived; a few preached caution and patience.

"There were some ups and downs," Carlisle said, "but the important thing was he was able to get involved."

Kidd said, "The big thing is just for him to get more minutes and to get more comfortable."

The next night, Dallas was in Phoenix to play its last game before the All-Star break, and Beaubois found his name alongside Kidd's in the starting backcourt. The inexperience showed again, however, as Beaubois managed to pick up five fouls in 19 minutes and finished with the worst plus-minus rating on the squad. During his time on the floor, the Mavs were a net minus-seven points in relation to the Suns.

The rest of the team performed well, particularly Nowitzki. Dirk warmed up for his All-Star appearance by drilling 13 of 18 shots on a 35-point night, his finest game yet since returning from the knee injury. The Mavs improved to 40-16 with a 112-106 road win.

"Dirk's back," Carlisle declared after the game. "He is all the way back, and it really is great."

Even Nowitzki remained encouraged about Beaubois' potential.

"For Roddy, the sky's the limit," Nowitzki said. "He's got to keep on working. Once he's healthy, I think he's exactly what we need: An explosive guy who can get the ball in the paint off the dribble, which is sometimes what we lack."

After the All-Star Game, four days remained before the league's trading deadline, so Cuban and Donnie Nelson were working hard to determine what else their championship contender might lack.

They couldn't find many holes. Their team had just won 13 of 14 games before the break, and the last two weeks saw two new starters added in the small forward Stojakovic and shooting guard Beaubois. Unless something big materialized, the Mavs would be happy taking this roster into the postseason.

A depleted Utah team came to Dallas the night before the deadline, having just traded franchise point guard Deron Williams to New Jersey a few hours before tipoff. The Mavs got all 12 of their players into the game and no one needed to play more than 31 minutes as they blitzed the Jazz, 118-99. Meanwhile, Nelson worked the phones but in the end found no deals to his liking.

"This group's got special chemistry, and they've really earned the right to make a run for the roses," Nelson told ESPNDallas.com. "We feel great about it, and we're looking forward to the playoffs. You've got to give to get, and we were not willing to give up any of our core rotation guys, because you've got a unique thing in that locker room. That's really what it came down to."

That meant Beaubois, coveted by some potential trade partners, was remaining in the Mavericks' plans. And to Jason Terry, who was not oblivious to how media, fans and even some teammates were fawning over Beaubois, that meant it was on.

Until now, Terry had been Nowitzki's offensive sidekick. That worked well when Terry was in one of his hot-shooting streaks, not so well when he wasn't. Terry knew Beaubois wasn't here to replace Nowitzki or Kidd. And while Terry continued to say the right things publicly, he knew that the next few weeks could be critical to keeping his postseason role significant. He needed to rise to the challenge and outperform the kid.

The Mavs embarked on a three-game Eastern trip, in which they collected victories in Washington (105-99), Toronto (114-96) and Philadelphia (101-93). In those three games, Terry hit 30 of 49 shots (61 percent) and scored 74 points. Beaubois shot 32 percent (6 of 19) and scored 13 points in those same three games.

Much of Terry's production was coming at crunch time, too, as he was stepping up as a true fourth-quarter leader. By the end of the season, Terry would wind up leading all NBA players in fourth-quarter minutes played (843) and fourth-quarter field goals made (189). Only New York's Amar'e Stoudemire finished ahead of Terry in fourth-quarter scoring (529-505) and fourth-quarter shot attempts (389-383).

The focus of so much criticism for postseason failings, Terry would become the Mavs' go-to scorer late in games. He finished the season with 44 more fourth-quarter field goals than Nowitzki. And in the entire league, only Chicago's Kyle Korver hit more 3-pointers in the fourth quarter than Terry (57-51). Terry was making it clear that his performance would determine when he was through, not the presence of a flashy and untested new teammate.

The Mavericks had another big injury scare during the March 1 game in Philadelphia, when Sixers center Spencer Hawes fell on Chandler's right ankle late in the first half. To the Mavs' relief, X-rays revealed no fracture, but the severe sprain would sideline Chandler for a week. Chandler was averaging 10.4 points and 9.4 rebounds, had tallied 16 double-doubles, and had an irreplaceable presence on defense.

After sweeping the road trip and beating Indiana at home, 116-108, the Mavs had won 18 of 19 and were 45-16. Since the trials of January, they had been defeated only once — on the last-second shot in Denver that beat them by a single point. They still trailed San Antonio by 5½ games in the Southwest Division standings, but had climbed above the Lakers in the race for the No. 2 seed in the Western Conference.

Nobody even noticed the dark storm clouds gathering on the horizon.

10

THE "SOFT" LABEL

(March 6-30, 2011)

There is a seldom-discussed secret of professional sports, one that would surely distress hard-core fans (and infuriate sports bettors). It is this: Not every team is trying to win every single game with all its might.

This is not to suggest teams are trying to lose. But, especially for winning teams with an eye fixed on the postseason, there are times when a coach might quietly experiment if the pressure to win each night has eased. Lineups, strategy changes, and just being mindful of minutes for key players might cost him that night's battle, but could provide valuable new insight to eventually win the war.

"Health is maintained when the minutes are right," Carlisle explained. "In my second year, we played Jason Kidd too many minutes. We got into that 13-game winning streak and were just trying to keep it going. He was playing great and he was playing in the high 30s, minutes-wise, and it was just too much. And we had to come up with a plan this year that helped facilitate him getting down in the low 30s.

"The other good thing that happened was we also got Dirk's minutes down significantly this year, which psychologically and physically really helped him. And Tyson plays so hard that it was clear to us that, when he played to exhaustion, you had to get him out of the game, too. Because when he was tired, he was prone to fouling and even injury. And he didn't miss a practice all year. Keeping the minutes down for our key players was at the top of our list as a staff, and it seemed to make a huge difference."

In pro basketball, as in most other sports, the objective is not to compile the most regular-season wins or best record. There are no trophies to be found there. Championships are won by getting a team to peak at the right time, staying healthy, drawing the most favorable matchups, and navigating successfully through the grueling thicket of postseason tournaments. For Carlisle, part of that mission included keeping one of the oldest teams in the league fresh enough to compete in the second season. In the NBA, the only team history remembers is the one that dances through the playoff minefield and emerges with 16 postseason wins. That team is handed a trophy and added to the rolls of basketball immortality. Everyone else is forgotten.

When Carlisle and his bosses decided to experiment to see whether Peja Stojakovic and Roddy Beaubois could make their team more dynamic and offensively potent, they knew the results could go either way.

Beaubois was the antithesis of his veteran teammates. He was young and inexperienced. While most of the Mavericks' core players had acquired the knowledge and battle scars from logging at least 10 years of NBA service time, Beaubois was a pup who had not played the sport at any level for more than six years. The Mavericks needed to find out what he could do. The only way to gauge his potential impact on the playoffs would be to give him plenty of minutes in February, March and April.

Carlisle is a coach known for using his entire roster. If there are 12 players on the bench, he considers them 12 tools in his toolbox. Certain situations call for particular tools to be utilized. But, over the course of a year, Carlisle wants to use all his tools plenty.

"He not only handles superstars well, but he knows how to handle his mid-bench and end-of-bench guys", Donnie Nelson said. "I don't think there are many guys who can look at an opponent and know which pieces he can use better. And, nine out of 10 times, he gets it right."

Carlisle expected each of his players to stay as prepared and ready as a professional should. And he spoke from personal experience.

Carlisle's NBA playing career spanned five seasons and 188 games. He started a game only once. His role, especially as a bench player for one of the best teams of all time (the 1985-86 Boston Celtics), was to be ready when the team needed him. Some nights, they needed 20 minutes. Other nights, they didn't need him at all. But he stayed ready and made impact plays when called upon. The last thing he wanted to do was disappoint Larry Bird, Kevin McHale or Dennis Johnson. He was part of a team trying to win a championship.

Therefore, as coach of the Dallas Mavericks, Carlisle wasn't asking Shawn Marion, DeShawn Stevenson, Brendan Haywood or Brian Cardinal to do anything he hadn't done himself. As a player, he stayed ready, because he knew Celtics coach K.C. Jones would need him at some point. And he prepared each day as if that was the day he would be needed.

So, as the Mavericks steered into March and the homestretch of the regular season, were they intent on fielding their best team at all times? No. Did they admit that to the media, their fans, their opponents or even to their own players? No. But management already knew what the veterans could do. It was time to see whether Beaubois belonged in the postseason toolbox.

Beaubois first had to play his way into shape and regain faith in his supposedly healed foot. If he could not trust his foot, he couldn't play with confidence. Next, he had to set aside the lofty expectations being placed upon him and learn to play the game without pressing. It wasn't that Beaubois wasn't trying, it was that he often was trying too hard. His performances could be spectacular, or just as easily erratic. Carlisle was trying to stay patient, even when Beaubois' play wasn't on par with that of the veterans who had been together since training camp.

Meanwhile, the passing of the trade deadline didn't mean Donnie Nelson's job was finished. The Mavericks saw an opportunity to add lanky forward Corey Brewer, a defensive specialist who had been acquired by New York from Minnesota and then released as part of the complicated maneuvering to land Carmelo Anthony from Denver.

Brewer, three days shy of his 25th birthday, signed a three-year deal with the Mavericks on March 2 after receiving offers from several contenders. Having won two NCAA championships with Florida, Cardinal's former Timberwolves teammate was just as eager to escape Minnesota and play for a winner. At 6-foot-9 and less than 190 pounds, the 2007 lottery pick (seventh overall) was a long, lean and young addition to one of the oldest teams in the league. Like Beaubois, he would be quickly tested for a potential role in the playoffs, while being youthful enough to be considered part of the team's future.

Brewer's debut in a 116-108 home victory over Indiana showed his "enthusiasm." He went scoreless but picked up five fouls in just 5:21 of playing time.

"I was a little bit too aggressive," he said sheepishly after the game.

Next up was a visit from Memphis, one of the troublesome first-round opponents the Mavericks could possibly draw. Like the Lakers, the Grizzlies caused matchup trouble with their big-man combination of Zach Randolph and Marc Gasol.

That duo combined for 43 points and 19 rebounds on this night, most of it in the paint. But it was an improbable 17-foot baseline jumper by Randolph with 3.1 seconds left that doomed the Mavericks to only their second loss in 20 games, 104-103. Carlisle was seething after seeing his team blow an 18-point lead at home.

It wasn't the best way to start another tough stretch of schedule. The Mavs were to play four game in five days in three cities, then return home to face the Lakers.

Stojakovic, bothered by neck issues that would ultimately cost him two weeks of action and his starting role, sat out the following night's game in Minnesota. So Cardinal stepped up to be the hero against his former team, hitting four 3-point shots for a season-high 12 points in a 108-105 victory.

Two nights later, the Mavs were back in New Orleans, where they would lose for the eighth consecutive visit. The Hornets were playing without leader Chris Paul (concussion), while the Mavericks had Tyson Chandler back from his sprained ankle. Chandler had 16 points and 13 rebounds, but missed two free throws with 17 seconds left. That enabled Jarrett Jack to make three free throws for the final margin of a 93-92 victory, after he was fouled by Kidd on a flailing 3-point attempt with 8.4 seconds left.

Nowitzki had one last chance to hit a game-winner, but his 18-foot jumper over Emeka Okafor bounced off the front of the rim as time expired. The Hornets had completed an 8-0 run inside the final minute to win.

"Just bad, bad execution down the stretch," Nowitzki said, shaking his head.

It was only the third loss in 48 days. But, like the other two, it happened because of careless play at crunch time. In each case, the Mavericks had blown leads that should have been safe, and Carlisle had reached his boiling point. He decided to send a scathing message in his postgame media session:

Reporter No. 1: "Were you disheartened the way these last two games have gone down, and the way even the Minnesota game was really nip and tuck and they had some big runs?"

Carlisle: "I'm sorry, am I what?"

Reporter No. 1: "Disheartened by the way…"

Carlisle: "Oh, I'm disappointed. Yeah. Yeah. Yeah."

Reporter No. 1: "Does that stem from ... do you feel focus has waned, or just ... out-manned?"

Carlisle: "Soft."

Reporter No. 1: "Soft?"

Carlisle: "Yeah, soft."

Reporter No. 1: "Why do you feel the team has been soft? Is there a reason for that at this point of the season, with so much on the line in terms of seedings?"

Carlisle: "Well, I think we've just got to be tougher. Just got to be tougher."

Reporter No. 2: "If those free throws go in, we are talking about a different game there."

Carlisle: "If cows were kittens, there would be a milk shortage. What do you want me to say to that? That's pretty obvious."

Carlisle had labeled his team "soft." In some places, that may not be a big deal. But for a Dallas team that had battled hard for a decade to shed that insulting perception, it was a place they never expected their own coach to go.

Word of Carlisle's damning remark quickly filtered back to the visitors' locker room, and players were not pleased. Once reporters were admitted inside, most went straight to Terry — the resident go-to quote machine — for a response.

"Who said that?" a surprised Terry asked. "I'm not soft, not me. I don't know where that comes from, but we ain't soft. We have to see how he meant 'soft' in that aspect. But I know he wasn't talking to me personally or any of my teammates, because I don't think none of these guys are soft."

Carlisle had been annoyed by the blown lead, no question. But it seemed two incidents in particular had driven him to use the "S" word. The first was a flagrant foul by Marco Belinelli, who had smacked Shawn Marion into a television cameraman on a transition layup attempt late in the third quarter. Marion had to leave the game with bruised ribs. The second was when David West pushed Nowitzki into the Mavericks' bench during a scramble for a loose ball.

It bothered Carlisle that in neither case did the Mavericks leap to the defense of their aggrieved teammate. Carlisle would face league discipline if he had flat-out called for physical retribution, but his intent seemed clear: If the Mavericks wouldn't send the message that such actions would not be tolerated, they would continue to be viewed as "soft" and have to endure plenty more such instances.

Carlisle, speaking later to newspaper columnist-broadcaster Randy Galloway, made a meager attempt to walk back his "soft" comment.

"I was shocked by the amount of play that thing got," Carlisle said. "I believe we are a tough-minded team, but we have to play together and aggressive. The thing we have to realize is that we went 20-3 against a favorable schedule. Now, we are headed into a stretch of much more volatile travel; much more physical, experienced teams; and a lot of potential playoff matchups — first-, second-round or whatever. Right now, it's all about improving and getting better."

The next night's 127-109 trouncing of the Knicks back in Dallas was no surprise, given the friction resulting from their coach's comments the night before. Marion went to the final 30 minutes before tipoff before deciding he could play despite the bruised ribs, and he scored 22. Nowitzki scored 23, Terry 21 and the Mavs set season highs for points in a quarter (41 in the second), half (72 in the first half) and game. The 18-point margin of victory was one shy of the team's best this season.

An ESPN.com reporter asked Terry afterward what impact Carlisle's critique had on the team's performance less than 24 hours later.

"None whatsoever," Terry said. "We know what kind of team we are."

========

With 17 games to play, the San Antonio Spurs had a firm grip on the No. 1 seed for the Western Conference standings. They led the Mavericks by six games and the Los Angeles Lakers by 7½. So when the Lakers came to Dallas on March 12, the stakes were high. Whichever team could clinch the No. 2 seed would have homecourt advantage over the other in a potential second-round playoff matchup.

"We want homecourt advantage against them," Lakers coach Phil Jackson said, "and that is important."

Mavericks partisans cringed at premature talk of a second-round scenario. Dallas had been booted out in the playoffs' first round in three of the last four seasons. The Lakers, two-time defending league champions, could look ahead if they chose, but the Mavericks knew to keep their eyes on their own paper.

This mid-March meeting served as a stark reminder of the matchup problems the Lakers posed for Carlisle.

Los Angeles center Andrew Bynum, at 7-feet and a listed 285 pounds, had at least a 50-pound weight advantage on Chandler. Bynum dominated with 22 points and 15 rebounds, while Chandler managed just four points and six boards. Bynum simply wore Chandler out.

The Mavericks' center wasn't the only one having problems. The absence of Caron Butler left Carlisle having to give too many minutes to "one-way" specialists. Terry, Barea and Beaubois could provide offense but were defensive weak spots the Lakers would exploit repeatedly. Defensive standouts Stevenson and Brewer could cause Kobe Bryant some problems, but on the other end of the floor were hardly worth guarding closely, not when double-teaming Nowitzki was a better use of defenders' time.

And in his first chance to strike fear (or at least healthy respect) in the hearts of the champs, Beaubois instead looked like the nervous rookie he probably was. He made just 1 of 7 shots from the floor and committed two turnovers. He had started the game, but wound up playing just 14 largely ineffective minutes.

It took an ankle injury to Bryant to keep the score respectable (though the Lakers went on an 8-0 run when Bryant went to the locker room late in the third quarter). Bryant returned with six minutes to play and helped finish off a 96-91 victory before 20,619, the largest crowd ever to see a regular-season game at the AAC. The Mavericks' lead for the No. 2 seed in the West was almost completely gone.

Three nights later, Nowitzki missed a potential game-tying 3-pointer from the corner in the waning seconds of a 104-101 loss in Portland. After going 18-1 from Jan. 22-March 4, the Mavs now had gone 2-4 in their last six games, with all four losses coming against playoff teams from the West.

Marion, still playing with a tender rib cage that was his souvenir from New Orleans, was performing well. Despite some rather unattractive release points (TV commentator Mark Followill described Marion's awkward shots as "an acquired taste"), Marion had evolved into the team's premier post scorer. They weren't always pretty, but Marion was delivering key baskets in critical situations.

The next night, March 16, saw the Mavericks return to Oakland's ORACLE Arena, the scene of Beaubois' dream 40-point night against Golden State one year earlier.

Carlisle extended the young guard's leash once again, and Beaubois responded with 18 points and just one turnover in a solid 37 minutes. Dallas had to rally from 18 points down (including a 15-0 run in the fourth quarter), but emerged with a 112-106 victory that moved them back into a tie with the Lakers for second place in the West with 14 games remaining.

Up next, however, were the conference-leading Spurs. They were coming to Dallas having had three days to prepare and lick their wounds from an embarrassing 110-80 thrashing by Miami. San Antonio coach Gregg Popovich had harshly criticized his team's defense in that loss and expected a far better effort in Dallas.

Popovich saw his team playing sloppy defense again, and called a timeout to share his disgust. The game was 42 seconds old and his Spurs were only trailing 2-0, but someone had failed to switch on Nowitzki quickly enough. Message received. The Spurs did not trail again in rolling to a 97-91 victory.

"When you have Pop in your ear for three days, it can be a long three days," Spurs guard Tony Parker said. "Tonight, we wanted to make sure we stayed in front of people and made sure their shots were hard."

The Spurs held the Mavs to just 49 percent shooting, including an ugly 6 of 23 (26 percent) from 3-point range. Chandler landed in early foul trouble and contributed just three points in 22 minutes. His backup Haywood, who had missed the previous two games with a stiff back, scored only two points in 19 minutes. Marion ran into a teammate just before halftime and had to leave the game for X-rays on an injured wrist, playing just 14 minutes.

And then there was Beaubois, having another "down" game in his up-and-down season. Beaubois scored eight points on 4-of-11 shooting (0 for 4 from 3-point distance) and continued a worrisome pattern. He played with confidence against the Golden States of the league. But against the powerful, playoff-caliber opponents of the West, Beaubois was a shrinking violet.

It was the Mavericks' fifth consecutive loss against potential playoff opponents, and Chandler would remain quiet no longer.

According to a story by ESPN.com's Jeff Caplan, a frustrated Chandler stood in the locker room after the loss and demanded to know where his teammates stood on changing their sorry postseason reputation.

"What are we going to do, fellas?" Chandler asked. "Are we going to go the opposite way? Because we can call it a summer real early. Or, are we going to buckle down and get things together defensively and do what we all said we can do? Accomplish what we all thought we could accomplish at the beginning of the year?"

It was what the team needed to hear. In their pursuit of more offense and versatility, they had started to lose the gritty defensive identity that had been so important earlier in the year. At closing time, they could not allow opponents to outwork them and prevail. Chandler, the anchor of that defense, was willing to accept his share of the blame. But it was time for all the Mavericks to be accountable on both ends of the floor.

Chandler, whom Carlisle would frequently describe as "the heart and spirit of the team," was a player whose acquisition the previous July drew scant attention. But with his willingness to give his all on the court, and to deliver the tough love needed off it, he was a priceless piece of whatever this team would be. He was a respected leader who could rightly challenge the manhood of the collective squad. He claimed he lost sleep when the Mavericks performed poorly, and the passion with which he spoke made you believe it.

Chandler backed up his words two nights later with 17 rebounds and stout defense in a 101-73 demolition of Golden State. His backup, Ian Mahinmi, was inspired enough to grab a career-high 13 rebounds. And Stojakovic returned after a six-game absence to hit five 3-pointers en route to 17 points. After 70 games, the Mavs were 49-21 and had clinched their 11th consecutive playoff berth.

Dallas had four days until its next game, but Kidd had a occasion to deal with on the eve of that visit from Minnesota. He had arrived at his 38th birthday on March 23.

There are a few professional athletes who defy odds and perform well at an advanced age. But there aren't many examples of ancient point guards pushing their teams deep into the NBA playoffs. Utah's John Stockton helped steer the Jazz into back-to-back Finals in 1997-98 when he was 35 and 36. But even though he continued playing well to age 41, Stockton retired without a championship ring.

Kidd was having a steady and consistent season, no doubt aided by the way Carlisle was carefully rationing his minutes (33.1 per game, the lowest average in his 17-year career).

"He averaged 36 minutes last season, and we needed to get him down to 33 or 34," Carlisle said. "If you think about it, 82 games played times three minutes played at complete exhaustion adds up to a lot of games, when you play at full bore. So those minutes are really important."

Still, the clock was ticking loudly, and Kidd was edging dangerously close to joining Stockton, Karl Malone, Elgin Baylor, Pete Maravich, Patrick Ewing, Charles Barkley, Dominique Wilkins, George Gervin, Alex English and Reggie Miller on the list of great players who never won an NBA title.

"When people doubt you, it motivates you," Kidd said. "The history of it all has never dawned on me. I am just happy to be in the right place at the right time. My game is definitely closer to the ground, and now I shorten the court where I just run between the 3-point lines."

He was joking (mostly) about his territory on the court. But there was no question Kidd's basketball I.Q. was helping him slow the aging process.

Minnesota arrived without injured All-Star forward Kevin Love, but still made a game of it, even taking a two-point lead with 3:17 remaining. But the Mavericks no longer were in the mood to let winnable games slip away.

"Dirk said, during a timeout, 'We can't lose this one,'" Terry recalled.

Carlisle called for a steady fourth-quarter diet of pick-and-roll plays between Terry and Nowitzki, and they combined for 19 points in the final period. The Mavs put together an 11-2 run in the final 2:38 and secured their 11th consecutive 50-win season, 104-96.

The milestone was both a source of pride and misery. Only three other teams in history had strung together 11 consecutive seasons of 50 wins or more, but the Celtics (nine), Lakers (five) and Spurs (three) all had punctuated their dominant eras with multiple NBA championships. Being the only team in that elite group without a trophy made the Mavs the recipient of more ridicule than respect.

"It is nice, but I'd rather trade it in for a championship," Nowitzki said. "Eleven 50-win seasons don't mean nothing."

A season-long road trip (six games in nine days) was next, and the Mavs opened it in style with a stifling 94-77 victory in Utah. The Mavs trailed 70-68 with 6:20 to play when Nowitzki was subbed out for what was expected to be a quick rest. But the unit of Kidd, Barea, Terry, Chandler and Marion went on such a tear (26-7 run to end the game), Nowitzki was not needed again.

The next night produced a 91-83 victory in Phoenix against a Suns team that was battling Memphis for the eighth and final playoff spot in the West. Chandler (16 points and 18 rebounds) and Kidd (two clutch 3-pointers in the final 1:11) were serving notice that with the Mavericks' improved arsenal, they might be a tough out this spring. They were now 12-1 against Pacific Division teams.

The winning streak reached five with a 106-100 victory over the Clippers three nights later in Los Angeles, but by then Terry was coping with a family tragedy. A beloved aunt had passed away between the Phoenix and L.A. games, and Terry had left to attend the funeral in Seattle. He had rejoined the team in time for a haphazard 2-for-11 shooting night against the Clippers. But that was nothing compared to what would happen the next night against the Lakers.

With only eight games left before the playoffs, the guy with the Larry O'Brien Trophy tattoo was about to fly off the rails.

11

THE JET COMES UNGLUED

(March 31-April 13, 2011)

With eight games to play in the regular season, the Mavericks trailed the Lakers by one in the loss column and were even with 53 wins. But things seldom went right when Dallas faced the Lakers in Los Angeles (at The Forum or Staples Center). In 23 visits since 1998 (the "Dirk Era"), the Mavericks were 4-19.

They led a 2002 game here by 27 points after three quarters, and still lost. In 2003, they unveiled their new silver road uniforms here on Opening Night, only to be pounded so badly (109-93 for their 26th consecutive road loss to the Lakers) they never wore them again. And there was the December 2005 game in which Kobe Bryant scored 62 against them — in just three quarters (33 minutes). Bad things happen here.

With the postseason on the horizon, Carlisle needed to answer a strategic question in this game. He needed to know whether Beaubois could defend Bryant. If these teams did advance to their expected second-round confrontation, solving the personnel matchups posed by the sizable Lakers would be critical.

Some matchups were established. Nowitzki guards similar 7-footer Pau Gasol. Chandler must try to handle Bynum. Marion would take on Bryant or small forward Ron Artest. Kidd and Beaubois were left to contend with point guard Derek Fisher and whomever Marion was not guarding. Kidd could contain Bryant in small doses, but not through 48 minutes. So if Kidd opened against Fisher, the slight Beaubois would have to take on either the 6-7, 260-pound Artest or Bryant, one of the most dangerous and dynamic shooting guards in the history of the game. Neither choice was optimal for Beaubois, and everybody seemed to know it.

But there was only one way to find out. When the 6-6 Bryant saw he was being defended by the 6-1, 170-pound Beaubois, he immediately backed him into the post to go to work. Bryant was 2 for 4 within the first three minutes.

Nowitzki was doing his best to counter Bryant, scoring 22 points in the first three quarters, but he was getting little support offensively. The Lakers ran up an 82-70 lead heading to the fourth. And that's when the two-time defending league champions began sending their message.

Dallas was treated to a 12-minute lesson in humility. The Lakers attacked the rim and dominated the paint. Lamar Odom started the fourth with back-to-back 3-pointers, and the lead grew to 90-73 in the blink of an eye. That's when Terry, who was following his 2-for-11 night against the Clippers with a 2-for-9 effort against the Lakers, snapped.

There was 9:23 remaining when Terry sent Lakers guard Steve Blake sprawling with a flagrant two-handed shove in the back as Blake drove to the hoop. Blake leaped to his feet and charged at Terry. They stood toe-to-toe, exchanging heated words, before Lakers forward Matt Barnes intervened from the side and shoved Terry.

Chaos ensued. Terry tried reaching Barnes and was bear-hugged by a referee from behind. Mavericks assistant coach Terry Stotts tried restraining Barnes, but was flung into spectators seated courtside. When order finally was restored, Blake, Barnes, Terry and the Mavs' Brendan Haywood had been ejected. The Lakers' Shannon Brown was ejected seven minutes later after a confrontation with Brian Cardinal, but Brown's team had the last laugh with a decisive 110-82 triumph.

It was the Mavericks' seventh consecutive loss to a Western Conference playoff team. After the game, Terry apologized for his actions and referenced the "tough week" he was having since his aunt's death. But his stretch of curious behavior was just getting started.

Terry was interviewed the next morning — April Fools' Day — on Colin Cowherd's nationally syndicated radio program and offered some interesting logic for the previous night's histrionics.

"For me, it was all about making a statement for my team," Terry said. "Anything to get them fired up. If we see these guys again, we are not going to be a pushover, literally."

He was asked whether Barnes was the perfect tough guy for the Lakers.

"We call him 'The Charminator,'" Terry replied. "Do you know what that is? A guy who is as soft as Charmin toilet paper. ... I don't think he is a tough guy. Barnes, I remember you at Golden State, Phoenix, Orlando. You are a journeyman. All of a sudden you put on the Lakers' uniform and you turn into Jerry West and Magic Johnson? Come on."

Amusing to some, perhaps. But not to Barnes, a veteran of the 2007 Golden State team that upset Dallas in the first round. After hearing of Terry's trash talk in the wake of a 28-point loss, Barnes responded via Twitter:

"NO ONES worried bout wat Jason Terry is talkn bout everyone remembers the 07 season. Me & the Golden St homies laid out the blueprint on how to beat Dallas.. 'PUNK'EM' Ain't s--- changed homey.. So enough w/the small talk"

It might not have been the most elegantly worded or properly spelled assessment of Terry's team, but Barnes certainly had reminded the Mavericks of their reputation around the league. They still were considered soft, and would be until they proved otherwise.

They tipped off the next night in Golden State, where Beaubois' 40-point night was an increasingly fading memory. He was still in the starting lineup, but his leash was shortened considerably. Beaubois got the hook early after a turnover and charging foul, and wound up playing just nine minutes of the 99-92 loss to the Warriors. Observers couldn't be sure whether Beaubois' foot was again damaged, but certainly the player's confidence was.

Carlisle also decided to return Stevenson to the starting lineup in place of Marion, who had started nine games in March. Stevenson had started 48 of the first 54 games. He also had sat out entirely six times in March. With a 53-23 record after 76 games, it appeared Carlisle still was searching for the right postseason rotation. And with only six games left, the Mavs trailed the Lakers by 2½ games in the race for the No. 2 seed.

The long road trip ended ingloriously the next night in Portland, where a potential first-round opponent ran up a 21-point lead against the sluggish Mavs before winning, 104-96. Chandler sat out with a sore back, and the rest of the squad just looked tired and ready to head home.

"This tells me we just have a weary team," Terry said. "We need to get home and get re-energized."

The gap between the Lakers and Mavs remained at 2½ games with five to play, and Oklahoma City was another 2½ games behind Dallas. The Mavericks were pretty much locked into the No. 3 seed.

Kidd admitted he "was exhausted after that trip," so the coaching staff decided to hold him out of the next two home games against the Nuggets and Clippers. That would give the 38-year-old a full week between games and the chance to return with three to play, refreshed and ready for the postseason. The veteran did not argue.

Beaubois got the chance to run much of the show against the Nuggets, but four turnovers and a 2-for-7 shooting night didn't help his cause. And even though the outcome of this game mattered little, Terry again lost his cool trailing by nine with 30 seconds to go. He got into a dispute with an official and continued until receiving a technical foul.

Carlisle scolded Terry in both the huddle and his postgame news conference, telling everyone that Terry should know by now that opponents would try to light his short fuse. Terry had left immediately after his team's fourth consecutive loss, a rare night when he had nothing more to say to anyone.

Two nights later, with Kidd still resting, the Clippers were blowing the Mavericks out of their own building, running up a 35-19 lead after one quarter. Two minutes into the second period, another Dallas turnover led to a breakaway layup for the Clippers and an angry Carlisle called timeout.

As the Mavs huddled, Terry lit into Barea for both the quality and frequency of his passing. Barea snapped back and Carlisle ordered both players to opposite ends of the bench, furious that they would cause such a scene in full view of the packed arena. This, according to one player in the huddle, caused "Jet to lose it" and start yelling at his coach.

"It seemed like everything was going to hell in a hand basket," said one Mavericks operative.

Cuban spent the next timeout speaking with Terry away from the rest of the team. But Carlisle had seen enough of Terry's recent erratic play and conduct. He sat Terry for the remainder of the game, which the Mavs roared back to win, 107-96, behind 20 points from Corey Brewer.

Carlisle was tight-lipped about the incident after the game.

"It's an internal matter," he said. "It's going to remain an internal matter. ... Emotions run high and sometimes things happen, and I'm going to leave it at that. Jet's a very important guy on our team. I was considering giving him a night off going forward, but I think tonight will be his night off."

Terry refused to discuss the incident after the game, but said the next day he saw no need for anyone to panic.

"It's over with and we're moving forward," Terry said. "Emotions are going to be high at this time of the season. The last couple of years, we've kind of been real lax and kind of went through the motions. But this year is totally different. ... Last night, I let it become negative. And so, going forward, it's just not going to be that. It's going to be all positive."

Barea said there was no lingering ill will, describing the conflict as "nothing big."

"That's my boy, my favorite teammate since I got here," Barea said of Terry.

Nevertheless, in the nine days since the death of Terry's aunt, the Mavericks' second-leading scorer had appeared to unravel. Besides the flagrant foul in the Lakers game, the technical foul late in the loss to Denver, and the blowup with Barea and Carlisle, Terry was shooting just 32.7 percent over his last six games. His scoring average in those contests plunged to 7.8 points per game, less than half his season average.

The Mavericks had genuine concern for Terry. He was a crucial piece of their puzzle, and now was not the time for him to come unglued.

Jet had always marched to the unorthodox beat of his own jazz-fusion drummer. He was outspoken, unabashedly emotional, and certainly the only Mavs player cocky enough to put a Larry O'Brien Trophy tattoo on his arm before actually winning one. His winged takeoff celebrations would rub opponents the wrong way and his streakiness could drive his own fans crazy, but he never backed down and could hit enormous clutch dagger shots that made it all better. For better or worse, the Mavs needed Terry and they needed him with his head right. At least as right as Terry's head could be.

The impact of the incident, and Terry's private response to the team the following day, could not be overstated.

"That was one of our turning points of the season," Nowitzki said. "We were going through a tough time there. And it was going the wrong direction, unfortunately, right before the playoffs. And that incident brought everyone back into the same boat. It happened, and it wasn't great and it wasn't pretty, but afterwards everyone came together.

"The next day, we had a meeting, talked about it, and Jet apologized to the team. Jet refocused himself to the team and not doing his own thing. I mentioned it a bunch of times — obviously not in the media, but amongst each other — that might have been the turning point of the season."

Through all of Terry's struggles and momentary lapses of reason, his coach never wavered in his belief in Jet.

"I chose to focus on emphasizing the importance of him playing the entire game," Carlisle said. "Not just scoring, but play-making, the efficiency, the defensive end and the leadership. I think too much was made of his struggles the previous year, and I knew our team and our chemistry was much better this year. Whatever was going on in March and April, I have been with Jet too long to worry about him coming out of it. He has never gone through an extended period that he doesn't come out of. He is too good of a player. He always comes out of his slumps."

As the Mavericks prepared for a home game with Phoenix on Sunday, April 10, only three games and four days remained in the regular season. Agonizing over playoff seeding seemed pointless, since the Spurs had run away with the top seed and the Lakers (despite a five-game losing streak since the Mavs left town) remained in control of the No. 2 spot by virtue of winning the season series with Dallas, 2-1.

Kidd returned and looked fresher against the Suns, as evidenced by his five points, three assists, two steals and one rebound in the first eight minutes. But the best news was that Terry looked like himself again. He hit 6 of 11 shots and scored 17 points in the easy 115-90 victory. His plus-20 rating while on the floor was easily the best on the team, and accomplished in just 25 minutes off the bench.

Dallas actually moved a half-game ahead of the Lakers with their 98-91 overtime victory in Houston the following night. The game was marred by 20 Mavericks turnovers and Dallas shot just 4 for 17 from 3-point range. But it was another bit of Terry intrigue that had some scratching their heads.

The Mavs trailed 86-85 with 10 seconds left when they called a play to put the ball in Terry's hands. It was a common set where Terry came off multiple baseline screens to receive the ball, then could either find Nowitzki in the post, kick the ball to another shooter up top or create a shot on his own. With Houston's 6-6 center Chuck Hayes picking him up on the left wing, Terry pump-faked, drew contact and missed but was sent to the line.

Terry's foot had been ruled touching the 3-point arc, so he would be shooting two free throws for the win. He made the first, tying the game 86-86. Terry missed the second, but still ran down the court smiling with arms raised in celebration — he clearly believed the Mavericks had won. When he realized Dallas was tied, he walked sheepishly to the sideline huddle to prepare for overtime.

Longtime Mavericks fans would remember a similar moment from the 1984 playoffs, when Derek Harper mistakenly celebrated when Game 4 of the Western Conference semifinals was still tied with the Lakers. This time, the Mavericks would outscore the Rockets 12-5 in overtime to bank the victory, but there were a lot of laughs and smart remarks coming out of the huddle to start the extra period.

"I couldn't believe it," Nowitzki recalled later. "I have been around basketball for close to 20 years, and I have never seen it where a guy didn't know the score. After the game, he told me, 'Oh no, I knew the score. I was just happy we went into overtime.' I said, 'Jet, I'm not that dumb. I might look dumb, but I am not *that* dumb.'"

After the game, Terry stuck to his ridiculous story. He insisted to reporters that he hadn't been mistakenly celebrating a win, but was just exuberant because the Rockets had not controlled the ball with a second left and the play some 80 feet from the Houston basket. Jet was being Jet, but at least everyone was smiling again.

Terry had inadvertently provided the trip's comic relief, but there was some serious discussion in Houston, too.

Nowitzki and Kidd had privately spent some time evaluating the team's numerous lineups, something both players enjoyed. They discussed that meeting back in November, when the Mavericks were trying to settle on a shooting guard to start next to Kidd.

"You can talk with (Kidd) for days about the team," Nowitzki said. "He has so much in his head. He will be a great coach someday."

The Mavericks' senior leaders were concerned about how the bigger shooting guards of the West would be contained when the playoffs began. Kidd couldn't play that level of defense for 48 minutes, and opponents were still exploiting Beaubois' lack of experience and size.

"Dirk and I talked a little bit during the Roddy period that we might need to do something different, toughness-wise," Kidd said. "That was the main focal point, so that I didn't have to guard the 2s so early in the game. I told Dirk, 'I don't mind guarding them for a short period, but I can't guard them the whole game.'"

Nowitzki and Kidd took their concerns to Carlisle, and found the coach equally worried. Carlisle was leaning toward starting J.J. Barea as a solution. But the players lobbied for DeShawn Stevenson instead.

"We went to Coach in Houston and he had his ideas, too, where he thought he might go with J.J. to start, because we had success with that lineup," Kidd said. "But Dirk and I were thinking D-Steve, because we thought the toughness of him guarding the 2s made us way better off. D-Steve took it to another level by shooting the ball, too."

Carlisle was not so proud or rigid not to listen to his players, especially these respected team leaders.

"I spent two years working for Chuck Daly, and he was a big believer in the idea that if you have a veteran team, you should find out what they think because they will often have good information and insights," Carlisle said. "It's obvious that involving them in decisions helps on many levels. It engages their investment with what is happening with the team. And more times than not, they have a lot of great ideas. It is my job to digest it and implement whatever we are going to do. But when you have Jason Kidd and Dirk and even Jet on your team, you have to listen to those guys because there is a lot of experience there. And not only do they know the game well, they know their teammates very well.

"Sometimes, they will have ideas that I never would have thought of, that don't necessarily sound like the right course to take. Oftentimes, I will roll with it just to put it out there. One thing you have to do is put trust in a veteran team. If it works, then great. If it doesn't, then you change course. We don't have meetings every day, but when there are critical issues, I talk to these guys to get their take."

They discussed the pros and cons of each lineup and opponent. Carlisle's first reaction was that he liked Barea in the starting role, because he could provide dynamic offensive penetration from the opening tip. But he agreed Stevenson was a far better option if stout defense was the primary objective. His two future Hall of Famers implored Carlisle to err on the side of defense and toughness for these playoffs, and the coach agreed. Stevenson, somewhat of a forgotten man during the Beaubois experiment, would start.

New Orleans arrived April 13 for the regular-season finale, and multiple playoff scenarios were still in play. Depending upon results around the league, the Mavs could still wind up facing Memphis, Denver, Portland or New Orleans in the first round. Having lost nine in a row to other Western Conference playoff teams, the Mavs weren't a popular pick to go far, no matter which opponent they drew.

But internally, spirits had been elevated. Carlisle's decision to listen to his most trusted players gave them a greater sense of ownership in the upcoming run. Beaubois' future was still bright, but his present needed to wait, either because of his foot or his flagging confidence. Stevenson, a 10-year veteran, was invigorated by his important new role and eager to prove correct those who had shown him such faith.

The finale began with Hornets star Chris Paul yapping early and often. According to witnesses within hearing range, Paul took to reminding the Mavericks' bench that the team was "soft" and, perhaps, anatomically lacking. Even in Game 82, the Mavs were still having their manhood questioned.

In the third quarter, Paul rammed his shoulder into a screen set by Chandler, knocking the Dallas center to the floor. Stevenson shoved "CP3" in the chest, drawing a whistle but sending a clear message that the Mavs were prepared to answer.

Moments later, New Orleans looked for Stevenson. Paul brought the ball up the floor against him, then led him toward a screen set by Emeka Okafor, whose blind-side shoulder blow left Stevenson wincing on the floor. But Chandler switched smoothly to Paul and was waiting for the little point guard. Chandler body-checked his former teammate into the scorer's table, sending even the official scorer flying.

"Oh, it's like that, huh?" Paul shouted angrily.

"Yep," Chandler said defiantly. "Just like that."

"I see. All right," Paul said, nodding as Hornets coach Monty Williams pulled him away.

Broadcaster Jeff "Skin" Wade was only a few feet away from the confrontation and nearly wet himself with excitement.

"If you folks at home could see the look on Tyson's face, you would be pumping your fist right now!" Wade gushed. "This is the right attitude. Take this on into the weekend."

This confrontation, Wade said later, appeared to him to be the critical moment when the team "came together" in a way the old Mavericks never had. They demonstrated a resolve previously missing, a willingness to battle and defend one another. Chandler had set a new tone by punishing an old friend, and it would be behind that iron-fisted banner that Dallas would charge into the postseason.

Equipment manager Al Whitley explained, "That sent a message from Tyson that said, 'When we are on the floor, I don't care who you are or that we were friends. I am playing for the Dallas Mavericks and will do whatever it will take to win.' It got everybody's attention and it got Chris Paul's attention. This was an ultimate team, where everybody sticks up for everybody. That was huge."

The incident spurred another big Dallas run. The Mavs led 75-68 with 4:15 left in the third quarter when the collision happened. Dallas outscored New Orleans 46-21 the rest of the way, winning, 121-89. And Paul didn't seem to have another word the rest of the night.

It was believed several of the teams seeded below Dallas were hoping for a first-round date with the Mavs. It was the ultimate disrespect, but then the Mavs had been one-and-done three times in the past four seasons. It would take two hours after the victory over the Hornets for the playoff picture to crystallize.

The Lakers needed a dramatic overtime victory in their 82nd game to finish above the Mavs on the head-to-head tiebreaker for the second seed. Dallas would claim the No. 3 seed, and Oklahoma City lost its finale to finish at No. 4.

The top-seeded Spurs would face No. 8 Memphis. Paul and New Orleans would face the Lakers as the No. 7 seed. Oklahoma City would play fifth-seeded Denver. And the third-seeded Mavericks would face the No. 6 Portland Trail Blazers, led by Dallas native LaMarcus Aldridge. The teams had split their four regular-season meetings, the home team winning each game.

It was time for the only part of the season Kidd said truly mattered, and the biggest question was whether this year truly would be different. Time would tell very soon.

12

PORTLAND GAMES 1-2

(April 16-19, 2011)

Having played 17 seasons in the NBA had taught Jason Kidd a thing or two about perspective.

"The longer you play in this league, the more you look at the regular season as a dress rehearsal," Kidd explained. "I'm not going for scoring titles or All-Star games or MVPs. I am trying to get ready for the real season — the playoffs.

"You want to be playing your best basketball going into that. Coaches don't want to hear that, because they want to win every game all year."

The trials of January and late March might have rattled less-experienced NBA teams, but the Mavericks opened the 2011 playoffs with a virtually clean slate. They were banged up from the grueling, 82-game regular-season schedule. But they were experienced enough to know this was what they had been playing for, and it was time to catch a second wind and go.

They were one of 16 teams qualified to play for a championship, but only one of those teams would get the 16 wins needed to complete the task. Kidd, Nowitzki and Terry knew how long and perilous the road would be to even reach the NBA Finals. They also had been on teams that had worked hard for months to secure a high seed and homecourt advantage, only to be ousted in a first-round upset.

Did this team have too much baggage, too much disappointing history, too much of that "soft" reputation to be a championship threat? Had too much self-doubt poisoned the well after so many years of falling short? Could the league's best road team this season (tied with Miami at 28-13) finally start winning playoff games on the road, after going 2-13 away from home in the last four postseasons?

After another long year of waiting, the Mavericks' next chance for redemption had arrived. But would this year be different?

The NBA media certainly didn't think so. Nor did many of the potential opponents, who openly admitted that they would enjoy a chance to play Dallas. Being listed as a favorable opponent is quite an insult. But recent history did not afford the team many public defenders. It was "show me" time for this franchise. And the Mavs believed they were ready to let their basketball do the talking.

On the final night of the season, Chandler spoke like a man ready to go to war.

"Everybody's saying, 'Same old Mavs, same old Mavs,' and that's a good thing," Chandler said. "I hope whoever we're facing is going to think we're the same old Mavs, too, a team that's going to come and get knocked out early. Because that will give us an advantage. Sometimes it's good to be the hunter instead of the hunted."

=========

Few in the local media thought Portland a favorable first-round matchup for Dallas. The Trail Blazers fit the mold of teams that had found playoff success against the Mavericks. They had a roster loaded with long, athletic bigs to harass Nowitzki, and played in a suffocating home arena that could be hostile and unsettling to visitors. Matt Barnes had claimed Golden State laid out the blueprint for beating the Mavs in 2007, and there seemed a lot of similarities with this Portland squad.

Carlisle's decision to heed his star players' wishes and return Stevenson to the starting lineup meant the Mavericks would open the postseason with their rotation fairly settled. Starting Kidd and Stevenson at guard, Nowitzki and Marion at forward and Chandler in the middle meant the first four players off the bench would still be Terry, Barea, Stojakovic and Haywood. Cardinal, Brewer and Mahinmi remained in deep reserve, and Beaubois went on the inactive list after tweaking a knee in the finale against New Orleans.

Local columnists puzzled over Carlisle's change of heart regarding Beaubois, who likely could have played by the second or third game of the postseason. But the coach was trusting in his own judgment and that of his floor leaders. The team was going to sink or swim with "D-Steve," and the Beaubois experiment was going to be put on ice for the year. Either Stevenson would work in his starting role or the Mavs might be one-and-done yet again.

Saturday, April 16
Game 1, Western Conference First Round
Dallas, Texas

It could have been easy for the Mavs to let Portland steal Game 1. Midway through the fourth quarter, it was the Blazers controlling the game's pace, style, momentum and score (72-66 with six minutes to play). Dallas' 3-point assault was off target, and Portland was ending more than a few possessions with players hanging on the rim after demonstrative dunks.

The Mavs had not followed their recipe for success most of the night. But, led almost exclusively by Nowitzki and Kidd, they converted enough possessions and won enough battles in the final minutes to emerge with an 89-81 comeback victory. Nowitzki scored 18 of his team-high 28 points in the fourth period (including 13 of 13 free throws) and Kidd nailed six 3-point shots (a personal playoff best) en route to 24 points.

NBA playoff games can essentially be divided into two segments: the first 43 minutes and the final 5. If you can't irrevocably put away your opponent in the first segment, you sure better be able to win the pressure-packed second one.

Soon after Portland held its largest lead of six points, Nowitzki brought the Mavs back within two (72-70) with a pair of free throws with 4:49 left. Kidd then rebounded an Andre Miller miss and found Nowitzki, who was again fouled. Two more free throws tied the game. Miller responded with a layup, but Nowitzki drilled a 3-pointer from the right corner with 3:40 remaining that put Dallas ahead to stay.

"The most important shot of the game," Carlisle said. "That really energized our building and energized our team."

It didn't hurt the Mavs' confidence knowing that Game 1 winners go on to win NBA best-of-seven series about 78 percent of the time.

Aldridge led Portland with 27 points, but 11 came in the first 7½ minutes of the game. In the final minutes, it was Chandler grabbing big rebounds on both ends of the floor and Kidd icily hitting the kill shot — his sixth 3-pointer — with 25.4 seconds to play.

Carlisle described Kidd's performance as "spectacular." The guard's 24-point eruption surpassed anything he had produced in the regular season (when his high was 21 against the Lakers in mid-January). He looked an entirely different player than the guy who was scoreless and missed all six shots (five from 3-point range) two weeks earlier in Portland before getting his week off to recharge.

"Every shot he made, every play he made was absolutely essential for us," Carlisle said. "His leadership is something you can't quantify."

Carlisle needed quality minutes from Kidd against Portland, because Miller and the other Blazers guards were making a point of attacking Terry and Barea. The 6-foot-2 Miller scored 18, posting up the smaller Barea at every opportunity. It was not a matchup favorable to Dallas.

Portland's other strategy was to try dominating the paint. Besides the 6-11 Aldridge, the Blazers started the 6-11 Marcus Camby and 6-7 Gerald Wallace up front, with 6-8 Nicolas Batum coming off the bench. Blazers coach Nate McMillan was intent on keeping at least three of them on the floor at all times, and each athletic big man played at least 29 minutes in the opener. They took turns guarding Nowitzki while working to keep the rest of the Mavs shooting from a distant perimeter.

Portland had outscored Dallas in the paint by a 46-18 margin. The Blazers returned to their hotel feeling confident the Mavs wouldn't be able to rely on hitting 10 3-pointers every game to survive, especially when the series shifted to the hostile Rose Garden.

Few in the Cuban Era have ever accused referees of being on the Mavs' side. But McMillan hinted at injustice that his team was outscored 19-2 at the foul line in the final period. For the game, the Mavs were 25 of 29 at the line, the Blazers 9 of 13.

"I just don't get that," McMillan said. "Our guys didn't know how to play (in the fourth quarter) with the way it was being called."

However, Portland had wasted a number of possessions, too. They shot 46 percent in the game, but only made 2 of 16 3-point attempts (12.5 percent).

Though Chandler and Haywood had brought a marked improvement, Dallas still didn't have the type of roster that would aggressively attack the basket and control interior play. Fans and media expressed concern about trading 2-foot shots for 22-foot shots against a quality opponent, but the Mavericks' coaches and players were comfortable doing exactly that. They had faith they had assembled one of the best perimeter-shooting teams ever, and that those snipers would get a number of open looks as opponents were forced to collapse on the superbly skilled Nowitzki.

Carlisle's plan was predicated on spacing and ball movement. Nowitzki would score when he could, which was often. But when defenses swarmed him, a few extra passes until the Mavs knocked down an open-look shot from distance would be just fine. It would take a while for the outside world to understand just how deadly this could be, so long as someone was hitting those jumpers.

In Game 1, that wasn't Stojakovic (2 for 7), Barea (1 for 7) or Terry (2 for 5), who combined to make just 5 of 19 shots (including 2 of 6 3-pointers, both by Peja).

Terry remained in an odd place mentally, scoring 10 points but taking only five shots from the field in his first chance to assure everyone that his previous playoff disappearances were behind him. Everyone knew how vital his scoring would be, particularly in the fourth quarter, but his first effort was rather underwhelming.

So, too, were starters Stevenson (2 for 4, five points in 19 minutes), Marion (2 for 6, six points in 35 minutes) and Chandler (1 for 1, four points and nine rebounds in 32 minutes). The moment the playoff lights went on, Kidd and Nowitzki stepped up to combine for 34 shots and 52 points. The other eight Mavericks who played took just 32 shots and contributed 37 points.

Nowitzki and Kidd out-executed Aldridge and his teammates in the closing minutes to secure the Game 1 victory. But both teams still believed they were in excellent shape to win the series.

Tuesday, April 19
Game 2, Western Conference First Round
Dallas, Texas

Winning postseason basketball games was not something the Mavericks had proven good at since being loaded up with the mental baggage of 2006. The mere mention of the 2006 Finals collapse still induced nausea throughout the organization.

Virtually every playoff opponent Dallas had faced since had seemed to take advantage of this team's wounded, gun-shy mentality and put the Mavericks to the sword over the course of each seven-game series.

In 2007, Golden State won the first-round series in six games. In 2008, New Orleans needed just five games to oust the Mavericks. Dallas scored a five-game victory over San Antonio in 2009 (the Spurs were missing injured Manu Ginobili), but then lost to Denver in five. The healthy Spurs beat the Mavericks in six games in 2010. This was never a case of a "bad matchup." The opponent didn't seem to matter as much as the mental block that would overtake and affect key members of this team when the postseason began. Talk of a two-month playoff run seemed silly when this franchise usually couldn't last two weeks.

Dating to Game 3 of the 2006 Finals, the Mavs had lost 21 of their last 31 playoff games before rallying to beat Portland in Game 1. Their reputation for having a fragile collective psyche had been proven real and was documented in postseason box scores.

That's why the Mavericks' stifling 101-89 victory over the Trail Blazers in Game 2 seemed impressive on several levels. The Mavs had played like a determined bunch. They fought as if the game meant everything to them. They battled as if they were the better team. They didn't fold when faced with adversity. Simply put, they played like a team without baggage and self-doubt.

There was internal concern before the opening tip, given that referee Danny Crawford would be officiating. The Mavericks were 1-17 in playoff games he called, and rarely felt the official gave them the benefit of the doubt on close calls. Add to that Portland's insistence that the officials had not called Game 1 fairly, and the pregame narrative was easy to predict. But instead of letting the officials become a factor, the Mavs instead played hard enough to ensure they wouldn't.

Portland trailed for only 36 seconds of the first half, but took a slim 52-50 lead into the break. Dallas cranked up the defense in the second half, allowing just 37 points over the final two quarters. The Blazers got only 11 points from their bench, none in the second half.

It's easy to talk big about defense being the new calling card of an organization, but it's a much harder thing to implement. And while regular-season statistics might illustrate improvement on the defensive end, it's another thing to prove it again and again over the course of a two-week playoff street fight.

But these Mavericks were displaying a determination and resolve that had been absent for years. Those who had picked the Blazers in this series — and they were the majority — were essentially picking against the Mavericks' fragile mindset and against Nowitzki in particular. They viewed the Dallas talisman as a fine player, but one whose credentials, history and skill set suggested his championship window had already closed.

So, to watch No. 41 play both ends of the floor with an intensity reminiscent of 2006 was something to behold. He had pulled Game 1 out of the fire with his fourth-quarter play (18 of his 28 points), and did it again in Game 2, scoring 14 of his 33 points in the final period. Dirk scored his team's final 11 points to personally tuck the game away, and was playing like a man possessed. Nowitzki clearly had shifted into a higher gear for the postseason, and the Blazers didn't seem to have a response.

Nowitzki had help earlier in the game. Kidd continued scoring with 18 points (including 3-of-6 shooting from 3-point range) and eight assists. And Stojakovic gave the Blazers more fits, scoring 21 points that included five 3-pointers, tying his personal playoff best. Despite being lost down the bench at times, Peja was another example of veteran depth and know-how that Carlisle could try in a given situation. If he helped win a game or two in the playoffs, his acquisition would be proven to be well worth the trouble. And his fingerprints were all over Game 2. Stojakovic did exactly what Donnie Nelson had hoped he would: Make an opponent pay for double-teaming Nowitzki in the post by taking the German's passes and nailing those open looks.

"We're never sure which two or three guys we're going to get hot," Carlisle admitted after the game. "But we need contributions from a lot of different guys to be successful, and that's what we got tonight."

Nowitzki had pulled down seven rebounds and showed he would not shy away from the punishment required to battle under the rim. His sacrifice sent him to the line 17 times, where he picked up 15 points on free throws. But even with a 2-0 lead and Portland struggling for answers as things shifted to the Rose Garden, Nowitzki warned, "This series is far from over."

No team understood the fool's gold of a 2-0 series lead better than these Mavericks. But in addition to Nowitzki raising his superb game to yet a higher level, they were encouraged by the difference their centers were making. Chandler had returned to the game with roughly six minutes remaining and wound up leading both teams in fourth-quarter rebounds. He clearly had his hands full with the dynamic LaMarcus Aldridge (24 points, 10 rebounds in 44 minutes). But with Chandler and Haywood battling in the paint for every rebound and loose ball, Aldridge was getting all he could handle, too.

And therein was the problem for Portland. It appeared Aldridge was the Blazers' only dangerous option in their half-court set, as shooting guard Brandon Roy did not seem to have the knees or rhythm to be an effective second scorer off the bench. Other than point guard Andre Miller (18 points) trying to abuse Barea, Portland's set offense looked like that of a typical No. 6 seed.

The Blazers' defense wasn't looking much better. They had no one capable of shackling Nowitzki down the stretch, were slow to react to the aged 3-point shooters carving them up from the perimeter, and seemed easily distracted and confused by Terry weaving through numerous screens.

Portland remained dangerous, but Dallas already looked far the better team. The question was whether the increasingly confident Mavericks could sustain the pressure in Oregon. Since closing out Phoenix in the 2006 Western Conference finals, the Mavericks were an abysmal 2-16 as a road playoff team. They had won twice in San Antonio when the Spurs lacked Ginobili in 2009. And they had lost every other road game — 16 in all — at Miami, Golden State, New Orleans, Denver and San Antonio again.

On the road in the playoffs, a team is isolated and on its own. It often receives no help from the outside. The crowd screams for the opponent. The officials seem to favor the home side. And in these situations, the Mavericks had crumbled for five years running. In many of those 16 road losses, the margins of defeat were in double-digits. It was no small challenge to overcome this obstacle. But, if they did not start winning on the road, the playoff campaign of 2011 would be short.

In Game 3, the Mavs would have a chance to demonstrate how far they had come. They were staying in the moment, not looking ahead, taking it a day at a time — all the appropriate cliches for a team that understood snakebite. Still, they climbed the stairs of their jet to Portland with confidence.

Little did they know the swagger was about to be knocked out of them.

13

PORTLAND GAMES 3-4

(April 21-23, 2011)

Playing in Portland posed a fabulous test for a team that struggles to win postseason road games. The Rose Garden sets the gold standard in the NBA for arenas generating so much crowd noise you can't hear yourself think. It is a point of jealousy league-wide, as teams in other cities wonder why their crowd cannot match the proactive manner of the Blazers' faithful. They don't wait for good things to cheer about; they scream to make good things happen for their team.

One player determined to ramp up that noise was Trail Blazers guard Brandon Roy. The league's Rookie of the Year in 2007 and a three-time All-Star, Roy had struggled the second half of the season after requiring double arthroscopic knee surgery in mid-January. His impact on the first two games of the series in Dallas had been negligible — two points in Game 1, none in Game 2. The career 19-points per game scorer had seen just 34 minutes of action in the series and made 1 of 8 shots. He had been relegated to a reserve role, and Blazers coach Nate McMillan wasn't seeing anything to change his mind.

Roy didn't help matters when he went public with his discontent after playing just eight scoreless minutes in Game 2. He had told Portland's newspaper, *The Oregonian*, "I just always thought I would be treated a little better. That was a little disappointing for me. There was a moment where I was thinking, 'You better not cry.'" Roy apologized for those comments at the morning shootaround the day of Game 3, and attempted to patch things up with McMillan in a private meeting with the coach.

It was the type of distracting, headline-grabbing controversy that could cause a team to implode, or to rally around its embattled teammate. Either way, most eyes were clearly trained on the Blazers' guard as the Game 3 tipoff neared.

Thursday, April 21
Game 3, Western Conference First Round
Portland, Oregon

Roy entered Game 3 to a standing ovation with 2:17 left in the first quarter. He had received dozens of encouraging calls and text messages before the game (including one from TNT analyst Charles Barkley), but nothing had lifted his spirits as much as this deafening home crowd showing its love.

"The fans were really supportive," Roy said later. "That's really big for me. We've been through a lot together, and to know that they still have my back was great for me tonight."

Not so great for the Mavericks, however.

Dallas had won the first two games of the series, in part, because Portland had come up empty finding a consistent perimeter threat to complement LaMarcus Aldridge's inside game. On this night, however, both Wesley Matthews (25 points) and Roy (16 points in 24 minutes) regained lethal shooting strokes to accompany Aldridge's bruising 20 points in the paint.

Matthews buried 8 of 12 shots, including 4 of 6 from 3-point range, and had scored 22 points by halftime. Roy went 6 for 10 (1 of 3 from long distance) and provided the bench-scoring spark Portland had been missing. Aided by Tyson Chandler fouling out with 7:24 to play, the Blazers repelled a late charge to win, 97-92. The victory improved their record against Dallas in home playoff games to 7-1.

Perhaps the biggest question facing this Mavericks team was whether it could win postseason games in hostile environments. It didn't seem to matter that Dallas had been the league's finest road team for two regular seasons running. The Game 3 loss left the Mavs a dismal 2-17 in their last 19 road playoff games.

It was unfair to tar the entire roster with the stink of that 2-17 number. Chandler, for instance, was playing his first road playoff game in a Dallas uniform when he fouled out of Game 3. That he was saddled so early by what some considered "ticky-tack" foul trouble only brought up another frequent gripe heard during the 2-17 run — the officials were out to get Cuban's team.

Carlisle didn't want to hear it. The coach preached accountability. He wanted his team to recognize the cost of self-inflicted wounds, handle the details within players' control, and stop worrying about the officiating. The five-point loss in Game 3 could just as easily (and perhaps more accurately) be pinned on the Mavs' 10 missed free throws and 16 turnovers than on Chandler's foul trouble.

Some of Carlisle's tactics raised questions, too. The coach believed in Barea, almost to a fault. And his determination to test the Blazers' ability to cope with "small ball" wound up backfiring.

When Barea checked in late in the third period, the Mavericks had a 69-68 lead. Five minutes later, they trailed by 13. Carlisle had Nowitzki and Haywood on the floor with the undersized Terry-Kidd-Barea trio, and the Blazers were relentlessly attacking the diminutive Barea. Yet Carlisle left Barea out there for all but 10 seconds of the final 13½ minutes of the game.

Kidd also couldn't maintain the brilliance of his first two playoff games. His 38 minutes in Game 3 produced eight points, six rebounds and only three assists. He committed five turnovers and hit just 2 of 8 shots from 3-point range.

With Kidd ineffective, the Blazers threw the kitchen sink at Nowitzki defensively. McMillan had Nick Batum guarding the German All-Star most of the time, but sent an array of switches and double-teams his way as well. Nowitzki missed more than half his shots (making 10 of 21) but still finished with 25 points and nine rebounds.

What excited the Mavericks most about the loss was that Terry seemed to be finding another of his vintage hot-shooting streaks, which would bode well for the rest of the series. Terry looked confident from the start and buried 10 of 13 shots (including 5 of 7 3-pointers) en route to a team-high 29 points.

Terry's volatile temper was tested once when a courtside fan stuck his hand near Terry's face as he chased a loose ball out of bounds. Terry showed restraint with the fan, but not with Batum when the Portland forward pushed him aside to inbound the ball. Terry slung Batum away and drew a technical foul, but Carlisle didn't mind the reaction. In a hostile atmosphere, he wanted Terry ready to push back all night long.

In the end, missed foul shots, too many turnovers and a starting center who couldn't stay in the game conspired to knock the Mavericks down again on the road. The glass-is-half-full crowd would be encouraged that even with those failings, Dallas only fell short by five points.

It would be a quick turnaround before Game 4, scheduled for Saturday afternoon, so there would be little time for rest or regret. But the Mavs knew they had to prove they could win at the Rose Garden, or risk playing a dangerous opponent in a decisive seventh game where anything could happen.

========

Saturday, April 23
Game 4, Western Conference First Round
Portland, Oregon

It was happening again.

A team haunted by its past was having another incomprehensible meltdown to sabotage all progress. This time, it was against the No. 6-seeded Portland Trail Blazers, but many were starting to wonder whether the opponent really mattered. The Mavericks' biggest issue this time of year might not be whom they were playing, but rather what was going on between their own ears.

When Peja Stojakovic stepped into another silky-smooth 3-pointer from the corner, the Mavs were running the Blazers out of their own building, putting up a mammoth 67-44 lead with 1:15 left in the third quarter. The Blazers had missed their first 15 shots in the period, finally managing just 14 points in the quarter. This, after they scored just 11 in the first. The Mavericks were cruising to a big road win in Game 4, one that would give them a chokehold on the series. And, perhaps just as importantly, it would demonstrate that this team could win in a hostile building in the postseason.

Then the avalanche began.

Brandon Roy, who hadn't made his first field-goal attempt until the final two seconds of the third period, somehow ignited himself and his team in the fourth. Roy made 8 of 10 shots in the fourth, scoring 18 points and dishing off four assists in the final 12 minutes. Portland shot 75 percent, did not commit a turnover and outscored Dallas by 20 points in the final period to storm back to an 84-82 victory over the stunned Mavericks.

"It still just doesn't feel real yet," said a grinning Roy, inadvertently also summing up the feelings in the snake-bit visitors' locker room. "It was just an unbelievable game and comeback."

It was a playoff comeback — or collapse — of historic proportions. Portland had become only the third NBA team in the shot-clock era to win a playoff game when trailing by 18 points or more heading into the fourth quarter. According to the Elias Sports Bureau, only the 2002 Celtics (down 21 against Jason Kidd and New Jersey) and the 1994 Suns (trailing by 18 against Houston) had staged equal or greater comebacks in the final quarter of NBA playoff games.

Portland had trailed by 18 at the end of the third (67-49), but had finished the game on a 40-15 run to overcome the 23-point deficit over the final 13:15.

"Did we let up?" Carlisle said, repeating a reporter's question after the game. "I think we let up, yeah. There isn't any question."

A 23-point lead should be good enough to survive any single-quarter onslaught. But as it slipped away like sand through their fingers, the Mavs appeared to be battling not only the resilient Trail Blazers, but their own demons from five years earlier.

It was Game 3 of the 2006 Finals, after all, when this epic streak of Dallas postseason road futility had begun. The Mavericks had taken a 2-0 series lead to Miami and looked in great shape to capture Game 3 when they led by 13 points with 6:33 to play. But they allowed the Heat to finish on a 22-7 run to win that game and change the course of history. Having lost virtually everything that has mattered since, the psychologically damaged Mavericks now looked like the golfer who plays wonderfully until finding he cannot sink the easy putt to finish the round.

The Mavericks had strewn playoff road losses from Miami to Golden State to New Orleans to San Antonio to Denver and now to Portland over their demoralizing five-year odyssey. Among their common threads were complaints about officiating, a tendency to shy away from the physical play near the rim (giving rise to their "soft" reputation) and an emphasis (or, critics felt, overemphasis) on the 3-point shot as their primary postseason weapon. If those long-range shots weren't falling, the Mavs were often quick to lose their composure in hostile road arenas.

On this night in Portland, they had fired up eight 3-pointers in the final period and hit just one. They attempted only two shots in the paint in the final quarter, and missed them both. And Shawn Marion, the defensive stopper, suddenly had been found lacking against the gimpy-kneed Roy in the minutes that mattered most.

"I'm going to take the blame for a lot of that," Carlisle said. "There are different things defensively we could have done."

There was an abundance of blame to go around. Chandler (six points, seven rebounds, five fouls limiting him to 30 minutes) was still being outplayed by LaMarcus Aldridge (18 points, six rebounds). Terry made just 5 of 16 shots and had been ineffective again. Barea (four points, three assists, three turnovers) was nearly invisible in his 19 minutes. Kidd and Terry each missed potential game-winning 3-point shots within the final 29 seconds.

But it was the fourth-quarter scoreline (Portland 35, Dallas 15) that was most infuriating in this two-point loss. One more basket and the Mavericks force overtime. Two more baskets (or a 3-ball) and they win. Instead, the game ate them alive and threatened to sear these proud veterans with the legacy of being nothing but playoff failures. The series was tied 2-2, but it surely felt as if the Mavericks were on the verge of early elimination yet again.

The Mavs' locker room was quiet, solemn and angry. Everyone affiliated with the team sensed that this was the pivotal night of the season. For some, perhaps, of their entire ringless careers.

"I'm pissed off," Marion told ESPN.com's Tim MacMahon. "I'm mad that we lost this game. It was in our hands. We let them come back. We just let our guard down. We thought it was over with. They were down by 23 and we let our guard down."

Nowitzki, the face of this title-less franchise, bore the burden of explaining the inexplicable in a news conference with international media. He admitted his team felt gutted, but said talk was cheap.

"You can always, after the fact, talk about what you could have done or should have done," Nowitzki said. "Afterward, you're a lot smarter, but that doesn't help anybody right now. We all have to take it and stay positive.

"This is definitely a tough one to sit on. Now, we have to fly home for four hours on that one, and frustration is definitely at a high level. We've got to win two out of three now, and we have two at home."

But behind the scenes, Nowitzki dispensed with the cliches, and showed a different, far more defiant side to his teammates. Kidd was sitting on a trainer's table having the tape cut from around his ankles when a very tall, steely-eyed German came in.

"After Game 4, I was thinking, 'Oh no, here we go again. Please don't let this happen to us again,'" Kidd recalled. "And then I felt better when Dirk told me, 'They are not coming into my house and getting a win. We are coming back here, up 3-2. And we are going to close it out up here.'"

Game 5 would be Monday back in Dallas, and no one was underestimating its importance.

"I remember coming back on the plane from Game 4, knowing that the entire landscape of this franchise could change with a loss in Game 5," Donnie Nelson recalled. "That was, at the time, the most important game since I had been in Dallas.

"I know that if we lose Game 5, there is a good chance we go back up there and lose Game 6. There was more pressure on Game 5 than any other game in the playoffs. Because that would have been another first-round exit — the fourth in five years."

The team would have a long flight back to Texas to consider that, with more worry and regret than could possibly fit in the airliner's overhead bins. The bus ride from the Rose Garden to the airport would begin as soon as Nowitzki completed his interview obligations. Most of the traveling party had downcast eyes, quietly reading messages on their phones or silently pondering the enormity of the loss.

Finally, Nowitzki stepped on the bus. He walked slowly down the aisle, extending his fist for a bump from each of his teammates as he walked all the way back. He was not rattled. He had seen it before. And he knew what they had to do next.

14

PORTLAND GAMES 5-6

(April 25-28, 2011)

Gut-check time.

Anyone with even a modicum of interest in the NBA playoffs got set to tune in April 25 for Game 5 in Dallas, when the Mavericks would reveal whether they had the hearts of lions or of mice. They were home for a crucial game in a series that could still go either way. Those with a grasp of history knew this was a good spot to see if these were the "same ol' Mavericks."

The NBA's playoff format allows for a dramatic crescendo that the NFL cannot match. NFL teams need only to win three or four games to be crowned champions. Each contest is a single-game battle they either win in three hours, or their season ends.

The NBA playoffs offer a deeper, more immersive experience. Each best-of-7 series takes nearly two weeks to complete. Between every game there are usually travel or practice days during which the questions, conjecture and outright panic attacks can escalate. Every game is a self-contained drama that can send the series lurching in a new, unexpected direction.

The Mavericks felt great after the first two games, confident they were the better team because they had outplayed the Blazers in "crunch time," the final 3-5 minutes when close games are won by the brave and bold.

Two losses in Portland, however, changed everything. Though the series was deadlocked, the nature of that gutting Game 4 loss had rocked the Mavericks and their oft-wounded, understandably skeptical fans to their core. It didn't matter that Dallas had outplayed its opponent for most of the two games in Oregon. Only the final scores count.

To some, suffering a complete blowout loss in Game 4 would have been preferable to finding a way to lead by 23 and still lose. It was a psychologically damaging slip by the Mavericks. And, if this team was cut from the same cloth as its predecessors, Dallas would cave under the pressure.

Nowitzki and Kidd spoke again in the training room on Monday, while getting taped up for the morning shootaround. Nowitzki's faith had not wavered. His determination in the wake of Saturday night's debacle had only grown.

"I didn't feel a great vibe there in the locker room that morning," Nowitzki recalled. "I said, 'They aren't going to beat us tonight — there is just no way.'

"Usually, I am a very negative, skeptical person. You know, Germans in general are very negative. And usually when we lose, then (I think) I am the worst player and we are the worst team. But, for some reason, I was confident that we were not going to lose Game 5 and they couldn't beat us in Dallas."

Kidd loved this Dirk.

Nowitzki had his detractors, people who conceded he was a superstar, but one they thought didn't dig as deep as true champions did each spring. Some felt Nowitzki would be bullied and pushed out of the playoffs when it was time to play for keeps. Kidd knew some had this perception of Nowitzki, and he found it absurd. The Hall of Fame-bound point guard had been legitimately concerned about the Mavericks' situation, until he saw the look in Dirk's eyes when the forward assured him everything was fine. That was all Kidd needed in order to believe.

Team owner Mark Cuban, meanwhile, had his own message for the doubting public.

"Anybody who wants to quit on us, quit on us," Cuban challenged. "We're not going to beg them. They can do what they want to do. That's why they call them fans and that's why they call everybody else talk-radio junkies. Obviously, we hate losing any game. Last I checked, it was just one game. They're a good team. We're a good team. It's a seven-game series. That's why we play all the games."

========

Monday, April 25
Game 5, Western Conference First Round
Dallas, Texas

Nowitzki wasn't the only Mavericks player who arrived to Monday's game truly inspired. There was also the team's big man, the new guy who wasn't carrying all those years of emotional baggage from past Dallas disappointments. The guy who arrived ready to live the motto tattooed on his shoulder: "Only the Strong Survive."

For Tyson Chandler, 16 points and 30 rebounds would have been a pretty special game. Unfortunately, those were his totals for the first four games against LaMarcus Aldridge and the Trail Blazers. Chandler wasn't proud of these first few performances. His minutes and production had been hampered by numerous ticky-tack and ill-advised fouls, but Chandler approached Game 5 with a decisive plan to be aggressive and active, come what may from the officials.

Chandler also had approached Carlisle at the morning shootaround with a suggestion. Rather than being anchored on the weak side of the offense, drawing large defenders away from the ball, he asked if he could get more involved by moving around the lane, pursuing rebound chances by instinct rather than by rigid spacing. Carlisle told him to have at it, a decision that would alter the series substantially.

Chandler, who had already proven his worth as the team's emotional leader during the regular season, hit Game 5 like a cyclone. The 7-1 center overwhelmed the Blazers and fired up his teammates with a barrage of rebounds, dunks, interior points, physical play and primal screams.

"Oh my God, he was so focused tonight," Barea told ESPN.com's Jeff Caplan. "He was controlling everybody. He was on everyone's ass. He made sure we won this game. It's hard to beat us when Tyson Chandler plays like that. Impossible, I think."

Chandler was tenacious from the start, racking up seven points and seven rebounds in the first nine minutes. And when Dallas broke open a tight game with a 15-5 run in the third period, Chandler made sure he was there at the end. The Mavericks built a lead as large as 17 points, and this time they protected it. Chandler yanked down seven more rebounds in the fourth quarter to help seal a decisive 93-82 victory.

"They played like they wanted it more than we did," Blazers guard Brandon Roy admitted. "I thought they played a little tougher than in the first four games."

Nowitzki handled the scoring load with 25 points, 11 coming in the third quarter when things were still tight. But this time, Chandler was big in support on both ends of the floor. He finished with 14 points and 20 rebounds (his career best for a postseason game). His 13 offensive rebounds were the most by anyone in an NBA playoff game since Shaquille O'Neal had 14 for the Orlando Magic in 1995, when Chandler was 12 years old.

He also gave Aldridge fits on the defensive end, limiting the big Blazers power forward to a series-low 12 points and nine rebounds.

"I really just want to do whatever it takes to win at whatever time," Chandler said. "In (Game 4), I was as much in shock as everybody else. I vowed to myself that I wouldn't let it happen again. ... I wanted to come out, bring energy and I was hoping my teammates would feed off of me, and they did."

And then there was Dirk, from whom many on the Dallas roster still take their cues virtually every night. When he stays somewhat passive and settles for nothing but outside shots, his teammates generally follow suit. When he blends his outside shooting with a willingness to go hard to the rim, take punishment and get to the foul line, he can be impossible to defend and his teammates often follow.

Nowitzki understood his role at this juncture better than he ever had. This would be one of the most determined games of his career. He would not settle. He took (and missed) only one 3-point shot, but drove hard inside or faked and hit shorter fall-away jumpers for 16 of his points. The balance came when he drew fouls and made 9 of 11 free throws.

Following his lead, the Mavs wound up drawing 35 foul shots and made 26, which offset their terrible 3-point shooting (3 of 17). The Blazers were only 14 of 19 from the line, which proved the difference, as both teams made 32 field-goal attempts.

The Mavs didn't need to just win Game 5, they needed to reclaim the court. Portland had owned the lane in Game 4 (an 18-0 edge in fourth-quarter points from the paint), and it was up to the Mavs to regain some territory. Behind Chandler and Nowitzki, Dallas scored 40 in the paint in Game 5 to put the Blazers back on their heels.

The Mavericks had morphed from the passive, timid, jump-shooting team that repeatedly proved inadequate for the bruising warfare that is the NBA playoffs. With Chandler in foul trouble and Nowitzki content to settle for 22-footers, Dallas looked vulnerable. But with Nowitzki getting to the foul line at least 10 times, the Mavs were now 14-0 for the season. That spoke volumes for the disposition Dirk needed to show in key moments, and the success that would follow.

Chandler staying on the floor certainly helped. He was proving to be every bit of the player and emotional leader for which Cuban and Donnie Nelson had hoped when they pulled the trigger on one of the most important moves in franchise history. The referees had seemed intent on keeping tensions low with quick whistles in Portland, but a bit more contact was permitted in Game 5, allowing Chandler and his team to thrive. It was an odd thing for a franchise that had never been fond of street fights, but Chandler was changing that mentality, too.

The Mavericks outrebounded the taller Blazers by a 49-37 margin. Their zone defense moved quickly and effectively, forcing 10 consecutive missed shots early in the fourth quarter. Even Roy conceded the Mavs played with "more of a sense of urgency."

Portland took a small bit of comfort knowing that, so far, the home team had won every game. Game 6 would be Thursday, back at the rowdy Rose Garden. But now the Mavs had history back on their side. Of the previous 157 series tied 2-2, the Game 5 winner had ultimately prevailed 83 percent of the time.

"We can't rely on being home as a cure-all," Blazers forward Marcus Camby said. "We have to play a whole lot better."

The Blazers would likely go as far as Aldridge could carry them, and it appeared the Mavericks were figuring him out, especially when Chandler was allowed to get a bit more physical with him. Aldridge's scoring output had diminished with each of the first five games (27, 24, 20, 18 and 12). No one in Dallas was suggesting the mission was accomplished, but Mavs strategists felt the Blazers were starting to wear down and lacked the bench depth of their Texas-based opponent.

The Blazers' bench primarily consisted of Nick Batum and the somewhat unpredictable Roy and Rudy Fernandez. So with Dallas figuring out how to handle Aldridge and Roy's health uncertain, Portland was relying heavily on Andre Miller, a journeyman point guard who in January 2010 scored a career-high 52 points against the Mavs.

Miller, 35, was proving to have a solid offensive game in this series, and his strength posed a problem for Barea. Kidd, however, matched up better with a point guard of Miller's ilk than with the quicker Chris Paul-types who become an issue over seven games. Miller led the Blazers with 18 points in Game 5, but his 16.8 ppg average thus far in the series was within the Mavs' tolerance.

Cuban would often say that Shawn Marion was the Mavericks' unsung hero. With Nowitzki, Terry, Chandler and Kidd doing most of the ball-handling and scoring, people often forgot about the fifth member of the lineup finishing up games. But while Marion was the fifth option on offense, he was the Mavs' primary defender when there was a dynamic scorer to shut down.

Marion felt responsibility for the Game 4 debacle, and he bounced back two nights later with tremendous energy at both ends of the floor. Four steals and two blocked shots only told part of the story of how disruptive Marion was to the Portland offense. And though Dallas never ran offense specifically for him, his contribution of 14 points spoke to his effectiveness converting loose balls, second-chance shots and running the floor in transition. Marion joined Chandler in fighting hard around the offensive glass. And even if he wasn't getting as many rebounds as the Mavs' center, his selfless grunt work blocking out kept Portland's frontline players at bay so Chandler could operate.

Through nine meetings between these teams in the regular season and playoffs, the home team had won every game. Their 3-2 series lead meant winning Game 6 no longer was mandatory for the Mavericks, but their 2-18 record over the last 20 road playoff games suggested something else. It was vital that Dallas start to establish a confident road mentality by winning on a hostile enemy floor. They had to prove they were not the "same ol' Mavericks" any more.

After Game 5, Mavericks trainer Casey Smith took Nowitzki aside and reminded the player of his morning pledge of victory.

"I have never heard you say that in all my years here," Smith said, perhaps sensing a corner had been turned in Nowitzki's career.

Portland's Game 4 comeback had been an enormous gut-punch for the Mavericks, and the entire league had been watching to see how they would respond.

The Mavericks had punched back even harder.

========

Thursday, April 28
Game 6, Western Conference First Round
Portland, Oregon

The Rose Garden crowd was going bonkers as Game 6 tipped off. The Trail Blazers' fans and players were supremely confident they could force a seventh game and take their chances in a 48-minute, winner-take-all brawl a few nights later in Dallas.

And the Mavericks seemed to be obliging. Portland's Gerald Wallace was running around the court like a madman, scoring 13 first-quarter points to spur the Blazers to an early 12-point lead. LaMarcus Aldridge was finding and knocking down shots again. Guard Wesley Matthews was even chipping in the occasional 3-ball. The place was rocking and the Blazers were rolling.

But with Portland leading 33-22, the game suddenly changed. Blazers backup center Chris Johnson, a seldom-used callup from Portland's NBA Developmental League team (the mighty Dakota Wizards of Bismarck, ND), figured it was his time to shine. Perhaps he had heard of Matt Barnes' tweeted blueprint of how to handle the Mavs and decided it was time to "punk 'em."

Nowitzki drove past Johnson to score a left-handed layup and drew contact, yelling, "And one!" This prompted Johnson, the D-League's Defensive Player of the Year, to leap to his feet and try facing down the 10-time NBA All-Star. To his credit, Nowitzki seemed oblivious to the rookie's strut. And after hitting his free throw, Nowitzki retreated to play defense.

At the other end, Nowitzki grabbed a defensive rebound, and started back down the floor. That's when the still-angry Johnson inexplicably reached out from behind and swiped at Nowitzki's face, drawing a flagrant foul and lighting the Mavericks' fuse. Nowitzki stayed down a few seconds, composed himself and calmly knocked down two free throws. They were the start of the nine points he would score during the Mavs' 13-2 run to tie the score.

"He kind of punched me in the face there," Nowitzki said later. "Hey, that was their thing. They wanted to be really physical with us. We talked about how that's not going to happen today. This is our moment."

History occasionally had shown that, over the run of the "Dirk Era," a cheap shot could turn Dallas timid. There was a reason their reputation was given, and more importantly, earned. But, the evolution from a fragile team to a hardened one on a mission appeared to be underway. Dirk took the blow, and his team decided to show a response that would ultimately end the series.

In the final 9:17 of the first half, the Mavericks roared through a 30-10 run, turning a 33-22 deficit into a 52-43 lead. Only the halftime whistle allowed the Blazers to catch their breath and regroup after Johnson had poked the bear. Johnson, who had played five minutes, was not used again.

Adding to Portland's troubles, Wallace had to leave the game with a sore back and missed much of the second quarter. He managed to return and finish with 32 points and 12 rebounds, and his rousing steal and dunk with 5:24 to play brought Portland back within one point at 86-85. Dallas had led by as many as 17 in the third period but now had to wonder: Could this seriously be happening again?

Absolutely not, decided Dallas' veteran guards.

Kidd answered with perhaps his biggest shot as a Maverick to date, drilling a 3-pointer that quieted the crowd and spread the lead back to four with 5:05 to play.

Portland missed two shots at the other end, then Kidd stole the ball from Aldridge. He looked up, found Terry rushing down the wing, and fed him for a long two-pointer for a 91-85 lead with 4:03 to play. The Blazers called timeout but never got closer than four points after that. Nowitzki made 8 of 8 free throws over the final 30 seconds to secure the 103-96 victory.

Dirk (33 points, 11 rebounds) and Jet (22 points, team-high eight assists), the longtime collaborators and sole uniformed holdovers from the 2006 Finals, had squeezed the life out of Portland and won this first-round series on the road, four games to two.

It was a bit early to say the Mavericks had rewritten their legacy and reputation.

It was a bit early to say definitively the Mavericks were able to win road playoff games again.

It was a bit early to say the Mavericks no longer could be bullied in the postseason with physical and intimidating play.

It was a bit early to say the entire NBA was on notice.

But closing out Portland in six games with such tenacity and courage after a devastating Game 4 loss was a nice start in that direction.

Winning a playoff series should never be minimized. It had been five years since they'd won more than one, and now their prize was a meeting with the mighty Los Angeles Lakers. But the Mavericks would have a few days to catch their breath before that marquee battle. They could take pride in having outwrestled a very competitive Portland side that dragged them out into deep waters, knowing they were the survivors to reach the next shore.

"Tonight, Nowitzki, Kidd and Terry weren't going to let us lose the game. It was simple as that," Carlisle said. "There wasn't going to be a miracle tonight. ... Walking in this place and playing a playoff game is no fun, brother. This is the loudest place I've ever been. For our guys to hang in and be able to win in this environment is huge for us. To go

135

through what we went through in Game 4, these things happen for a reason. But we feel our work has just begun."

Nowitzki had both talked the talk and walked the walk. He scored 164 points in the six-game series — 60 more than his next-closest teammate, and never fewer than 20 in a game. With scoring totals of 28, 33, 25, 20, 25 and 33 against the Blazers, he was proving to be as deadly a weapon as in any point of his career. He had become that rare breed of player who could go on the road and make an entire arena groan when he released an open shot. When he started rolling, there was often no stopping him.

But Dirk would still need support. Perhaps his most dominating playoff series since 2006 had been in the Western Conference semifinals against Denver in 2009. Then, he amassed 172 points in just five games (28, 35, 33, 44 and 32), but Dallas lost the series. Nowitzki had delivered many times in many situations, but he could not single-handedly drag his team to victory. Neither could the Lakers' Kobe Bryant before he was given proper help in 2008.

But perhaps this year truly was different. Nowitzki had battle-hardened, playoff-tested help. When his shot is falling, Terry can terrorize any opposing defense. Marion could lock down most top scorers and provide the loose-ball intangibles under the glass or in transition. Kidd's vision and passing wisdom remained almost unparalleled. And then there was the big guy — Tyson Chandler — whose acquisition back in July 2010, frankly, disappointed many locals. Sure, he seemed to be an interesting player when healthy, but how excited could fans really get about a starting center who had started just 72 games in two years?

Well, they were excited now. And not just because Chandler wasn't Erick Dampier. In the final two games of the Portland series, Chandler had realized all the potential that Cuban and Donnie Nelson had envisioned 9½ months earlier when they finalized the trade with Charlotte, beating Toronto to the punch. He not only had provided the best post play on both ends of the floor of any Dallas center in the "Dirk Era," but he also appeared to be the William Wallace element the Mavericks always lacked. Chandler's passion was undeniable, genuine and infectious.

Was he the alpha male? No, that was Dirk. But was he the guy who kept the bullies away from his buddies? Yes, he was.

A strange thing happened as Nowitzki left the court after Game 6. Many of the Portland fans who had been rooting so hard against him suddenly showed their admiration and wished the big German continued success.

"They were great," Nowitzki told Eddie Sefko of the *Dallas Morning News*. "When we won and were walking off the court, a lot of them were yelling, 'Go beat L.A.!'"

Earning opposing fans' respect and a ticket to the conference semifinals was nice, but Nowitzki had much more on his agenda.

"It's a nice win, but, I don't really want to overrate this win," he told reporters. "Our goal the last five or six seasons was always a championship. When I first got to the Mavericks, our big goal was making the playoffs. That goal obviously changed. Once you've been in the playoffs a number of years, you want to win it all.

"We understand that to win it all, you've got to take the first step, and that's winning the first round. So we feel good about that. But we know we have a long way to go."

That Nowitzki and Terry could play such big roles in dispatching the Blazers seemed especially fulfilling to their coach.

"These guys have been here a long time," Carlisle said. "It is so meaningful for them both to help us move on. ... I have grown to love these guys so much, and what they stand for, and what they've been through over a period of time that extends long before I got here. ... Our team is a true team."

The Blazers had been stout first-round opponents, certainly no pushovers. Their team wanted a fight and offered one. Their arena set the benchmark for what loud could mean. They forced the Mavericks to come together as a squad and see just how much agony and heartbreak they could stand. This series had been an ideal proving ground for what was ahead.

15

LOS ANGELES LAKERS
GAMES 1-2

(May 2-4, 2011)

"One of the things I wanted to remind the team is that this is a team that can beat us in the postseason. And, for whatever reason, whenever we play Dallas, it doesn't have that same energy as when we play Oklahoma (City) and San Antonio. It's important for us to understand that this team is a serious contender, and that we don't approach them lightly."

— Kobe Bryant, March 2011

The Western Conference semifinals brought an entirely new vibe to the Dallas Mavericks' playoff run.

Before a shot was taken, the Mavs were transformed from a dangerous team on a roll into a haggard old squad facing insurmountable odds. When you beat Portland, people raise an eyebrow and apologize for doubting you. When your reward is facing the Los Angeles Lakers in the very next round, many of your fans begin drawing up concession speeches.

The Lakers needed no introduction. They had been to the NBA Finals three straight years, lifting the trophy in both 2009 and 2010. Led by the alpha male of the sport, Kobe Bryant, they had now assembled a team so big, athletic and talent-laden as to almost seem unfair.

Contending teams throughout the league had spent the past year building squads they hoped could compete with the Lakers when they finally met.

The Boston Celtics had added more "bigs" in the offseason — 7-1 Shaquille O'Neal and 6-11 Jermaine O'Neal (no relation) — with Los Angeles in mind. When Oklahoma City traded for the 6-10 Kendrick Perkins in February, it was to potentially cope with the Lakers. And when the Mavericks packed their roster with essentially two starting centers (Tyson Chandler and Brendan Haywood), it was because they knew, at some point, the Lakers would be waiting.

And those Lakers were beasts.

Their mammoth frontcourt featured Andrew Bynum (7-0, 285 pounds), Spanish forward Pau Gasol (7-0, 250) and Khloe Kardashian's lesser-known husband Lamar Odom (6-10, 230). Joining them in the forward rotation was 6-7, 260-pound Ron Artest, a master at defending, rebounding and instigating. Derek Fisher was still a capable playoff point guard at 36. And then, of course, there was Kobe.

Bryant, 32, was the benchmark of modern NBA superstars. He was intent this year on equaling Michael Jordan's six NBA titles. And if, like Jordan, he could cap off a second "three-peat," he would quiet any remaining doubters as to his legitimacy as heir to Jordan's throne.

The Lakers' coach, Phil Jackson, also had irons in the fire.

Jackson needed one more championship to finish off his *fourth* "three-peat." It was a poorly kept secret that Jackson, 65, was likely to retire after these playoffs. Doing so with a 12th ring (three more than Red Auerbach, seven more than Pat Riley and John Kundla) would pretty much end the debate about where Jackson ranked among the league's greatest coaches.

In short, the Mavericks would likely never face an opponent more loaded, experienced, prepared and driven to destroy anything in their path.

The Mavericks went about their preparations quietly, with Carlisle paying Jackson's team its proper respect publicly.

"When you're playing a team that's defending champs, everybody's wondering how these guys can possibly be beat," Carlisle said. "We've got to play our game at an extremely high level. It's as simple as that."

With the exception of TNT's resident contrarian Charles Barkley, it was hard to find a prognosticator who thought the Mavericks had enough to deal with the Lakers. They were, after all, the Lakers. If benefit of the doubt was required, their opponents would not receive it.

Even in Dallas, most analysts agreed that if the Mavericks played really well and could extend the series to six games, there would be no shame in having made the Lakers work for their victory. Nobody conceived a path that would lead to the invincible Lakers' demise.

Usually when the situation looked dire, Mark Cuban would take to the airwaves, social media and newsprint. He would challenge fans, needle opponents, perhaps be kind enough to prep the referees on what they should be focusing on. But this time, Cuban remained suspiciously quiet. So did most of the Mavericks before the ball went up at the Staples Center for Game 1.

If the Mavericks had anything to say, they planned to say it during the game.

Monday, May 2
Game 1, Western Conference Semifinals
Los Angeles, California

Thirty-two days had passed since the Lakers and Mavericks had last met, that testy affair in the Staples Center that had resulted in five ejections after Terry's flagrant foul on Steve Blake.

The sense of rivalry had intensified that night, and bloomed the next day with Terry's "Charminator" assessment of Matt Barnes and Barnes' Twitter response. Lakers coach Phil Jackson said of that March 31 skirmish, "It's just a buildup, a buildup for what we can see down the road."

Well, "down the road" had now arrived. This was the first postseason meeting between the teams since the 1988 Western Conference finals (a seven-game war won by Magic Johnson and Los Angeles). And the Mavericks knew it was incumbent upon them to keep their composure and use their heads against a formidable opponent with a proven knack for getting under their skin.

They almost accomplished that for the first half of Game 1. Then, in a baffling turn of events, Dallas managed to turn a five-point deficit into a nine-point gap by gifting the Lakers four points in the final 0.7 seconds before halftime.

Just before the halftime buzzer, Lamar Odom had the ball near halfcourt and threw up a 50-foot desperation heave. Inexplicably, Terry felt the need to contest this shot, leaping at Odom and fouling him on the arm. Odom was awarded three free throws, and made them all.

Making the bad situation worse, Nowitzki got into a skirmish under the hoop with Ron Artest following one of the free throws, and was slapped with a technical foul for throwing an elbow at the Lakers forward. Perhaps Dirk was trying to send a message, but it appeared to be another unforced error that cost a point when Bryant made the resulting free throw. The chuckling Lakers trotted into the locker room leading 53-44 with two quarters to go. The Mavericks limped into halftime with a smoking hole in the top of their shoe.

If composure was the theme of Carlisle's blistering halftime remarks, the Mavs paid little heed. They started the second half with three ugly turnovers resulting in seven more quick Los Angeles points. In just 1:22, the Lakers' lead had widened to 60-44. The Game 1 rout, it appeared, was on.

That could have been the end of the story. But it wasn't.

Instead, partly because the Mavericks did not panic and partly because the Lakers went on autopilot, Dallas began climbing back into the game. The Mavs' shots began falling, their defense made stops, and a determination to attack the rim helped build a 20-6 scoring run.

Part of the comeback resulted from a stellar contribution from Corey Brewer. Carlisle was looking for any defensive spark from his bench, and thought he would try the newest tool in his toolbox, a swingman who had played just four minutes in the entire Portland series. Brewer was able to cause some stops and then hit a clutch 3-pointer from the corner that prompted Jackson to call timeout. And after Chandler made 1 of 2 free throws just over a minute later, the Lakers' lead had been cut to 66-64 with 4:03 left in the third.

Bryant didn't like what he was seeing, and started demanding the ball. He scored the Lakers' next eight points which, along with four free throws from Pau Gasol, gave his team a seven-point edge at the end of the third (78-71). Dallas had only outscored L.A. by two points in the period.

But the Lakers had abandoned what got them their big early lead. In the first half, they had used their size advantage well, asserting themselves in the paint. They had taken 25 of their 42 first-half shots within 10 feet of the basket. In the second half, only 15 of their 42 shots were taken from such close range.

Bryant was doing damage from the perimeter, but his teammates were not, and the Mavericks were coming on strong. Nowitzki buried a deep 3-pointer with 9:03 left to get the Mavs within 80-79. The Lakers could not extend their lead beyond five points the rest of the way, but the Mavs couldn't take the lead away, either.

Not until the final minute, that is.

Nowitzki brought his team back within one (94-93) when he nailed another of his left-footed fadeaways with 40 seconds left. Bryant rushed downcourt to draw defenders and tried kicking the ball back out to the perimeter. But Terry read his pass like a defensive back and jumped the route for a hugely important steal, drawing an open-court foul from Derek Fisher.

The Mavericks brought in 3-point threats Stojakovic and Barea (for Marion and Chandler), but wisely worked the ball into Dirk's hands on the critical inbounds pass. Nowitzki went to meet the ball and drew a foul from Gasol, as the Spaniard's defense was overly aggressive. Dirk would shoot for the lead from the line, allowing Carlisle to hustle Marion and Chandler back out in exchange for the perimeter threats.

Nowitzki made both free throws, giving the Mavs their first lead since late in the first half at 95-94. A few seconds later, Kidd stole the ball from Gasol and was fouled. He made 1 of 2 free throws for a 96-94 lead with two seconds to play.

That set up the moment that perhaps determined both teams' fate for the 2011 postseason.

Carlisle knew Kidd would be his best defender against Bryant for a one-possession, winner-take-all scenario. The veteran guard had the strength, savvy and enough respect from officials to perhaps earn the benefit of the doubt if a close call was to be made.

Jackson called a play that had Bryant starting near the baseline. Fisher would inbound the ball and Bryant would scrape off a double screen at the top of the free-throw circle, as Bynum and Gasol were guarded by Chandler and Marion.

As Bryant tried to rub Kidd off a pick, Bynum moved backwards into the Mavericks' guard. It would have been judged an illegal moving screen at just about any other point in the game. But officials are not likely to blow the whistle and decide the game on a call off the ball, so no one was surprised when there was no call at this juncture.

The screen freed Bryant from Kidd, giving the Lakers' star the open look envisioned by Jackson in the huddle. Bryant rose in the air and fired the 3-point shot that would win the game for Los Angeles. The ball looked good in the air, but bounced harmlessly off the back of the rim. The Mavericks had survived, and both Bryant and Jackson looked dumbfounded.

The league's premier assassin had missed his kill shot. Interestingly, it marked the fifth consecutive time that Bryant had missed a potential game-tying or lead-taking field goal in the final 24 seconds of a postseason game or overtime. Perception did not always match reality.

And the perception of the Mavericks would not change with one game. The Mavs had again proven to the public, and to themselves, that they could win a road playoff game, this time by outplaying the defending champions in crunch time at the Staples Center. It was no small feat.

However, they also knew the New Orleans Hornets had just stolen Game 1 on the Lakers' home floor in the first round, before being drummed out in six games.

Nothing was won yet, but these Mavericks had entered May playing with great purpose and resolve. In a five-day span, they had won as many playoff road games (two) as they had in the last five years. Were all things now truly possible?

"This team can beat us," said Bryant, who finished with 36 points but needed 39. "It's clear."

Surrendering that 23-point lead nine days earlier in Portland had been a catalyst for change. Adversity used to bring Dallas to its knees, but in this instance seemed to have brought the team together in unity and determination heretofore unimagined. So much so that a 16-point deficit at the Staples Center rattled the Mavericks not a whit.

"You've got to make plays, and you've got to dodge some bullets," Carlisle said after the game. "We did both."

Jackson made it clear he felt his team had given the game away. And while that could be construed as insulting to the Mavericks, his point could be seen from the Lakers' perspective. Artest, in particularly, hurt his team in the third quarter by taking and missing three unnecessary 3-point shots in the span of three minutes. Los Angeles had built its comfortable lead with gritty interior play, then started settling for long-range shots, which ultimately took the boot off Dallas' throat. It was the same recipe for disaster the Mavericks had followed in their Rose Garden debacle.

The Mavericks, meanwhile, reiterated their game plan in the third quarter and stuck with it.

"We talked about it in the huddle — stick with it and get stops," Nowitzki said. "Let's get a shot up each time and not turn the ball over and put them in transition. And to only give up 15 points in the fourth quarter, that's big. J-Kidd trying to keep the ball out of Kobe's hands was huge, and everyone scrambling around … It was fun to watch."

Dallas' defense played a significant part in the comeback. The Mavericks generated eight steals, eight blocked shots, forced 11 turnovers and held the Lakers to 42.9 percent shooting in Game 1. The smaller Mavs were only outrebounded by a 44-40 margin, and with 35 defensive boards, they made the Lakers earn their points. In the final 1:43, Chandler's block of a Gasol post shot and the steals by Kidd and Terry were three huge defensive plays. For the first time in several postseasons, there was a "D" in Dallas.

Some had snickered before the series when Terry had suggested this Dallas team was "built to play the Lakers." The Lakers liked to attack with their tree line of Bynum, Gasol and Odom as complements to their wings of Bryant, Artest and Barnes. But Chandler, backed by a fresh Brendan Haywood, enabled Dallas to protect the rim reasonably well. And in Kidd, Marion, Brewer and DeShawn Stevenson (still starting and setting a defensive tone, as Kidd envisioned), Dallas had nice rotation of defenders to throw at Kobe. Each would face the Lakers' superstar for a few minutes at a time, making him size up a new opponent and work for everything he could get. Perhaps the little extra touch of fatigue this caused sent Bryant's final shot astray.

This is exactly what Terry meant.

Wednesday, May 4
Game 2, Western Conference Semifinals
Los Angeles, California

The buildup to Game 2 revolved around what the Lakers had done wrong. Few in the national media extended much credit to the other team in the series. If Los Angeles took care of its business, Dallas surely would not last long.

In an odd way, the Mavericks' deplorable history was serving them well. Their annual compilation of disappointment provided a bleak track record of which their opponents were well aware. It gave their rivals a false sense of security, one that might be exploited for an ambush, especially early in a series.

Among the Lakers, only Bryant seemed to understand this. He had sensed, and warned against, his team's penchant for taking Dallas more lightly than San Antonio or other league heavyweights. The Lakers always had their game faces on against the Spurs. Bryant seemed to feel it was harder for his teammates to take the Mavs' threat as seriously, which he thought explained their letdown after running up a 16-point lead in Game 1.

Both sides knew Game 2 would reveal plenty. Would the Mavericks play greedy and chase hard after a result, or would they play without urgency, content to have already secured a road split of the first two games? They would have to play with conviction, because there was no question a different Lakers side would be on display.

From the opening jump, the Lakers were ready to rumble in Game 2. But so were the Mavericks. All they had heard for 48 hours were warnings of the impending tornado of fury the Lakers would bring down upon them. But, with Nowitzki, Kidd and even Stevenson hitting big shots early, Dallas established a tone of calm to counter the Lakers' desperation. The Mavericks withstood the opening salvo, and finished the first quarter with a 26-20 lead.

Once again, the Lakers inexplicably ignored their formidable inside game and got caught up trying to outgun the Mavs from distance. How did that work out? The Lakers missed their first 15 3-point attempts. Los Angeles didn't make a 3-pointer until Bryant finally hit one with 2:43 left in the game, and the host team finished a dismal 2 for 20 from behind the arc.

Dallas didn't have its greatest shooting night either (42 percent from the floor), but made 17 of 21 free throws and 8 of 25 3-pointers to fuel a surprisingly easy victory. Nowitzki hit a 13-foot jumper with five seconds left before halftime to give Dallas a 51-49 edge, and the lead never changed hands again as the Mavs gradually pulled away to win, 93-81.

That doesn't mean there was no late drama, however. This game would be remembered for the fourth-quarter damage inflicted by the shortest player in the game, the Mavs' J.J. Barea, and the Lakers' self-destructive reaction to it.

Barea certainly isn't a player depended on to take over a game, or sometimes to even contribute much. Some matchups work for him, others don't. But his fourth-quarter effort in Game 2 immediately found its way into Mavericks lore. In a four-minute stretch that marked the Lakers' last stab at evening the series, Barea dominated the ball and frustrated the living daylights out of Phil Jackson and the Los Angeles defenders.

His appearance didn't start well. A poor pass by Barea was stolen by Bryant, who pushed it to Fisher for a layup that brought the Lakers within 75-69 with 6:47 to play. Nowitzki yanked out his mouthpiece and gave Barea an earful about the reckless play, demanding the guard raise his game.

It was a demonstration of leadership Nowitzki might not have been comfortable with in years past. But now, quite clearly, when Dirk had something to say he was direct about it. And the manner in which Barea responded to the challenge was a testament to the young guard's confidence and fortitude.

Barea brought the ball back downcourt, faked left and drove right, and hit a tough running jumper in the lane. Bryant missed two shots at the other end and Barea pushed it again, this time finding Haywood to finish a drive-and-dump dunk. The Lakers called timeout, now trailing 79-69 with 6:05 left.

Odom missed a layup and Barea raced downcourt to drive the lane hard again. This time, Bynum was waiting and blocked Barea's layup attempt. But Haywood grabbed the rebound and kicked it out to Kidd for a 3-pointer before the Lakers' defense could get set. Spurred by Barea's speedy transition, the Mavs led 82-69 with 5:18 to go.

The Lakers' Shannon Brown missed a 3-point attempt. Haywood rebounded and found Barea, who darted through the L.A. defense yet again, scoring a driving layup for a 15-point lead (84-69) with 4:39 left. He had sucked the life out of the two-time defending champions.

With 12 points and 4 assists, Barea had put his name on the national map and sent both Dallas and his native Puerto Rico into a frenzy. The petulant Artest decided to do something about that.

The volatile Lakers forward showed his frustration with Barea by clotheslining the smaller guard as he dribbled in the backcourt with 24.4 seconds left. It was a stupid, gutless play made all the more indelicate as Artest kneed teammate Lamar Odom in the groin in the process. Odom clutching himself in discomfort proved a fitting metaphor for what the Lakers were feeling after losing the first two games at home.

Television announcers immediately predicted the league would suspend Artest. Jackson conceded "there's a good chance" he wouldn't have Artest for Game 3. He would be correct.

Nowitzki had again led with 24 points and 7 rebounds, the Mavs winding up 15 points better than their opponents while he was on the floor. Barea's 12 points matched the entire output of the Lakers' bench. Barnes and Blake, who would now have to assume some of Artest's minutes in Game 3, had shot a combined 0 for 7 from the floor. But there was no overlooking the energy and determination being exhibited by Dallas' finest player.

Nowitzki had always scored his points and displayed a remarkable shooting touch. But his game was ascending to another level. His new fall-away spin move appeared utterly indefensible. He was barking orders and directing traffic, even having verbal exchanges with opponents and their fans. He appeared more ruthless and determined than ever, with a look in his eye that said he was on a mission that required 16 wins. This was the Dirk of which his fans had always dreamed — unrivaled skills now combined with an unquenchable desire.

"If you would have told me before that we were going to win both games (at the Staples Center), that would have been hard to believe," Nowitzki said. "But I think we earned it."

Indeed they had. And now, taking a 2-0 lead back to Dallas, the Mavericks were starting to be viewed in a much different light.

"I have never seen a team take it to the Lakers at home in back-to-back playoff games," Los Angeles Hall of Famer Magic Johnson tweeted from the TNT studios where he was working as an analyst. "The Mavs have the Lakers pointing fingers at one another. It's going to be a tough climb to come back, and I think their chances are slim."

Terry told ESPN.com's Marc Stein, "We've heard all the talk about how we're a regular-season team, how the Mavericks fold mentally, all that stuff. And we've had situations in the past where we've lived up to that. But it's not even about that. We're not trying to prove anything to you (media) guys or anyone else.

"We're just trying to prove to ourselves that we belong."

The oldest cliche in sports might be that "defense wins championships," but it is said with good reason. For years, when Dallas chased its championship dream, it did so with playoff teams rarely equipped to play title-caliber defense. That wasn't the case anymore, as the Lakers were finding out.

Bryant had still managed 23 points and five steals despite a gimpy left ankle, but the Lakers' atrocious outside shooting left them unable to spread the floor. They could not penetrate the Chandler-led defense as the Mavs controlled what Nowitzki called a "tight paint." For the fifth time in eight playoff games, Dallas had held its opponent under 90 points.

The Lakers scored more than 20 in a quarter just once in Game 2, and their frustration was boiling over. Center Andrew Bynum spoke cryptically after the game about dissension within the ranks, saying, "It's obvious that we have trust issues. ... And unless we come out and discuss them, nothing is going to change."

It was the kind of mysterious statement the media would seize on for the next 48 hours, along with the story of Artest's impending suspension. The Lakers appeared to be unraveling, but Carlisle was quick to remind his players of the task before them.

"It's one win of 16 that we need," Carlisle told reporters. "Right now, we have 10 more wins to get to our goal, and that is what we are focusing on."

Nowitzki wouldn't even look that far ahead.

"This series is far from over," he said. "I've been around a long time. I've been up 2-0 and ended up losing the series. And lost both games at home to Houston a few years ago (the first round in 2005), been down 0-2, and have come back to win in seven. We've seen a lot of things. Stay focused and stay together, let our home crowd ride us on Friday. And, hopefully, get another one."

The Lakers would need to win four of the next five games, with three of the next four in Dallas. It was a formidable task, but Bryant wasn't near ready to concede the series.

"Just gotta win one game," Bryant reasoned. "Everybody's tripping. Just win one game. Win the next game, and then go on to the next one. Simple as that."

Nowitzki found a private moment to give his teammates a simple message, too.

"Dirk is not the most talkative guy and he isn't going to give you a rah-rah speech," Mavs forward Brian Cardinal said. "But there were specific times when he said something. J-Kidd and myself would encourage him to speak up, and tell him the guys needed to hear from him more.

"After Game 2, he made sure he said something to the team. He said, 'We have to approach Game 3 the same way, and stay focused. … 2-0 or 0-2 doesn't mean anything. We have to bring it back in Dallas.'"

16

LOS ANGELES LAKERS
GAMES 3-4

(May 6-8, 2011)

Many expected talkative Mavericks owner Mark Cuban to be boasting loudly as his team took its 2-0 series lead back to Dallas.

Cuban had always enjoyed the limelight, and in the past had delighted in needling Phil Jackson, jousting with Kobe Bryant or Shaq, and of course criticizing game and league officials until he'd been fined nearly $1.8 million. Would the brash owner be so bold now as to warn NBA Commissioner David Stern to practice handing him the trophy instead of another fine?

Not a chance.

The media expecting Cuban to fill their off-day stories and recordings were disappointed to learn they would have to work instead. "Both teams played hard," was all the 52-year-old billionaire had to say.

As was his custom, Cuban had made himself available to reporters on the floor about an hour before tipoff in Los Angeles. He was swarmed by local media wanting either to grill him about possible interest in purchasing the Los Angeles Dodgers baseball team or hoping to reignite past quote feuds with Jackson and Artest. Neither line of questioning appealed to Cuban, so he shut the media down. And after two unexpected wins on the West Coast, the superstitious owner now saw no need to change. He kept his mouth shut, except to drink another "good luck" Diet Coke.

Nowitzki didn't know what was behind his team owner's sudden vow of silence. He just knew it pleased him.

"That (motive) is a question mark to me, too," Nowitzki admitted. "But, I loved it. I don't know who told him, or if he just decided to do it. But I have told him a million times, 'Mark, I don't know if you doing that is helping us.'

"Not talking to the media was a big step for him. He didn't do it and stayed quiet, and I thought it was a big key for us. Just not saying anything or firing up the other teams, or shooting back at teams when they say something … I just think that was great."

Even without Cuban, Mavericks Nation promised to be in full voice for Game 3. It was being promoted as Dallas' chance to go for the kill, and fans lucky enough to hold tickets were encouraged to arrive early to the AAC, wear blue, and be prepared to get very, very loud.

It would become that first night of Mavericks basketball when, suddenly, everything truly seemed possible.

Friday, May 6
Game 3, Western Conference Semifinals
Dallas, Texas

Fourth quarter, 5:07 remaining. Lakers 85, Mavericks 78.

Though it won't say so on the ticket, entry into an NBA playoff game between elite teams usually gives you two games for the price of one.

The first game starts at the opening tipoff and runs about 40-45 minutes. In this game, benches matter, secondary scorers are important, and even bit players can find ways to impact the contest.

Then there is the second game, the "game within the game," covering the final 3-5 minutes of regulation. Also known as "money time" or "crunch time," this is when the best players in the world square off over the course of five or six possessions each. The team that can score three or four key baskets and manage a few critical defensive stops will get the win.

This is where the NBA playoffs get their special cachet. Magic versus Larry. MJ and Scottie against Stockton and Malone. And, in this series, Kobe versus Dirk.

The Lakers desperately needed to win that matchup in the final 5:07 of Game 3, and they would go into it holding a seven-point lead.

Somehow, this didn't seem to faze the Mavericks, especially not the guy wearing No. 41.

The Lakers' Achilles' heel in this series seemed to be their inability to switch coverages quickly and rotate defenders when a double team was required. Doubling leaves one man open, and when the offense finds him in the corner, the defense must react quickly or there will be problems. It was a basic building block of any modern NBA defense, but the Lakers repeatedly appeared too slow or too confused in their reactions. All it took was a moment's hesitation or lapse, leaving Nowitzki an extra instant to compose and release his shot, and the deadly swish seemed inevitable. Of all the players to leave open...

Dirk buried an open 3-pointer to get his team within 85-81. Kobe answered with a tough 18-foot shot at the other end to make it 87-81. The next time down, Nowitzki drove the lane but was called for a charging foul, giving the ball back to the Lakers with a six-point lead and 4:23 left to play.

This is when the Mavericks asserted their new defensive identity. They got a stop on the Lakers' next possession, something they would manage on eight of L.A.'s final 10 trips downcourt. Unbeknownst to him, Bryant already had scored his last points of the night.

Undaunted by the previous charging call, Nowitzki again drove the lane in anger. This time, as the Lakers' Bynum and Gasol rose to meet him, he kicked the ball out to a wide-open Peja Stojakovic waiting outside the arc. Odom and Fisher tried to disrupt him, but his 3-pointer flew through the rim. The Mavs trailed 87-84 with 3:48 to go.

Next it was Kidd's turn. The Lakers predictably went back to Bryant, but Kidd (with help from Nowitzki) forced him to change his mind mid-air about the 17-foot shot he was about to fling up. Bryant tried a desperate pass to Gasol underneath, but the Spaniard already had turned, looking to rebound. The pass bounced off Gasol's back and was grabbed by Chandler, who flipped it upcourt to Kidd. Bryant fouled Kidd, and the 38-year-old sank two free throws to get the Mavs within one at 87-86.

Bryant demanded the ball once more, but again found himself being hounded by Kidd as the shot clock ticked away. Bryant had to settle for a fall-away jumper from 23 feet that bounced off the front of the rim. Terry rebounded and found Nowitzki, who again drove hard to the rim. He was fouled by Bynum, sank two free throws, and listened to the crowd go wild as the Mavs led 88-87 with 2:40 left.

A running 9-footer by Fisher put the Lakers back on top, 89-88, setting up the decisive moment of crunch time. Nowitzki was double-teamed on the high post and the Mavs' outstanding ball movement kicked in. Nowitzki found Kidd open on the wing. Fisher charged out and Kidd hesitated an instant to let him get closer. That left Terry open in the corner and Kidd hit him with a sharp pass. Bryant was already gesturing to Bynum for blowing this rotation assignment as Terry buried his 3-pointer, putting Dallas up 91-89 with two minutes left. Pandemonium erupted from the stands.

Bryant wanted the ball again, but this time Odom took charge and made a tough shot over Stojakovic and Chandler, tying the game at 91 with 1:39 to play. The crowd groaned, but was getting its money's worth with this finish.

Every possession was crucial. The Mavs again went to Nowitzki on the high post and the double team again was a half-step slow to arrive. Nowitzki drove left on Gasol and, before Bynum could interfere, tossed in a cheeky left-handed jump hook for a 93-91 advantage with 1:23 left.

Any stop now could decide the game, but there hadn't been a whistle to allow Carlisle to put Marion back on the floor. Consequently, Odom wanted to take on Stojakovic again, with Bryant drawing attention on the weak side of the court. Odom backed his defender down, but missed his 8-foot shot and couldn't beat Stojakovic to the rebound. The Mavericks had their lead and the ball with 1:01 left, and their arena had never been louder.

Once again, Nowitzki drew double coverage but managed to find the open man. The ball whipped to Kidd, then to Stojakovic, but this time his 17-footer went long. The rebound wound up in the hands of Terry, giving Dallas a fresh 24-second shot clock with 39 seconds to play. With 18 seconds remaining, Fisher bumped Terry for a foul. Carlisle utilized this chance to swap Marion for Stojakovic, and Terry calmly sank both free throws for a 95-91 lead with 18 seconds on the clock.

Terry was back at the line two seconds later, after Fisher turned the ball over with a poor pass and then had to foul immediately. Two more free throws by Jet cranked the Mavs' lead to 97-91 with 16 seconds to play.

Bryant still couldn't shake Kidd. The Lakers star tried a 3-pointer but Kidd blocked it. The rebound was batted around and found its way back to Bryant, but this time he missed from 28 feet. Gasol rebounded but missed a layup. He grabbed his own missed shot and was fouled by Chandler on his put-back attempt, but made only 1 of 2 free throws. The Lakers trailed 97-92 with eight seconds left.

Kidd rebounded Gasol's missed free throw, and was quickly fouled by the Spaniard. Kidd made the first of his two free throws to restore the six-point lead, 98-92. The Lakers' last gasp was a running 3-point jumper by Bryant from 26 feet that missed with three seconds left. Terry grabbed the rebound and the clock struck 0:00.

An amazing final five minutes filled with composure and precision execution had given Dallas a 98-92 victory. And, despite a strong 43 minutes of road playoff basketball, the Lakers' poor decisions and play in the final five left them disconsolate with an 0-3 series deficit, the first one Jackson ever had faced in his distinguished coaching career.

"It was a slugfest game," Carlisle said, "but we hung in there and kept battling. Dirk Nowitzki made it happen. Just about everything that happened down the stretch was a direct result of him either scoring the ball, or making a play to get somebody a shot, or making a pass for an assist. You've got to give our crowd a lot of credit, too. It was every bit as loud as it was in Portland the other day, and that was a difference maker."

It was difficult to comprehend the Mavericks' position after three games. It would be foolhardy to consider the reigning world champions in their grave until you actually saw the casket lowered into the ground. Yet, history said that in 98 previous series, no NBA playoff team had come back from an 0-3 deficit.

Some Dallas fans who had forgotten the heartbreak of 2006 might be hitting the local hardware stores to price brooms. Others, however, felt hairs stand on the backs of their necks when Bryant said in his postgame news conference, "I might be sick in the head or crazy or something like that, because I still think we're going to win this series."

The Lakers twice had proven unable to protect a late lead. It was the Mavericks displaying the poise and veteran savvy befitting a champion in those critical final minutes. The Lakers had played without the suspended Artest (some felt his absence worked against the Mavs, since he was shooting 5 for 18 in the series), but had still outscored Dallas in the paint by a 56-20 margin. Yet the Mavericks claimed the win, almost through sheer will.

"We treated that game like it was the seventh game," Donnie Nelson remarked weeks later. "There was some blood in the water, and we sensed we might be able to take down the champs if we could get that one. That was the linchpin game. Another case of our best players stepping up at the end."

The allure of sports is that no scripted drama can replicate the twists and turns, the heights and plunges, the complete emotional roller coaster a beloved team can put you through while pursuing a championship dream. Year after year, the disappointments pile up for every team but one, and faith can waver. And just when you think there is no chance of seeing the happiest of endings, a team can tease with fairy-tale results once again.

The NBA world had been rocked by seeing the two-time defending champions shoved to an 0-3 brink by a Dallas team few thought could ever match (much less dominate) Kobe Bryant, possession for possession, when the chips were down. But Nowitzki, looking and sounding weary after Game 3, wasn't worried about other people's outdated perceptions of his team.

"We've just got to go for it," he said of Game 4. "We're not good enough to coast or relax or anything. We've got to go for it on Sunday with the same hype from the crowd."

Carlisle was asked about the Nowitzki-Terry tandem but cut the question short.

"It's not just those two guys," he said. "Everybody is focused. We're all trying to do something that we have never done. So the focus, the determination, the discipline and all those things is crucial.

"Dirk is one of the all-time greats, there's no doubt about that. But we're going for the ring, and that's the one thing he hasn't done in his career. He's one step closer, but we have a long way to go. Getting one more game from Los Angeles is going to be a lot of hard work, and we're going to have to stay humble and stay hungry."

Bryant was still trying to sound defiant, even if it seemed few were buying what he was selling.

"I don't know, I might be nuts," he said. "(But) let's win on Sunday, go back home, and see if they can win in L.A."

========

Game 4 was to be played on Mother's Day. And on the day before, Terry wanted to make sure Mavericks fans — moms included — would have their priorities in order come Sunday.

"If you don't give us as much or more energy tomorrow (as in Game 3), we'll be disappointed," Terry said. "We know, deep down in our mind and our hearts, they're going to come cheering loud as soon as warm-up starts. As soon as the music comes on, they're going to be fired up. (The Lakers) are still the champs. Until you beat them, they hold the crown.

"We definitely know if we take care of business tomorrow, we put ourselves in great position. We definitely want to get the job done."

Terry had scored 20 points or more only twice in the final 17 games of the regular season, but had his wheels back on after a tumultuous time in late March and early April. He had regained his composure and touch, and had hit some major shots late in Game 3.

He and his teammates surely felt the air of confidence inside the American Airlines Center, but knew the series still could turn on a dime if they were to let Game 4 slip through their grasp. Should that happen, with Games 5 and 7 in Los Angeles, the fragile psyche of the old Mavericks could re-emerge. The directive in the locker room was crystal clear: Put the Lakers to the sword.

=========

Sunday, May 8
Game 4, Western Conference Semifinals
Dallas, Texas

The arena's scene was both bonkers and tense for this Mother's Day matinee. The Lakers looked ready to play for survival and the first quarter ended with Dallas holding a slim 27-23 edge.

Then Terry ended the series before halftime, dominating as he never had before.

Consider some of this second-quarter marksmanship:

11:30 — Terry 3-point shot, Dallas 30-23
9:33 — Terry 3-point shot, Dallas 37-27
8:21 — Terry 3-point shot, Dallas 42-30
7:07 — Terry 3-point shot, Dallas 47-32
6:41 — Stojakovic 3-point shot, Dallas 50-32
3:06 — Stojakovic 3-point shot, Dallas 56-38
0:31 — Terry 3-point shot, Dallas 63-38

"A couple of those shots, I didn't even see the rim," Terry said. "I was just letting it fly."

You almost had to see the onslaught to believe it. It was as if the Mavs were playing a video game and had entered a cheat code. They simply could not miss.

The Lakers hit five 3-point shots in Game 4. The Mavericks tied NBA playoff records with 11 3-pointers in the first half and 20 for the game. Dallas struck from behind the arc four times in the first quarter, seven times in the second and four times in the third. They added five more triples in the fourth quarter, which they started with an 86-62 lead.

Terry was 9 for 10 from long distance, tying a playoff record previously set by Rex Chapman, Vince Carter and Ray Allen. Stojakovic was 6 for 6 from behind the arc. Five other Mavs, including Brian Cardinal, hit 3-pointers as Dallas hit more in one game than the Lakers managed for the entire series (15).

With their astonishing 122-86 rout, the Mavericks ran up a 36-point margin of victory, the biggest ever in an NBA playoff game that finished off a four-game sweep. Take Dat Wit Chew into retirement, Phil Jackson.

"I don't think I've seen a team play to that level in a series in a game like they played this afternoon," Jackson said. "You'd like to have an opportunity to challenge, but we didn't."

Rarely is an NBA playoff game won in the second quarter, but the Mavericks' second period of Game 4 was one for the ages. They outscored the Lakers 36-16 in the period and hit 7 of 8 3-point attempts, including 5 of 6 by Terry.

Jackson implored his defenders to charge at the snipers, forcing them to dribble into two-point range, but his pleas went unheeded. According to ESPN's statistics, the Mavericks comfortably hit 20 of 33 jump shots (60.6 percent) without taking a dribble, including 19 of 30 (63.3 percent) from beyond the stripe.

For years, it seemed, an overzealous fascination with the 3-point shot had proven to be the Mavericks' undoing. But with this cast of sharpshooters, the long-range ability was clearly paying dividends. For them, the 3-pointer was a dagger, not a crutch. This team was making you rethink everything you thought you knew about Mavericks basketball.

The Mavericks had swept an opponent in a best-of-seven series for only the second time in franchise history (Memphis, first round of 2006, was the other). That it would happen against the two-time defending world champions, the team with the NBA's highest payroll ($91 million), was more than remarkable. According to STATS LLC, it was only the fourth time in history that an NBA champion defending multiple titles had been swept. And in 21 postseasons over his decorated career, Jackson had never seen one of his teams swept out of the playoffs.

Terry had led the way with 32 points on his remarkable shooting night (11 for 14), surely the best of his career considering the opponent and the stakes. Barea had scored 22 and Stojakovic 21. With 75 points, those three Dallas "bench" players nearly outscored the Lakers themselves.

"Their depth hurt us," Bryant admitted. "Every night, it was another bench player (who) stepped up and made plays. ... They just made three after three after three. We could never get back in it. You've got to put the credit in the right place, which is the Mavs' locker room."

In many ways, the allure of the 3-point shot is what started this era of Mavericks basketball.

That a 7-footer could reliably shoot from such distance is what got a 20-year-old Dirk Nowitzki on the Mavericks' draft board ahead of a more typical college star such as Paul Pierce in 1998.

Three-point range also helped explain the Nelsons' less-successful experiments with Wang Zhizhi, Raef LaFrentz, Marquis Daniels, Keith Van Horn and others. But when the right shooters employed the weapon, it had helped spur the Mavericks toward much regular-season success.

Yet, year after year in the postseason, the 3-point shot became something for Dallas fans to lament. When the opposition got too physical, the Mavericks would seem to retreat behind the stripe and take their chances. They would almost always fall short trying to exchange 23-footers against opponents' shots from the paint.

It was somewhat ironic, therefore, when the death blow against the Los Angeles Lakers was delivered with a 3-point exhibition that matched the best ever seen in an NBA postseason game. The Mavericks had proven they no longer were a passive team that shies from contact. They had struck the proper balance of physical interior play, smothering defense and a devastating perimeter-shooting attack.

"We had a lot of guys play great," Carlisle said. "Jet's shotmaking was breathtaking, really. The 3-point shot is a big part of the game now. It's been a big part of the success that we've been able to have.

"But, more importantly, we guarded. That fueled a lot of the good things that happened for us offensively. It was basically, 'Be more persistent, play harder, move the ball, and defend and rebound.' That's as simple as it comes."

The Lakers were made frustrated, then disheartened, and finally unraveled in an ugly display of poor sportsmanship. Both Odom and Bynum got themselves ejected within a span of 45 seconds, having no stomach for finishing the second-worst playoff defeat in their proud franchise's history. Odom was tossed after throwing a flagrant elbow at Nowitzki with 9:06 to play and his team trailing by 26 points. Less than a minute later, Bynum was ejected for slamming his elbow into Barea's ribs while the guard was in mid-flight on a layup.

"For me, it was embarrassing having the smallest guy on the court keep running down the lane and then making shots," Bynum explained to the Los Angeles Times. "So I just fouled him."

But the Mavericks would not be bullied, not anymore. Something had changed between Brandon Roy's fourth-quarter exhibition in Game 4 of the Portland series and the start of Game 5, which had kicked off this remarkable six-game postseason winning streak. They would not give satisfaction to those doubters who kept waiting for the "same ol' Mavericks" to crumble under the pressure and weight of their history and emotional baggage.

A trophy still sat a distant eight wins away, but the Mavericks were now halfway there. Knocking off the Lakers put them squarely on everybody's radar, but their confidence was growing.

For the second series in a row, the Mavericks had advanced in part because of a demonstrably deeper and more productive bench. Carlisle's directive that the entire roster needed to stay ready was paying dividends, and the coach expressed his gratitude for the depth of talent at his disposal.

"You've got to give Mark Cuban all the credit," Carlisle said. "He's kept this core team together. He's spent the money to get guys like Tyson and Jason Kidd. Jason Terry has been here a long time. The fact that he has continued to embrace the sixth-man role just sets a tremendous tone. This year, our job was to make sure that those efforts were fruitful.

"Coming into the playoffs, we knew it was going to be tough and that we would probably play Portland, a tough matchup. There were multiple teams that didn't play their guys down the stretch of the season to avoid the possibility of playing L.A. We did not do that. We kept playing, we kept winning. Because we felt that winning games and gaining momentum was the best way to win a championship."

17

OKLAHOMA CITY GAME 1

(May 17, 2011)

The passing of the sports calendar often seems to accelerate with the arrival of the playoffs. Teams spend all year working toward their postseason tournament, and then it can pass in a blur, leaving them stunned at what just transpired.

The Los Angeles Lakers surely felt that way as they returned to California. The two-time defending NBA champions had been, in the minds of most, ceded a spot in the NBA Finals opposite Boston or Miami since the season began. Then, in the span of six days, they had met and been swept aside by the Dallas Mavericks.

Their dissection had been so clinical and clean, no Lakers could offer any quarrel or dispute the results. But that didn't mean any of them could believe it. Swept? By the Dallas Mavericks? On the very rare occasions that these Lakers ever lost, it took a titanic effort that left both teams exhausted. Somehow, these Mavericks had made it look easy.

After Game 4, Mark Cuban walked out of the locker room toward a throng of media waiting outside. The reporters raised their cameras, recorders and notepads in anticipation of the human quote machine about to provide them all with "content," in the media parlance of the day. But Cuban nudged past them all, continuing his vow of silence. He wasn't about to change his conduct before this run ended.

But Cuban still had to be Cuban on some level. He stopped, turned and offered the media two words on the record: "We Believe."

Some speculated whether Nowitzki was responsible for Cuban's locked lips. When asked about his mostly silent owner the next day, Nowitzki said, "It should be about the players, never about the owner. We played a great series and fought hard and battled. That was fun. I haven't really seen Mark since then, and that's probably a good thing."

Cuban was correct: Belief was spreading. The number of believers had grown slightly after the Mavericks had survived the Portland series, then dropped sharply as soon as many realized the Lakers were up next. But after witnessing the six days of hard-nosed, emotional and dramatic basketball that had ousted Kobe and Co., the belief dam was bursting.

The Mavericks were looking like a team capable of all things. They were deep, confident and composed. Their defense was aggressive and sturdy. Their offense was varied and dynamic. Their coach was prepared and cool under fire. And, for the second straight round, the Mavericks wore down down their foe as the series went deeper. Whether it was depth, strategy or both, as the days went by Dallas had sorted out its challenge with increasing ease.

With the mighty Spurs (a six-game upset victim to eighth-seeded Memphis in the first round) and Lakers now slain, Dallas fans, media and even players were allowing themselves to appreciate they were now four wins from a chance at redemption in the NBA Finals and eight wins from basketball immortality.

"I thought Game 5 against Portland was a turning point for us — Are we going to continue to push this thing to the end or are we going to fold tent?" Jason Kidd recalled later. "After we won Game 5, we proved we are battle-tested and are going to stay together. So, at that point, we had a chance.

"But the next opponent was the Lakers. After (winning) Game 1, now we have made it a series and can make it go seven games. And then, after we swept them, I started to think this could go the distance. But there was always doubt to not look too far ahead."

Such was the mindset for most Mavericks fans. They would admonish each other to stay in the moment, lest they awaken the bad juju that had followed the franchise for decades. They wanted to believe their eyes — that they were seeing a well-constructed team capable of going all the way — but they could not tempt the Fates and risk another brutal heartbreak. They had been conditioned to live the Bruce Springsteen lyric:

"You end up like a dog that's been beat too much

'Til you spend half your life just covering up..."

Still, there was now plenty of idle time to dream. Because the Mavericks finished off the Lakers on May 8, the other Western Conference semifinal was only three games old. With Memphis holding a 2-1 lead over Oklahoma City at that point, the Mavericks would be getting a well-earned rest while awaiting their next opponent.

The Mavericks needed no reminding that they were an old basketball team. The physical and mental fatigue of the postseason would exact an enormous toll on even the youngest and freshest of players, and the only way the Mavericks could reduce it was by playing fewer games. That they had disposed of the Lakers so quickly and efficiently, earning a rest after just four games, might prove to be the most important factor of their playoff run. The Mavericks had seen how well their 38-year-old point guard had responded to a week off near the end of the regular season, and were delighted to give Kidd another one now.

Carlisle kept his team sharp with light midweek workouts. But with such a veteran group, there was no need to harp on them about the opportunity that was coming next.

"I don't have to preach much. These guys are very experienced," he said. "We've all been humbled too many times to not respect where we're at and how we got here and how we need to proceed.

"Things are very fragile in this league. We all understand that. Whoever your opponent is this time of year is going to be a terrific team, and nothing's ever guaranteed. So, we've got to stay in the present and kind of deal with each moment as it comes."

But Carlisle did want to poke the Mavericks' fan base, ensuring its readiness whenever the next series arrived.

"The thing that I want to make sure, and this is an important part of the next series, is that our fans don't lose their edge," Carlisle said, "that our building stays just as lively as it was in Game 3 and Game 4 for L.A. Because, this time of year, Oklahoma City is going to be wild, Memphis is going to be wild. And our building has to be up to the same standards as the L.A. series, because that really helps us."

Carlisle wanted his team's fans maintaining a fever pitch, but North Texas already was captivated. Dallas had enjoyed football success for decades, the hockey Stars had won a Stanley Cup in 1999, and the downtrodden Rangers had finally reached a World Series. But local fans had spent more than a decade following the career arc of the unassuming but hugely popular Dirk Nowitzki. And they yearned to see him win.

Nowitzki's bond with Dallas fans seemed to transcend accomplishment. He was a curiosity at first, this gangly German youngster with purported shooting range and a bad haircut. At first, it seemed no one but the Nelsons had ever heard of him, but 13 years later he had become a genuine city treasure.

His skills were magnificent and his work ethic superb. Fans adored him because he never attempted to leverage his importance to demand a trade, force a contract renegotiation, demand extra privileges or get a coach fired. He spent his summers adding to his game, not shooting commercials and chasing starlets. Despite his team's many defeats and disappointments, Dirk was back every year, ready to work hard and build again. He required virtually no maintenance. He just played basketball.

But for one embarrassing instance, Nowitzki also maintained a serene personal life. He had endured with dignity a rather public humiliation in May 2009. As the Mavericks flew back from Denver after Game 2 of their playoff series with the Nuggets, a 38-year-old woman to whom he had been engaged was arrested at his Dallas home on outstanding warrants and a parole violation.

Known to Nowitzki as "Crystal Taylor" and "Crissy Travino," the woman had claimed to be of Brazilian heritage. In reality, she was an ex-con from St. Louis named Crista Taylor who had outstanding arrest warrants in two states, at least 20 known aliases, and a long rap sheet for forgery and theft convictions. Her deceptions were revealed by private investigators looking into her past, part of a prenuptial agreement urged by Nowitzki's friends and advisers.

Taylor was returned to Missouri and jailed, and Nowitzki was left with his business all over the papers and airwaves. The private life he carefully had guarded suddenly was opened to public scrutiny. But despite the whirlwind of intrusive media coverage and well-wishes from sympathetic fans, Nowitzki maintained his focus and played fantastic basketball. Any suggestion of mental fragility seemed to be put to rest as he raised his game amidst the chaos.

That summer, Nowitzki told the German magazine Bild that the experience left him "very down and disappointed, sad and furious." But the way he handled the entire messy affair, including averaging 34.4 points and 11.6 rebounds as Dallas' lone threat during the five-game loss to the Nuggets, only made Mavericks fans love and wish the best for Dirk even more.

Would a man who had worked so hard and endured so much get one more opportunity to crown his career with the ultimate achievement of a championship? Dallas fans wanted another shot at The Finals for the sake of civic pride, sure. But perhaps more than anything, they wanted to see this dream come true for Nowitzki. He wanted it, too. Every night of the week between series, Nowitzki was in the gym with Geschwindner, working to keep his shooting touch sharp. The stakes were getting too high for anything less.

Entrepreneurs were getting in on the swelling Mavs fever as well. Bootleg T-shirts were popping up all over town and across the internet. One Nowitzki-loving fan named Jordan Rogers was frustrated that he couldn't find more Dirk-centric gear through official channels, so he created his own designs and launched a web-based storefront called Newdirkshirt.com. His most popular design featured a dictionary-style entry for DIRK with three acceptable definitions:

1. 7 ft. manbeast, prone to drop daggers
2. 4th quarter horse w/wide shoulders
3. UNGUARDABLE

"I wanted to design of Dirk, our hero here in Dallas," Rogers said. "Before long, an entire order of 100 were gone. And, by the end, almost 1,000 were sold."

At most Dallas-area chain stores, it was easier to find LeBron James and Kobe Bryant shirts than Nowitzki gear. It seemed crazy, but the big athletic clothing companies design what they think America wants to buy. A 7-foot jump shooter from Germany wasn't at the top of their list. Dirk demand, however, was spreading like wildfire.

It would be a tortuous nine days before the next series would begin. But the Dallas Mavericks' dream was still alive, and the city could think of almost nothing else.

========

On Sunday, May 15, Oklahoma City held off Memphis, 105-90, to finish the other Western Conference semifinal. It had gone the maximum distance of seven grueling games, and homecourt advantage for the finale seemed to have played an important role.

Oklahoma City was not yet a town awash in NBA basketball tradition. But in the three short years since the Seattle SuperSonics had relocated there as the Oklahoma City Thunder, there was no doubt that the populace had taken quite a shine to its only major-league sports franchise. The Oklahoma City Arena had become a very loud and difficult place in which to play.

The Thunder were led by former University of Texas star Kevin Durant, already a two-time NBA scoring champion after just four seasons in the league. A two-time All-Star at age 22, Durant was the leader of a young, athletic team of which five of the top six scorers were 23 or younger. As much as the graybeard Mavericks were defying the odds this postseason, it was arguably more remarkable that a team so young and inexperienced as the Thunder could now be four wins away from the NBA Finals.

The Thunder had played four taxing playoff games since the Mavericks had last been on the court, and Oklahoma City's players would get just one day of rest between series as opposed to the Mavericks' nine. The old legs were fresh and rested, the young legs perhaps tired. But the final showdown in the West would begin Tuesday night in Dallas.

Tuesday, May 17
Game 1, Western Conference Finals
Dallas, Texas

Any concerns that rust would have accumulated on Nowitzki's game because of the long layoff were quickly put to bed. The big German greeted the Thunder with one of the finest games of his career, unleashing a 48-point onslaught in a 121-112 victory that put the Mavericks up 1-0 in the series.

Certainly, 48 points speaks for itself. But, the demoralizing manner in which he went about his scoring in Game 1 is what took the performance to the next level. Time after time in front of the sellout crowd, he planted himself down on the blocks and called for the ball. This was not going to be a night for settling.

Nowitzki had 21 points by halftime. He hit 10 of his first 11 shots from the field, finishing 12 for 15. He was an amazing 24 of 24 from the free-throw line, setting an NBA playoff record for most foul shots without a miss. He scored 48 points without even attempting a 3-point shot (by choice), overshadowing a 40-point effort by Durant.

Peja Stojakovic, a man who knows a thing or two about shooting technique, called it "the best performance I've ever seen. The best I've ever seen any of my teammates play."

The man continued raising the bar of expectations.

Oklahoma City coach Scott Brooks was left shaking his head and shrugging in disbelief.

"Dirk was pretty good tonight," Brooks said, laughing. "He's a great player, one of the best I've ever seen offensively. A lot of shots, you don't think he has a chance to make it, but he does."

"Hopefully he misses a shot now and then, but tonight he had a rhythm. I don't know if the ball even hit the rim."

Nowitzki took hold of the game almost from the opening tip. He frustrated a series of would-be Thunder defenders, either embarrassing them with an array of slick, spinning post moves or attracting enough contact (drawing 16 fouls) to put virtually the entire Oklahoma City front line in foul trouble. It was a display of such dominance and precision, surely even the gruff Holger Geschwindner had to smile.

The Thunder had coped with Memphis' Zach Randolph using single coverage in the previous round, and had taken note of how Dallas' open 3-point snipers had carved up the Lakers when they ran a second man at Nowitzki. So they rather stubbornly refused to double-team Nowitzki, and he ate five different single defenders alive.

Serge Ibaka was first. Then Kendrick Perkins. Then Nick Collison, Thabo Sefolosha and even Durant tried. Five guys with different size, skill sets and physical tools each tried to deal with Dirk near the baseline though his 41 minutes. It didn't go well for any of them.

Between his field-goal and free-throw attempts, Nowitzki released 39 shots and 36 went through the hoop. It was shooting performance worthy of comparison to Bill Walton's for UCLA in the 1973 NCAA Final against Memphis State. In that game, the Bruins center was 21 of 22 from the floor and 2 of 2 from the line for 44 points.

Despite this infusion of industrial-strength Dirk, the Thunder weren't far from pulling off a Game 1 upset. Dallas only led by six points with both 2:53 and 48.5 seconds to play, as the Thunder (37 of 43) actually managed to outscore the Mavs (34 of 36) from the foul line. But the Mavericks also felt fairly comfortable. After a 13-0 run late in the second quarter erased a nine-point deficit, the Mavs never trailed again.

This Dirk was the best Dirk we had ever seen. Performing at an All-NBA level was nothing new for him. What was different, it seemed, was that he had attained a new level of ruthless, merciless, cold-blooded postseason savvy. Nothing mattered to him but picking up the eight final victories this championship would require. It mattered not whether he made 12 of 15 shots or missed 12 of 15, so long as the result was right for his team.

"The main thing is, we found a way to win," Nowitzki said. "That's what it's all about."

It was only the third time in NBA postseason history that opposing players had scored at least 40 points in a playoff series opener. But Nowitzki was so good, Durant's 40 was almost an afterthought. Durant's output managed only to keep his team close. What killed the

Thunder was point guard Russell Westbrook missing 12 of 15 shots, including 10 of his first 11. Late in the third quarter, Westbrook had taken more shots than Durant. So many empty possessions tended to add up.

Nowitzki's signature moment might have come late in the fourth quarter. Ibaka was down to his last idea on how to defend the Mavericks star, who had the ball on the baseline about 18 feet from the hoop. Ibaka began desperately waving his hands in Nowitzki's face to discourage him from shooting. Nowitzki simply waited, then lifted to pop another clean jumper in Ibaka's face. It was a true show of dominance.

But even if others didn't notice, Nowitzki knew he wasn't doing it alone. Oklahoma City found it had no answer for Barea, either, when the diminutive guard got rolling late in the game. Barea led the Mavericks in fourth-quarter scoring with 12 points, the bulk of the 21 he scored in just 16 minutes. Terry also came up big with a 24-point supporting effort.

"We are a good team," Nowitzki said. "And if we are attacking from all angles, then we are a tough team to beat."

Barea's quickness gave Carlisle a devastating secondary offense to employ late in games. Barea and a big man (either Chandler or Haywood) would be used along with three shooters from a group that included Nowitzki, Terry, Stojakovic, Stevenson and sometimes Kidd. Leave any of those shooters open and Barea kicks the ball back for the open 3-pointer. Guard the shooters tight, and Barea darted through space to the rim. This array had to be used judiciously, because if not in small doses Barea could become a defensive liability for opponents to attack. But for a few minutes at a time, it was proving lethal.

The Mavericks were learning they would have some difficulties as well, and containing the electrifying Durant was chief among them. The 22-year old phenom finished Game 1 with 40 points, eight rebounds, five assists, a steal and two blocked shots. He was 10 of 18 from the floor (including 2 of 5 on 3-point attempts), and nearly matched Nowitzki by making 18 of 19 free throws. He was going to be a handful, especially if Brooks could convince the sometimes selfish Westbrook to distribute the ball better. But it would seem foolish to suspect that Durant might not win a game or two in this series almost by himself.

The series also would have a physical element. It took just 70 seconds before Tyson Chandler and Kendrick Perkins would have their first confrontation, each drawing a technical foul as they tussled, attempting to stake their early claim to interior real estate. Perkins had built a solid postseason resume during his years in Boston, and his tough-guy persona is no act. Chandler, meanwhile, may only have contributed three points and eight rebounds, but his determination to challenge every shot fueled the Mavericks' defense and overall swagger. If he could stay out of foul trouble, his impact could be profound.

The Thunder took some solace in their ability to keep the game close late, despite the sub-par performance of Westbrook. Durant would be Durant, and sixth man James Harden was a dangerous guard who could erupt beyond his 12-point scoring average if conditions warranted it. Fatigue could have been a factor, but the young Thunder still had another chance to attain their goal of a road split if they could win Game 2.

The Mavericks, meanwhile, had bagged their ninth postseason victory and had not lost since April 23. If they could continue getting production from their bench and ride the back of their determined superstar, they felt this series could go just fine. A scoreboard video during a timeout had shown a montage of highlights before ending with the message "This Year is Different."

It sure was starting to feel that way.

18

OKLAHOMA CITY
GAMES 2-3

(May 19-21, 2011)

The Game 1 eruptions of Dirk Nowitzki and Kevin Durant had NBA fans buzzing. The Eastern Conference final between Miami and Chicago held more star-power cachet, perhaps, but this Western Conference duel might hold the greater entertainment value.

But besides the next impending shootout between the teams' superstars, there were other tasty subplots heading into Game 2.

Jason Terry had outscored Oklahoma City's entire bench in the series opener, 24-22. Dallas had gotten 53 points from its bench to support Nowitzki's 48, and looked to have another big advantage on the depth front. If they could keep up anything close to those numbers, this series would end quickly, and both sides knew it.

The Kendrick Perkins-Tyson Chandler struggle also looked captivating. The league as a whole was starting to recognize the real differences Chandler made to the Mavericks. Neither of these strong, rugged big men looked willing to give an inch. Chandler had finished third in the NBA Defensive Player of the Year voting behind Orlando's Dwight Howard and Boston's Kevin Garnett. That, in effect, made him the winner of the Western Conference Defensive Player of the Year voting, didn't it? He had helped transform the Mavericks from a nice team to a title contender. And Perkins, with his wealth of playoff experience with the Celtics, was doing his best to neutralize Chandler's impact after seeing what he'd done against the Trail Blazers and Lakers.

But the most column inches before Game 2 seemed to zero in on Russell Westbrook, and the Thunder point guard's inability (or refusal) to acquiesce and let Durant be the primary attacker. Westbrook's play in the Memphis series already had some wondering whether he understood that All-NBA first-teamer Durant was the best player on the squad and needed more touches on the offensive end. Westbrook, a third-year player who had just made the All-NBA second team, didn't always seem interested in deferring. Not even when his own shots weren't falling, as they clearly weren't in Game 1, when he hit just 1 of 12 shots coming off pick-and-rolls. It seemed a classic case of two alpha males on the same roster — something that the NBA seldom has seen work.

Thursday, May 19
Game 2, Western Conference Finals
Dallas, Texas

Rick Carlisle and Scott Brooks go way back, having played and even lived together while members of the Albany Patroons of the Continental Basketball Association. Brooks told reporters before Game 2 that Carlisle was a great teammate and roommate, even if he never bought Brooks a meal.

"Things haven't changed," Carlisle replied with a wry smile.

But even Carlisle had to appreciate his old friend's daring coaching gamble that helped even the series. Brooks entrusted a one-point lead to a lineup of Durant and four backups at the start of the fourth quarter, and they made a meal of the Mavericks en route to a 106-100 victory.

It had been 26 days since Dallas last tasted defeat, in that memorable Game 4 collapse in Portland. And they might not have tasted it again tonight, but for Brooks' bold and courageous decision to let his rolling reserves keep rolling while starters Westbrook, Perkins and Ibaka watched from the bench.

Brooks opened the fourth period with a lineup of Durant, shooting guard Daequan Cook, point guard Eric Maynor, forward Nick Collison and heavily bearded guard James Harden, whose four-point play (a trey plus a foul) had put the Thunder up 77-76 at the end of the third. Brooks hoped to get about four solid minutes from this group before getting Westbrook (18 points, four assists) and company back on the floor.

What Oklahoma City got was a 14-5 run for a 10-point lead (102-92) with 3:15 to play. The Thunder scored on 11 of their first 15 fourth-quarter possessions and Brooks was wise enough not to tinker or concern himself with Westbrook's ego.

"We had a good start to the fourth quarter," Durant said. "You can't mess that chemistry up. Coach made a good decision by doing that."

Nowitzki was still getting his. After a scoreless third quarter, he scored 16 of his 29 in the final period. But this time, he only got to the line 10 times and even missed one. It was a big miss, too, a foul shot that would have pulled Dallas within three with 36.7 seconds left.

But the big story was the turnaround in bench scoring. The Mavericks' reserves had outscored the Thunder's by a 53-22 margin in Game 1, but this time Oklahoma City's bench prevailed, 50-29.

"Their reserves came out swinging and really took it to us," Nowitzki said. "We were never really ready for their reserves."

Durant demonstrated early in Game 2 that he did not plan to go quietly from the Western Conference finals. The wiry scorer drove the lane late in the first quarter around the soft edge set by Peja Stojakovic. Durant turned the corner at roughly the free-throw line, saw nothing but daylight, and the result was a ridiculous dunk that begged for a place on closet doors everywhere. Durant had "posterized" Brendan Haywood by leaping to eye-level with the rim before slamming home a loud and clear message that Oklahoma City didn't plan to be a pushover.

The ferocity of the dunk was eye-opening to the Mavericks, a stark reminder of what the lively young legs of Durant and his friends could inflict if their defense became lax. It was a prime topic of the halftime discussions, and the Mavericks did pick up their defensive intensity quite a bit. However, the dunk and resulting momentum already had restored the Thunder's confidence. They now truly believed they could even this series, and they did.

For the most part, the Thunder were forced into taking tough, well-defended shots the Mavericks didn't mind conceding in that final period. But Harden (10 of his 23 points in the fourth) and Durant (24 points) were hitting them, even from distance. Maynor penetrated for a couple of scores, Cook hit a big 3-pointer, and Collison added a dunk and some big defensive stops. Sometimes, when dealing with NBA shooters, there is little more you can do.

Meanwhile, four of Oklahoma City's starters watched from courtside seats, with occasional glances toward Brooks, and each other, wondering when they'd get back in the game.

Westbrook had not had a bad game this time. He was 7 for 15 from the floor with 18 points, three rebounds and four assists through three productive quarters. Perkins and Ibaka had four fouls each, but seemingly would be essential to keeping a certain 7-foot German from driving the lane with impunity at crunch time.

But Brooks held fast with his lineup. With seven minutes to go, thoughts of changes crossed his mind. The offense was fine, but the defense was not stopping Nowitzki and Barea. Inside six minutes, it was still a one-possession game, and past the time when most coaches would cash in any winnings from his bench and get the starters back in to finish up.

Brooks opted to roll the dice again, keeping this unit on the floor and risking terrible ridicule if the decision backfired. How could he keep Maynor and Collison on the floor if he had better options on the bench? But Cook nailed a 3-pointer off a Durant assist with 5:16 to play, igniting a 7-0 run over the next 2:01 that proved decisive for the Thunder. Maynor added a running jumper and Harden buried a 22-footer from near the top of the key, forcing a Dallas timeout to ponder a 102-92 deficit.

Brooks stuck with his gut and the bench players rewarded him for his faith. Ibaka (37 seconds) and starting guard Thabo Sefolosha (13 seconds) returned in the final minute, but Westbrook and Perkins sat the entire fourth quarter.

"We've got 10 guys that can play," Collison said. "We don't lose confidence when other guys are in the game."

Sometimes you give away a game, sometimes one is taken from you. For the Mavericks, this felt like the latter. In this fourth quarter, Oklahoma City had made tough decisions, tough shots and had earned the right to return home with the series tied 1-1.

"Sometimes you get your butt kicked," Carlisle said. "You've got to take it like a man. Hey, we've got to respond."

Carlisle already had been pondering a response. He had been wrestling with how to address what he considered a vulnerability, even during his team's successful run of seven consecutive playoff wins.

The Mavericks had a deep roster, undoubtedly. But the coach was concerned about having too many "one-way" players in the current rotation. Too much Stevenson or Haywood helped the defense, but could stagnate the offense. Too much Barea or Stojakovic could open up points in transition, but also give away too many easy scores when opponents attacked those players at the other end. Choosing when and where to use each would be one of Carlisle's biggest challenges going forward.

Stojakovic, the legendary long-range marksman, was the toughest one to figure out. Assistant coach Terry Stotts had told ESPN how the team would marvel at his 3-point exercises in practice. How, in consecutive days, Stojakovic had hit 94 of 100 3-pointers, followed by 96 of 100, including one stretch of 48 in a row. Some players, even professionals, couldn't make 48 layups in a row.

Using a weapon such as Peja was enormously tempting, as he could help spread the floor like few others. But Carlisle had to weigh the sharpshooting against the defensive deficiencies Stojakovic would bring over the same number of minutes. Even the Mavs employing their zone defense wouldn't prevent the younger, quicker Thunder from finding an attractive matchup with Stojakovic on the floor.

Their long-range shelling of the Lakers had naturally increased the Mavericks' confidence in shooting from distance. They fired up 27 3-pointers in Game 2, but this time made only nine. Terry and Stojakovic only mustered eight points apiece. When Dallas' shooters are hitting their shots, the team is nearly unstoppable. But when they (Terry in particular) regress, the results can be messy. When Stevenson compounds the problem by flinging up six 3-pointers (making only one), they get even worse.

Harden's 23 points marked a career playoff high, and the Thunder were a net 14 points better than the Mavs this time when their sixth man was on the floor. That was a matchup the Mavericks needed Terry to win if they hoped to advance. Terry could be an up-and-down player, and Carlisle needed more up right now. The maddening pull-up 3-point attempts with no one in position to rebound wouldn't cut it.

Only two Dallas players (Nowitzki and Barea) managed to score in a fourth quarter in which the Mavericks were outshot 65 to 41 percent. For the game, the Thunder hit 62 percent of their two-point attempts and 56 percent from the floor overall.

"It's a dangerous team when they start to make shots. You can't let them believe. You can't give a young team hope," Chandler said. "This was one game that we didn't have to lose. We made too many defensive errors out there, and we are playing for too much right now to let that happen.

"In the Lakers series, we played with an edge because we were afraid of them and thought they could beat us. I feel like we took these boys too lightly. There is a reason why they are in the Western Conference finals."

Brooks' coaching strategy late in the game was clearly the headline of Game 2. As a coach, you seldom want to flirt with "losing your team" over a decision. When you sit your starters and roll with far less-prominent players in a playoff road game of great importance, any deviation from the script better work. And it did. The Thunder were back in this series.

For Dallas, the wake-up call had been heard. Not much else would be heard, though, when Game 3 tipped off Saturday at the raucous arena 200 miles north on I-35. But the Mavericks had recently buried their playoff road curse, and they knew Terry usually played better in a hostile environment.

It would be interesting to see how Dallas would respond to a defeat. The last time it happened, the Mavericks answered with nearly a month of fantastic basketball before they lost again.

Another chance to test that newfound playoff resilience would present itself on the weekend.

========

The Mavericks watched game film the day before Game 3, a session that would later be called the "Marion Meeting."

There was little question that the NBA's leading scorer was going to get his points, but the Mavericks still wanted to examine how they were defending Kevin Durant. Containing him could well punch their ticket back to the NBA Finals. There was too much at risk to allow anything less than each Mavs defender giving his all.

When the lights came on, a few players were ready to challenge the effort and approach of Shawn Marion, in particular, against Oklahoma City's scoring whiz. They felt Marion, the best and primary defender on the squad, was giving Durant too much room to operate, and that he appeared to be too concerned about picking up fouls to guard Durant tight.

"We were watching film and seeing something," Terry said. "We hold everyone accountable on this team — Dirk, Kidd, anyone. There were situations on the tape in Games 1 and 2 where we were giving them too much space. We have to be into Durant, and that's Shawn's assignment. And, to his credit, he let us know he was up to the challenge."

Like any professional worth his salt, Marion didn't enjoy being called out, but the team leaders felt it was needed. Accountability would supersede egos in the Mavericks' room, because so many respected veterans knew what was at stake. The message had been received, and Durant would find things a bit more difficult in Game 3.

Saturday, May 21
Game 3, Western Conference Finals
Oklahoma City, Oklahoma

It took 1:42 for either team to score in Game 3, but once DeShawn Stevenson's 3-pointer put Dallas up 3-0, there would be no more lead changes in this game.

Dallas proved again it could ratchet its fine defense even tighter when the group set its collective mind to the task. And with the Thunder appearing to start a bit nervous and indecisive inside their own rocking building, the Mavericks put forth a defensive surge that was swarming and decisive.

The Mavs built a staggering 23-point lead that Oklahoma City eventually whittled down to four with 24 seconds left. But that comeback took everything the Thunder had, and it wasn't enough to crest the summit of the early wave the Mavericks had thrown at them. Dallas hung on to win the pivotal contest, 93-87.

The Mavs opened this game determined to regain their homecourt advantage, and did so with a staggering show of force. They had the superior energy from the start, blocking shots, rebounding, stepping into passing lanes and reacting quickly with double-team defense to make things difficult. There seemed to be little Durant, Westbrook or their mates could do about it.

There was renewed determination on offense, too. After Stevenson's wide-open 3-pointer opened the scoring, Dallas scored its next six baskets from within a range of 4 feet. The Mavs were taking the ball hard to the rack and jumped to a 15-6 lead before some Thunder fans had even unwrapped their hot dogs.

Marion responded to his teammates' constructive criticism by coming up big at both ends of the floor. As was usually the case when the Mavericks were playing well in transition, Marion was cleaning up broken plays and finishing off fast breaks with high-percentage shots at or near the rim. He made 9 of 13 shots in Game 3, en route to 18 points with four rebounds, two steals and two blocks.

More important was his improved defensive work against Durant. Oklahoma City's franchise player still finished with a respectable 24 points and 12 rebounds, but this time the total required 22 shots and 11 free throws. Durant enjoyed few easy possessions as he went 7 of 22 from the floor, including 0 for 8 from 3-point range.

The "Marion Meeting" had left The Matrix with a chip on his shoulder. Whether upset with himself, or humiliated by teammates pointing fingers at his work against Durant, Marion played Game 3 angry. That was exactly what his teammates wanted to see.

"We've got to have him pissed," Chandler told Tim MacMahon of ESPNDallas.com. "We've got to have him slashing all over the place and being aggressive. We don't want the 'Happy 'Trix.' I like the angry one.

"He can be pissed off at all of us if he gives us the results. He took some criticism, and he's man enough to get out there and accept it the way he did. He didn't tuck his tail between his legs and go hide. He stood up like a man and went out there and gave us a great effort tonight."

Stevenson readily agreed.

"In the first two games, (Marion) wasn't really up on him, and he let Durant get to where he wanted to go. We watched that, and everybody came with focus and ready to play tonight."

Kidd also was magnificent (13 points, eight assists, six rebounds and four steals), with cerebral play on both ends of the court. While Marion was making things difficult for Durant, so too was Kidd treating Westbrook to a bit of finishing school. The old man pestered the young star into having an 8-for-20 shooting night with seven turnovers.

That the Mavs were where they were with a 38-year-old playing the point was difficult for some to understand. But not when you watched Kidd operate, baiting defenders into sending him to the foul line or looking off backside help with a glance just convincing enough to open up another lob pass and dunk. He seemed to see the game unfold a second or two before most on the court and always knew where to be and why. He still had to execute, either by making the shot or pass or defending the man. But it seemed his basketball I.Q. more than compensated for any loss of foot speed.

The beauty of the best-of-seven series is that it forces a team to prove itself superior four times. Any player or team can have a hot shooting night, or cause an opponent to have a poor one. Doing that once is enough to see a Goliath fall in single-elimination formats such as the NCAA's "March Madness" tournament. But the NBA requires the success to be repeated four times in two weeks before letting a team move on. That irons out a lot of the anomalies.

The Mavericks were confident that the format favored them. Oklahoma City's youthful quickness could prove the difference if a game hinged on who could reach a loose ball faster. But if the games were decided by winning the mental battles of patience, precision and execution, Dallas' elder statesmen felt their experience gave them a calm composure the exuberant and excitable Thunder couldn't match.

On a night when Nowitzki had uncharacteristically poor shooting (7 of 21) and committed seven turnovers, and when his main sidekick Terry was only 3 of 12 from the floor, the Mavericks still led wire to wire in Game 3 and kept their cool long enough to outlast the Thunder's late charge.

They did themselves no favors early in the fourth quarter when, just as in Game 4 of the Portland series, they lapsed into a stretch of conceding easy shots and free throws on defense and settling for low-percentage 3-point attempts on offense. Dallas still often displayed an uncomfortable demeanor after building a large lead. But the Mavs snapped out of it late with some clutch shooting from Nowitzki (10 of his 18 points in the fourth quarter) and Terry (6 of his 13 in the fourth). Neither was dominant, but they combined as reliably as ever to get the biggest points in the closing minutes.

The Dallas defense, meanwhile, managed to get stops on five of Oklahoma City's last nine possessions, preserving enough cushion to emerge with the 2-1 series lead.

"The difference," Carlisle said, "was that we played better defense tonight."

The result ensured the Mavs of at least a split in Oklahoma. As they looked forward to Monday's Game 4, they wondered whether reclaiming home-court advantage would speed up the end of this youthful rebellion, or merely tilt the odds slightly if this series took seven grueling games.

Either way, they now were only two wins away from returning to the NBA Finals.

19

OKLAHOMA CITY
GAMES 4-5

(May 23-25, 2011)

The day off Sunday in Oklahoma City provided another chance for Holger Geschwindner and Dirk Nowitzki to head back to the Oklahoma City Arena for another nighttime shooting session. No matter the city, if the Mavericks had a night off during the playoffs, Nowitzki was spending it being put through his shooting paces by his personal coach.

The television networks had caught wind of the routine. So, instead of working in complete solitude, Nowitzki and his mentor now had camera crews documenting part of their diligent work on one-footed shots and spin moves. But they were no distraction, as Nowitzki was locked in solely on the next game and how to overcome the tough defending of Nick Collison. And even if the Oklahoma City forward got a televised peek at what might be coming, that didn't mean he'd be able to stop it.

Nowitzki never allowed himself the luxury of thinking his shot was locked in. His only focus was on the next game. It only changed when a game ended, and his focus would shift to the game coming next.

"I just think you learn this from so many years in the playoffs. And it is why having our veteran roster counts even more in the playoffs," Nowitzki explained later. "After a win, you think, 'Oh my God, we have to win the next game, because we cannot give the momentum back to them.' And after a loss, you think, 'Oh my God, we have to win. We have to stop them and get the momentum back!'

"So, really, for two months — win or lose — you are always on edge. I think people don't understand that. It isn't the physical drainage only of playing every possession harder. It is the mental drain that you have to carry through the playoffs. And I learned that over the course of so many playoffs. You can never get satisfied or happy. And it just drains you."

The next game provided a rare opportunity to break the will of the young Thunder team. Oklahoma City had not lost consecutive games in the 2011 playoffs. Monday would offer the Thunder a chance to square the series at 2-2, or suffer a second consecutive home loss that would push them to the brink of elimination.

Monday, May 23
Game 4, Western Conference Finals
Oklahoma City, Oklahoma

The Thunder had not lost back-to-back home games for six months, and victory seemed all but assured when they ran their lead to 15 points over Dallas (99-84) as Durant buried a 3-pointer with 5:05 to play.

The lead was still 10 with 2:22 left in the contest. The series was destined for 2-2, based on all the evidence at hand.

"There's times and situations where they are going to test the courage and the mental inner strength of your team," Terry said. "This was one of those times."

Was it ever. But just as the courtside reporters were finishing off stories about a tied series and preparing to hit "send," the Mavericks staged a comeback so improbable that the moniker "team of destiny" began working its way into the rewrites. This was the win that you had to see to believe. And those who did see it still seemed dumbfounded when trying to wrap their arms around the rally. A sellout crowd trudged out like silent zombies into the Oklahoma City night.

Durant had celebrated his big 3-pointer by gesturing as if he was a pro wrestler donning a championship belt. The Mavericks took note, limited the Thunder to just one basket the rest of the way, and tied the game at 101 when Nowitzki made two free throws with 6.4 seconds left.

Nowitzki had scored 12 points during Dallas' incredible 17-2 closing run. It was enough to force overtime, after Marion (now fully engaged in his mission to crowd the NBA's leading scorer) managed to block Durant's 3-point attempt from nearly 30 feet away with two seconds on the clock.

Overtime belonged to the Mavericks. They outscored the Thunder 11-4 in the extra five minutes, taking their first lead of the entire game when Nowitzki made two more free throws 16 seconds into overtime. Dallas never let Oklahoma City regain the lead in overtime, and only allowed Durant two shots (both 3-pointers that missed) in the extra period. They emerged with a mind-boggling 112-105 victory for a 3-1 series lead.

The contrast in body language in the extra session was remarkable. The veteran Mavericks could smell blood and the young Thunder appeared to be coming apart at the seams. They could not believe they had blown their golden opportunity.

"We kept believing," Nowitzki said. "In the last couple minutes, we got great stops and finally got some rebounds. ... That was big down the stretch."

Indeed. The Mavericks trailed 99-84 with 4:48 to play in regulation, and were being manhandled inside. The Thunder outscored the Mavs in the paint, 54-34, and had an enormous 55-33 rebounding edge. According to the Elias Sports Bureau, it was the biggest rebounding advantage for a team in a playoff loss since April 18, 1986, when Philadelphia lost to the Washington Bullets despite outrebounding them by 29.

Rebounding advantage, especially accrued on the defensive end, is one of the more important statistics to a coaching staff. Many coaches will champion a number between 70-75 percent as their team's goal for all available defensive rebounds. But through three quarters of Game 4, the Mavericks had only secured 52 percent of the available defensive boards. Collison, Ibaka and Westbrook were repeatedly finding gaps in the defense to pull the ball back out for another chance. The Mavs, meanwhile, had managed to claim just four of a possible 24 offensive rebounds (17 percent). It was demoralizing. After such a determined effort in Game 3, the Mavericks appeared either tired or satisfied with heading back to Dallas tied 2-2.

Statistics often tell an important story, but sometimes they can mislead. Because as dominant as the Thunder were in many of the "hustle" categories, they still had not pulled away. Instead, the Mavericks steadily reeled them in over the closing minutes of regulation and then blitzed them in the overtime.

How bad was it? League researchers scrambled to determine that this was the first time in at least the last 15 seasons that a team came back to win a playoff game after trailing by 15 or more points with five minutes left in the fourth period. Astonishing.

Oklahoma City had tried hard to blow Dallas off the court early. The Thunder hit their first nine field-goal attempts and pushed their lead to a dozen points in the first half. But the Mavs kept hanging around, and by halftime trailed only by five, 59-54. They were within 79-77 in the final minute of the third quarter.

Still, it appeared the Thunder just wanted it more. They continued to dominate the glass, beating the Mavericks to rebounds at both ends. They outscored the Mavs 15-7 to start the first half of the final period. And with just over five minutes left in regulation, Westbrook missed a three, Collison grabbed the rebound and found Durant. He buried a majestic 3-pointer for a 99-84 lead. To most everyone, that shot looked like the fatal dagger. The crowd went wild as Carlisle called timeout.

Chandler later recounted what was said in that Dallas huddle:

"Even after that three, I looked up at the clock and the score and said, 'We still have time. Down 15, but we still have time.' I told the guys, 'Everything that went wrong tonight, there is still time. We are not giving up. There is still time on the clock and we are going to play this out.'

"I felt if we could put together a few stops, we would win. And the closer we got, the tighter they would get."

Chandler was exactly right. While Dallas should get plenty of credit, the Thunder were not above self-inflicted damage at crunch time, either.

Oklahoma City's fortunes turned when James Harden fouled out with 4:33 left in regulation. The Thunder were still leading by 13 at the time, and their sixth man had only managed seven points and six rebounds. But he was the outside shooting threat the Mavs had to respect. Once he was gone, the Thunder no longer were able to spread the Dallas defense as they had previously. They had run 25 pick-and-roll plays before Harden fouled out. They tried the tactic only twice and were outscored 26-6 after his disqualification.

The Thunder missed their next five shots and committed a turnover before Westbrook hit a field goal to push the lead back to

101-91 with 2:32 left. And over those final 2½ minutes, the Thunder went 0 for 4 from the floor, 0 for 2 from the line and turned the ball over once again when Marion stole it from Durant with 1:07 left. Poor clutch shooting and turnovers proved to be Oklahoma City's undoing. Durant committed nine turnovers, Westbrook six and the Thunder 25 as a team, to just 13 turnovers by the Mavs. No stat better illustrated the difference between veteran poise and youthful panic.

And there should be no overlooking Nowitzki, who morphed fully into "Beast Mode" to force the overtime. Dallas scored the final 10 points of regulation in the last 2:21, getting a free throw by Marion and nine points from Nowitzki, who finished with 40. Dirk nailed a straight-on 3-pointer over Collison, a shot that always seems truer when he is jogging forward than when pulling up. Then, trailing 101-94 with two minutes remaining, Dirk hit one of the most memorable shots of his amazing playoff run.

It was a well-guarded, double-pumped, fade-away attempt that seemed prayer-like upon release. But it swished through the rim with such majesty the entire crowd collectively gasped. He appeared to be fouled in the motion, but there would be no call. Next time down, of course, Nowitzki would do it again. This time, he converted a driving, spinning 5-footer over Collison after starting at the high post. Collison, who had troubled Dirk earlier in the series, was at a loss over what strategy to try next. He clearly was the main course at a Nowitzki barbecue, and did not appear to be capable of escape.

Finally, with six seconds left, Nowitzki was fouled by Collison. He made the two free throws to tie the game, the biggest of a night when he was 14 of 15 from the line.

The Thunder had one final possession in regulation, but there was Marion, playing Durant tougher and closer as his teammates had implored. He forced Durant to retreat near the time line just to get the pass. Then Marion made the high-risk decision to leap out at Durant as the star scorer launched his long 3-ball. The slightest contact against Durant's arm or hand would have put the homecourt hero on the line with three free throws to hit a game-winning point. But Marion hit nothing but ball, blocking the shot an instant after it was fired.

Not to be outdone, Kidd provided a gigantic moment of his own in the overtime. With the score tied at 105-105 with 1:01 left, Kidd stripped the ball from Durant as he went up for a shot. Kidd fed the ball to Nowitzki, who was quickly covered. He kicked the ball back to Kidd in the right corner. The savvy veteran pump-faked to get Westbrook in the air, then calmly hit a 3-point bomb that proved to be the game-winning points. It was simply another in a series of gigantic clutch shots from the oldest man on the court.

"Everybody asks questions about the age and all that other stuff," Carlisle said. "But the thing I'd say to anybody is, 'Never underestimate greatness.'"

"There's no doubt it was a tough loss," Thunder coach Scott Brooks said. "If this loss did not hurt, there's no such thing as a loss that can hurt you."

"It's not over yet," Durant said after the game, but it appeared obvious to most that his young team had just had its heart ripped out. The Thunder were constantly answering questions about their youth. Now, they were indeed performing at crucial moments like a team still in need of seasoning when faced with the high-leverage moments of late spring.

The Mavericks had their faults, but had again showed they also had incalculable will and resilience. It was too soon to know whether they would be worthy of a championship. But if they could beat this demoralized opponent before their home crowd in Dallas on Wednesday, they would take the Western Conference crown and get their chance to see.

What a ride this had become.

========

As they prepared for Game 5, the Mavericks took pride in how difficult they were making Kevin Durant's job. He had made 21 of 41 shots (51 percent) and scored 64 points in the first two games, prompting the "Marion Meeting."

Since then, Marion and his tag-team partner Kidd had held Durant to 16-for-44 shooting (36 percent) and 53 points in the next two games, with no increase in foul trouble. Durant had gotten to the line 22 times in the first two games, and 21 times in the next two. He also had made just six turnovers in the first two games, but had coughed it up 10 times under the tighter defense of Games 3 and 4. There was truly no stopping a player of Durant's caliber, but they were making him work much harder.

Thus far in the series, Marion and Kidd had combined for 23 steals. And from a production standpoint, the point guard battle was being dominated by the Mavericks. Kidd and his backup, Barea, had amassed 43 assists with just 12 turnovers. Westbrook and his backup, Maynor, had 25 assists and 23 turnovers.

What had gotten to Durant the most was that Kidd seemed to have solved his "rip move," a favorite technique in which Durant would take the ball and rip through his defender's arms, often drawing a shooting foul. Carlisle argued it was a "non-basketball movement" that the rules committee needed to outlaw, as when the league prohibited players from kicking their legs to draw a foul on jump shots.

Kidd had studied Durant's technique, and now often had his hand waiting for the ball. Even if he missed, Kidd usually earned the benefit of the doubt from officials. He had handled his dealings with officials with great respect over the years, and pitching few tantrums over the course of 17 years in the league helped earn comparable respect back.

"I guess it's not going to get called anymore, so I guess I'm going to have to throw it away," Durant complained at the morning shootaround. "I'm not going to try it again, because they didn't call it last game. I'm just going to try to make a stronger move and try to get to the rim or make the shot instead."

The quotes found their way into the Dallas locker room, making some veterans smile. They realized they had gotten into Durant's head a bit, and his inexperience was becoming an issue.

Wednesday, May 25
Game 5, Western Conference Finals
Dallas, Texas

The Western Conference finals ended the only fitting way — with Dirk again putting the Mavericks in the lead.

Dallas trailed 94-92 with 96 seconds to play when Nowitzki stole the ball. Russell Westbrook thought he saw Nick Collison open down low, but Dirk stepped in the path of the ball and was able to get his right hand on the pass.

The first priority as they crossed halfcourt was for Jason Kidd to find Nowitzki on the left wing against Collison, another isolation sequence seen over and over in this series. This time, Dirk got the edge on Collison and headed to the hoop, while the Thunder defense collapsed on the Dallas star. Nowitzki spotted Jason Terry in the corner for a go-ahead 3-pointer, but his pass was deflected out of bounds. The Thunder were in position to keep the series alive if they could last 84 more seconds with the lead.

Jason Kidd looked to inbound the ball, with all four Mavericks teammates starting the play near the free-throw line. As Kidd looked for options, first Terry and then Tyson Chandler screened Collison as

Dirk dropped back behind the 3-point line. Because of the double screen, Dirk was free for a split second. Kidd put the ball in the German's hands and time seemed to stand still as his shot flew toward the goal.

But it didn't go in. It rimmed out. And Westbrook grabbed the rebound in a battle with Chandler down low. In the scramble, Westbrook lost his balance and tried keeping the ball in play as he fell. In another stroke of Dallas good fortune, he basically rolled the ball right to Terry. Terry passed crosscourt to Marion. At the point Marion caught the ball, Dirk already had dropped back on defense and was actually on the midcourt timeline. He reversed direction back into the play.

Marion saw Dirk rush back and found him right as the Mavericks' leader was in position for another try. This time, there was no screen and Collison challenged the shot. But this time, there was no mistake. The ball ripped through the cords, giving the Mavericks a 95-94 lead. With 1:14 to play, the sellout crowd of 21,092 roared in grateful unison.

Like the 3-pointer he hit Monday night in the historic Game 4 rally, his 3-point shot in Game 5 marked the moment the tides finally turned all the way.

On the next possession, the Mavericks buckled down hard on defense and forced an airball from Eric Maynor from the paint. Collison collected the rebound as he was falling out of bounds. With no other option, he also attempted to send the ball in the general direction of his teammates and hoped for the best. Terry and James Harden grasped for the ball and somehow it tipped over to Marion, who always seemed ready to get a loose ball when needed most.

Marion had nothing but open court ahead of him and was about to make a one-point lead bigger inside the final minute. Durant tried to chase him down, but Terry pulled another veteran move and blocked his path for a step. That gave Marion all the space needed to dunk and draw a desperation foul from Durant. The crowd roared, sensing the end was near.

Moments later, when the five-game series was done and dusted with a 100-96 Mavericks victory, Nowitzki tried to look pleased, if only for the benefit of the fans cheering wildly all around the American Airlines Center. He couldn't fake it. He just wasn't interested in hoisting the Western Conference championship silverware. But, he also wasn't the type of guy to deny a request of his mates. So, with a forced smile, he lifted the trophy high for the fans to enjoy.

"We've got one of those trophies already," Nowitzki explained after the celebrations had subsided. "This is nice, for a day, but we set our goals in October to win it all. We haven't done it yet."

Such was the focus of the man who, once again, practically willed Dallas to a comeback victory with another clutch fourth quarter.

This time the deficit wasn't quite as daunting as Game 4's challenge of 15 points with five minutes left. But the Thunder held a seven-point lead with 5:48 left in Game 5, only to be outscored 17-6 the rest of the way to see their playoff dreams extinguished.

Nowitzki scored nine of his team-high 26 points in the final period, including seven in the decisive final four minutes. Crunch Time was Dirk Time, and he was now leading the NBA playoff participants in fourth-quarter scoring average with an impressive 11.4 points per quarter (11.8 if including overtime).

The Mavs outscored the Thunder 28-20 in the final period, and Nowitzki had help. Of the remaining 19 points Dallas scored in the fourth, 14 were from Marion, who was energetic again at both ends and a consistently solid finisher of the Mavs' transition chances. Marion was 10 of 17 from the floor, matching Nowitzki's team-high 26 points, and scored seven of his baskets within 5 feet of the rim. He also had eight rebounds and three blocked shots.

The last time the Mavericks reached the NBA Finals (2006), they advanced with a victory in Phoenix. This time, they got to celebrate the moment with their own fans on a stage quickly erected atop the AAC floor. Even franchise founder Don Carter joined the party, trading his signature white cowboy hat for one of the black baseball caps featuring the Mavs' logo, the O'Brien trophy, and the inscription "The Finals 2011."

"Their time will come, but it's not now," Carlisle said of the Thunder. "We feel like now is our time to move on."

The Thunder had gotten 31 points from Westbrook and 23 each from Durant and Harden. They had outrebounded the Mavs again (49-44), outshot them from the floor (42.7 percent to 41 percent), and only committed one more turnover than Dallas (13-12). But they were outscored by 10 points at the free-throw line (31-21 in 11 fewer attempts) and did not execute as cleanly in the critical final minutes.

"It's tough now, but we can learn from it," Durant said. "The only way to get better is to keep pushing. I just think we played hard and just couldn't come up with the win."

Ending the series in five games meant the Mavericks' creaky legs would get at least six days of rest before the start of The Finals. Kidd, especially, realized the importance of that.

"Any time you can get rest this time of year is a bonus," he said. "For us to close it out here is huge."

If sports fairy tales come true, Dallas fans would see Nowitzki truly celebrating within a few weeks' time. Just as Denver Broncos quarterback John Elway proved critics wrong with two Super Bowl victories in his final two seasons, now Dirk would get another chance at basketball immortality.

This series had demonstrated that veteran grit and know-how could supersede youthful energy and athleticism, at least at the crucial moments. Dallas had appeared superior in very few ways during most of the series. But when you examined the final five minutes of each of these five games (plus the one five-minute overtime), you found the Mavs outscored their opponent by a composite 29 points when things mattered most. And that, quite simply, was the only difference there was.

Dallas knew how to make shots, how to get stops, how to calmly sink important free throws, and how to get loose balls. Not all of them, but most of the ones that really mattered.

There was a ton of experience and resolve on the Mavericks' roster. The other three teams in the NBA's Final Four — Oklahoma City, Chicago and Miami — could discuss bright futures and the confident belief they would be back this deep in the playoffs many more times before all was said and done. This aging Dallas team did not have the same luxury, and that gave the Mavericks an urgency the others didn't share.

Their window was open, right now. In a few weeks, it might slam shut forever. For these Mavericks players, the thousands of practices and flights and hotels and games and injuries and victories had been part of lengthy careers. But those careers would still feel somewhat hollow if not crowned by the chance to be called NBA champions.

Nowitzki certainly felt this as he lifted the Western Conference trophy to show jubilant fans. And then owner Mark Cuban, in a now-rare moment of public speaking, took the microphone to convey his and Dirk's thoughts.

"All I can say is there's 20-some-thousand people in this building who believed in us when nobody else did," Cuban said. "There's all the guys in this organization and on the court who believed in us, and in Coach, and fought every game — every minute of the way.

"And all I can tell everybody is: We ain't done yet!"

As ESPN's coverage team moved in to interview Cuban and Carlisle, panicked producers saw something unexpected happening. Nowitzki, staring blankly, turned and left the stage. He was done with this moment. He wasn't interested in giving anyone the impression that his mission was accomplished. He was ready to move on.

Nowitzki headed to the seclusion of the locker room, and his teammates did what they had done this entire postseason. They followed their leader. They headed back to the room to symbolically move on, too. It was the moment that best demonstrated how much Nowitzki had changed over the years. The unassuming fellow who just loves the sport had grown into that William Wallace figure his detractors said he never would be.

Dirk said it. He had been this far before.

"We talked about it after the game," Nowitzki said. "This is a great moment, but we got one of those (Western Conference) trophies already and it didn't mean anything at the end. I think, once you get to The Finals, there is no second-place finish. I was already thinking about The Finals."

Cardinal couldn't believe what he saw happen next.

"They tossed the trophy in a laundry basket," Cardinal recalled, "and said, 'We want The Finals trophy.'"

Nowitzki later said he had only one regret about his decision to leave the stage prematurely, and that was standing up ESPN reporter Doris Burke for her expected live interview.

"That kind of looked bad, and I felt bad afterwards," he said. "I didn't know she would want to talk to me again."

But Nowitzki was in the moment, and participating in what he considered mini-celebrations no longer appealed to him.

"If you look at the playoffs, you have to win four rounds to win the championship. Winning three rounds is just not going to cut it," he said. "So, for me, winning the Western Conference was just another round to The Finals. That's how I looked at it. And that is why I left early."

Nowitzki had wanted to send a message to his team, his fans, and even to his yet-to-be-determined Finals opponent that he wasn't done. That Western Conference trophy was simply a marker along the road to the Mavericks' destination, which is why it was later photographed by a reporter's camera phone sitting alone on a taping table in the team's training room.

Nowitzki sent fans a Twitter message from his @swish41 feed the next morning that said:

"Big thx to all the mavs fans everywhere. On to the finals. Aac was a madhouse yesterday. Gotta stay humble and hungry once more. Bleed blue"

But his real message to teammates had been sent the previous night with the casual discarding of the Western Conference ceremony and silverware.

"Dirk summed it up," Terry said. "We got one of those. Now, let's go get the real trophy."

20

MIAMI GAME 1

(May 31, 2011)

The day after the Dallas Mavericks won the right to play for the NBA title, they were joined in The Finals by the Miami Heat.

In the Eastern Conference finals, the Heat had needed just five games to eliminate the Chicago Bulls, who had finished with the best record in the league (62-20) during the regular season. The decisiveness of Miami's victory over 2011 league MVP Derrick Rose and the Bulls was at least as impressive as the Mavericks' over the Thunder. The Heat lost Game 1 to the Bulls by 21 points, then drummed out Chicago with four consecutive victories. The winning margins were 10, 11, 8 and 3 points and the Heat had utilized the same formula as the Mavericks — domination at crunch time.

It's possible that no team ever had employed two closers the caliber of LeBron James and Dwyane Wade in their primes. And in Chris Bosh, Miami even had a third star who had taken most of Toronto's big shots for a number of years. Most prognosticators found it hard to envision the Mavericks owning crunch time in this series the way they had against Portland, Los Angeles and Oklahoma City. There was just too much Miami firepower to contain.

The Heat certainly were not popular nationally. The egomaniacal nature of James' televised "The Decision," coupled with the team's over-the-top unveiling of the star trio in the summer, had for most NBA fans cast the Heat in villain roles before the season began. But Miami eventually seemed to embrace the "heel" persona, playing well in the black hats. The Heat had overwhelmed Philadelphia, Boston and Chicago in Eastern Conference playoff series that each ended in five games. They might lose once in a series, but the notion of losing four times in one seemed pure fantasy.

Miami was roaring through the postseason despite one of the oddest, most counter-intuitive rosters in NBA history. James, Wade and Bosh were eating up $47.5 million of the Heat's $65.3 million payroll (73 percent). Each was making at least $15.5 million in salary (not including outside endorsement deals), while only one other Heat player (Mike Miller, $5.4 million) was earning more than $3.78 million. Miami had seven fairly anonymous players (the Seven Dwarfs?) getting paid less than $1.4 million. It truly was King James and His Court, surrounded by serfs.

There wasn't much opportunity for any of those role players to improve their worth, either. James, Wade and Bosh combined to take 62.3 percent of the Heat's shots during the regular season, and scored 65.6 percent of the team's points. If anyone else touched the ball, it usually was by accident.

With such dependence on that trio, even Heat coach Erik Spoelstra was looked upon as little more than a cheerleader with a clipboard. What power did he really wield, compared to the "Super Friends," "Miami Thrice," "The Three Amigos," the "Three Kings," the "James Gang," "MV3," "Miamma Slamma Jamma," "The Brothers Rim" or any of the other countless nicknames by which the triumverate had become known?

This was no team in the traditional sense, where chemistry, unity, attack diversity, bench impact, etc., were considered of great value. The tried and true pillars of building a championship team did not seem to apply to this group. This was a new paradigm for the YouTube-reality TV-social networking generation, a poster team for the "Hey, look at me" age of unchecked ego and personal branding. But nobody had been able to stop them yet.

The excitement in Dallas was rising to fever pitch as Dirk and the boys were on the brink of running down their dream. It seemed deliciously perfect to meet Miami in the final showdown, for there would be no better way to exorcise the ghosts of 2006. It would be sweet revenge or the cruelest, most agonizing defeat yet. But so many Dallas teams had found heartbreak in South Florida (the Cowboys lost the

Miami-hosted Super Bowls V, X and XIII), it reminded many to be careful for what they wished.

Most Mavericks players suggested they did not care who they would meet in The Finals, but one suspected the opponent held extra meaning for 2006 Finals holdovers Terry and Nowitzki. Terry, remember, recorded that video of the Heat's championship banner during the Mavs' December visit. He seemed obsessed with setting things right, and even promised reporters that he would have his O'Brien Trophy tattoo removed if the Mavs lost.

"It symbolized the fact we had a realistic shot of getting there," Terry said. "If I didn't think we had a chance, I definitely wouldn't have put that on there. … For me, it's something I have to sleep with, something I wake up with. I definitely know it's going to hurt worse if I have to take this thing off. It means it was bad luck."

Terry went on to mention how, over the weekend, he slept in Miami team shorts worn by former Heat guard Gary Payton in 2006. He thought it not strange at all, his professed habit of sleeping in the shorts of the next opponent the Mavericks are to face. His logic and motivation never was fully explained, it was just Jet being Jet.

Things were never boring when Terry had a microphone in front of him.

========

Game 1 would not arrive until Tuesday, May 31, which left the media four long days to milk whatever mileage it could out of the few "newsworthy" tidbits available.

Besides the clamor over the future of Terry's tattoo, reporters jumped on the following stories:

- The Mavericks would have to borrow the Phoenix Suns' jet to take the team to Miami, because Cuban's plane was inoperable due to hail damage.
- Miami backup center Erick Dampier had been part of the Mavericks' losing team in the 2006 Finals. This particular story had little pizazz, given Dampier's remote prospects of ever stepping onto the floor during The Finals.
- Mavericks backup point guard J.J. Barea had attended high school in Miami and was hugely popular with the city's Puerto Rican and Latin communities.

- Terry and Heat guard Mike Bibby had been college teammates for two years, including on the 1997 University of Arizona NCAA title-winning team.
- And (shudder) the Mavericks planned to use the same South Beach hotel that former coach Avery Johnson made them abandon in the middle of the 2006 Finals, when he thought the players had become distracted and were not focusing on the most important task of their careers.

"None of that matters," Nowitzki told the *Dallas Morning News*. "Wherever we stay is where we stay."

Nowitzki's thoughts were more occupied by what would happen on the court. Each team caused some matchup problems for the other. But in the back of his mind, Nowitzki sensed that much of this series could be decided by the battle of wills between himself and his 2006 nemesis Wade.

Most of the NBA's star players share a respectful (if not outright friendly) rapport. Not so with these two. It seemed as if some genuine bad blood had developed between rivals Nowitzki and Wade.

"I think we were the first All-Star starters who didn't shake hands before a game," Nowitzki said, recalling the 2007 All-Star Game in Las Vegas. "The whole thing started after The Finals (in 2006), when I said that we gave the championship away and that it was all us. He was upset that I didn't give them any credit at all. Then he said I wasn't a leader, and it just went from there."

But the hard feelings eventually subsided. Nowitzki even remembered bumping into Wade in a restroom before the February 2010 All-Star Game at Cowboys Stadium, where the Heat guard praised the Mavs' recent acquisition of Caron Butler.

"This year was fine," Nowitzki said of their relationship. "Before Game 1, J-Kidd and I ran into him in the hallway as were all doing media, and we shook hands and congratulated each other on getting to The Finals. And before Game 1, on the court, we shook hands.

"But once a series starts, I don't like to shake hands anymore with anyone."

========

Tuesday, May 31
Game 1, NBA Finals
Miami, Florida

Dallas was within striking distance, trailing 77-73 with 3:44 to play, when Miami once again found an extra gear at crunch time. An 8-2 scoring burst over the next 57 seconds widened the gap to 10 points, and the Heat held on for a 92-84 victory in the opener.

Two free throws by Bosh, a 3-pointer by Wade, and a spectacular dunk and free throw by James fueled the late Miami run. Wade and James embraced after the final whistle while Bosh stood nearby, holding up three fingers to the crowd. The Big Three just needed three more wins to secure the first of their many expected championships.

James had scored 24 points to help win his first NBA Finals game in five tries. Wade had scored 15 of his 22 points in the second half, to go with 10 rebounds and 6 assists. Bosh had 19 points and 9 rebounds. Miami's other two starters (Bibby and center Joel Anthony) did not score, and four bench players combined to add 27 points in 86 minutes of play.

Miami's continued lack of balance didn't seem to concern anyone, however, not when the Heat's defense held the Mavs to their second-lowest scoring total of the postseason.

"The difference in this game," ABC analyst Jeff Van Gundy enthused, "is that Miami has James and Wade and Dallas doesn't!"

The Mavericks had not been outplayed in the final minutes of the fourth very often in these playoffs, but it was true that the superior shot-making abilities of James and Wade might pose a new reality in The Finals. This was Dallas' first road loss since the Game 4 debacle in Portland more than six weeks earlier (April 23), but it still was tough to swallow. And now, for the first time this postseason, the Mavericks would have to come from behind to win a series.

"You can't get down with a loss," said Nowitzki, who scored a game-high 27 points. "If you're the road team, you're happy with a split. So we've got another opportunity Thursday to get one. Obviously, we don't want to go home down 0-2."

Nowitzki had arrived a few minutes late to his postgame media session, delayed by the need for X-rays on his left middle finger. He had injured the digit on his non-shooting hand (well, usually non-shooting) while stripping a ball away from Bosh. It soon was revealed that Nowitzki had torn a tendon in the finger and would have to play in a splint for the remainder of the series.

Marion finished with 16 points and 10 rebounds and Terry added 12 points in a game dominated by the defenses. Going in, there were many questions about the Mavericks' ability to defend Miami, but right to the end, they had the answers. Dallas had held Miami to 38.8 percent shooting, the Heat's second-worst showing of the playoffs. But the Mavs had their worst shooting night of the postseason (37.3 percent) and were outrebounded, 46-36.

"You hold a team to 38 percent shooting and 92 points," Marion said, "for us, that's usually a victory."

But this Miami team appeared to be an animal different from anything the Mavericks had seen.

Surprisingly, it was the offensive side of things that had the Mavericks concerned. Miami was a challenging team to defend because of the individual scoring prowess of the Big Three, but Dallas coaches were encouraged by their team's effort in Game 1. The Mavs had forced the Heat into many low-percentage shots, and the results showed.

But it was Miami's ability to make Dallas shooters uncomfortable that had Carlisle worried. The Mavericks' offense had been operating with impunity for weeks, but suddenly had found quality shots tough to come by. This was particularly true for scoring leaders Nowitzki and Terry, whose production was crucial. If they were stopped from scoring with their usual efficiency, the Mavs' entire offense could grind to a halt.

Was it simply a poor shooting night that saw Nowitzki and Terry combine to go 10 of 28 from the floor? Was it a case of nerves as their long-awaited chance at redemption was upon them? Or was it something the Miami defense was doing that needed to be counteracted quickly?

The Heat had done a good job of harassing Nowitzki, making him work hard for everything he got in Game 1. But as dangerous as Dirk was, it was apparent that the Heat looked at defending Terry as the key to the series. In Game 1, they held Jet scoreless the entire second half on 0-for-3 shooting. When there was no confident secondary scorer supporting Nowitzki, the results usually were poor for the Mavericks.

Whatever most of the nation now thought about James, there was no denying he is a tenacious defender, one good enough to be named to the league's All-Defensive first team three years running. The Mavericks had expected James would cover Nowitzki in the fourth quarters of this series. Instead, Spoelstra dispatched James to suffocate Terry late in the game. Udonis Haslem stayed on Nowitzki, with occasional help from Bosh and Wade.

Spoelstra was praised for this tactical decision, which seemed to catch the Mavericks a bit by surprise. Carlisle had seen most opponents focus their best defender(s) on Nowitzki, and had all manner of countermeasures up his sleeve. But, given Carlisle's preferred fourth-quarter lineup, if the Heat could nullify Terry, this could be a problem.

Dallas still had the defensive-minded Marion, Chandler and Kidd on the floor to get stops. But with Terry unable to maneuver against the much taller and more athletic James, there was no one left to help Nowitzki keep the offense alive late in the fourth. It seemed a very shrewd idea for Miami and it worked as brilliantly as they could have hoped.

Adding to the Mavericks' offensive woes was the fact that Haslem and James were defending Dallas' favored high pick-and-roll with Nowitzki and Terry as well as anyone had. The Mavs needed Terry to hit shots over much taller defenders for their strategy to work in this series. Carlisle could use Barea to open things up with his penetration, but then who could the little man guard at the other end, especially when the Heat used a larger lineup without a true point guard?

Carlisle was going to need some radical ideas to find a counterpunch. He could employ Stojakovic as shooter the Heat would (hopefully) have to respect, but who would come off the court? Marion's superb defense was essential against James or Wade. Pulling Chandler would give the Heat carte blanche to attack through the lane. Kidd's savvy made him essential at both ends of the court late in games. But only five players were permitted. If the Nowitzki-Terry pick-and-roll was being neutralized, the headaches that would cause were obvious. The Mavs would need more fourth-quarter offense from Kidd, and somehow find a way to get Terry better looks.

Early foul trouble had kept Chandler to 34 minutes in Game 1, and he produced only nine points and four rebounds. More was needed from him.

Dallas had gotten only 17 points from its bench, with 12 coming on an off-night from Terry. Stojakovic had missed a trio of 3-point attempts and gone scoreless in 15 minutes. And in 18 minutes, Barea had shot a pathetic 1 for 8, all inside the two-point area. Carlisle hoped this was simply a case of early nerves from the hometown kid playing in his first NBA Finals game.

Jitters may have been a factor, certainly, but as the Mavericks examined their poor shooting performance it was folly not to consider the tenacity of Miami's defenders in the equation. They consistently make their opponents miss shots. Miami finished the regular season tied with Boston for the second-lowest opponents' field-goal percentage (43.4 percent) among NBA defenses, trailing only Chicago (43 percent). For the Mavericks to survive, they would have to hit shots under duress, something Boston and Chicago could not do often enough.

The good news was that Dallas' zone defense had its desired effect, pushing the Heat further back and outside their offensive comfort zone.

During the regular season, the Heat averaged just over 18 3-point attempts per game, a number that dropped to 16.8 per game in the earlier playoff rounds. In Game 1 of The Finals, Miami took 24 3-point shots, hitting 11 (45.8 percent). It had been an impressive long-distance display, but one not likely to be repeated. The Heat shot only 37 percent from 3-point range over the course of the season. That included just 33 percent from James, who somehow canned 4 of 5 3-pointers in this series opener.

"The zone was OK, pretty good," Carlisle said. "I thought it got us through some matchups that were ... challenging, to say the least."

But even that came at a cost. Dallas conceded 16 offensive rebounds to Miami, a number that was way too high. One of the drawbacks to playing a zone defense is a team's diminished ability to account for every opponent when it was time to box out under the glass.

The Mavericks knew this final round of the postseason would pose their stiffest test. The last opponent in their way was clearly the most menacing. But theirs was a veteran team that understood Game 1 did not make a series, only a disappointing start. There was still a long war ahead, but winning Game 2 now took on added importance.

"We'll play better," Carlisle pledged. "I'm very certain of that."

21

MIAMI GAME 2

(June 2, 2011)

Beyond the reactions and over-reactions from a disappointing Game 1 result, news of Dirk Nowitzki's finger injury sent an additional wave of dread through the hearts and minds of most Mavericks fans. If LeBron James was going to have such success shutting down Jason Terry, then Dirk was going to have to do even more heavy lifting than usual. Would he have to do it without the use of his left hand?

A torn tendon sounded bad — really bad — to most lay people. But Nowitzki sounded reassuringly unnerved by the diagnosis while discussing the injury after Game 1.

"It was just a freaky play," Nowitzki said. "(Chris) Bosh got a bounce pass and I stepped in. I thought I stripped him clean, and then I kind of looked down and I couldn't straighten my finger out anymore.

"I guess it will be all right. I have to wear a splint, probably for the rest of the playoffs, a couple of weeks. But it will be all right. It's on my left hand, so I'll be all right for Thursday."

"He's right-handed. He'll be all right," concurred a smiling James at his own news conference.

So, with no surgery or amputation on the horizon for Nowitzki's injured finger, attention turned to the statistical importance of the upcoming Game 2. A couple notes were of particular interest to the Mavs and their fans:

- Since 1984, the Game 1 winner had gone on to claim the championship in 20 of 27 NBA Finals. The last team to lose The Finals after winning Game 1? The 2006 Mavericks, who beat Miami in Game 1, 90-80, before losing the series in six games.
- Under the current 2-3-2 format, a team with a 2-0 lead in the NBA Finals wins the title 93.3 percent of the time. Only three teams in NBA Finals history have fought back from an 0-2 deficit to win the title. The last to do it? That same 2006 Miami team that beat the Mavs in six games.

As if they needed reminding, history makes sure Nowitzki and Terry never forget 2006.

========

Thursday, June 2
Game 2, NBA Finals
Miami, Florida

Game 2 was an absolute mess for Dallas.

There had been one demoralizing Miami moment after another. One monster dunk after another. The Mavs looked beaten. Downtrodden. Even a bit whiny about the way they were being bullied and pushed around on the court.

With 10:15 left in the fourth, James re-entered the game for the final time. Miami led, 75-73, and then the Heat floored the gas pedal.

In the next 3:01, the Heat steamrolled Dallas in a show of force that nearly blew the roof off their American Airlines Arena. Dunk, layup, free throws, dunk, free throws, and finally a 3-pointer from the corner by a preening Wade. The deficit widened from two points to a virtually unmanageable 15 at 88-73 with 7:13 to play.

The Mavericks had overcome giant leads many times. They already had won four playoff games in which they trailed entering the final period. But this wasn't Oklahoma City. This time, a comeback seemed more unlikely, given the architects of this lead were superstars virtually without peer on the planet.

The Mavericks' veterans had one thing in common — no trophies, save for the one tattooed on Terry's arm. The 2011 NBA Finals, billed as Dallas' shot at redemption, looked to be hanging in the balance on a night when the Mavs' best players were struggling.

Now, in their moment of truth, the effort was coming unhinged. Nowitzki appeared to be bothered by his finger injury, and had made only 3 of 10 shots in the first half. Terry, nursing a bone bruise on his right (shooting) wrist, was just 2 for 8 midway through the fourth quarter. And Kidd, uncharacteristically, had as many turnovers (four) as assists.

It looked as if Wade's 3-pointer, putting the Heat up by 15 with 7:13 to play, would be remembered as the kill shot of Game 2, and perhaps of the whole series. Miami appeared just too strong for the feel-good Mavericks. Wade certainly seemed to think so, striking something of a showboat pose right in front of the Dallas bench by holding his follow-through high in the air for several moments after his shot fell.

Carlisle called timeout. And as the Mavericks began to gather for their huddle, James rushed over to nearly the same spot to celebrate with Wade. To some, it sure seemed they were rubbing the Mavericks' noses in it.

Wade and James would later dispute that they had meant any disrespect. Not even all Mavericks would agree on how much they took offense. But some believed this was the incident that lit Dallas' fuse.

"Nobody likes a showoff!" Terry shouted to teammates in their huddle. "Nobody likes a showoff!"

The Mavericks took note, Chandler recalled.

"When you got a guy showboating in front of your bench with seven minutes remaining, you say 'The game is not over. I don't care what they say, the game is not over,'" Chandler said. "I think it angered a lot of us. We came out there and we responded."

Did they ever.

Dallas would allow Miami only one other field goal the rest of the game, a Mario Chalmers 3-pointer with 24 seconds left. The Mavericks came out of their timeout to start a remarkable 22-5 run, and many thought they had Wade to thank for the inspiration.

"The first thing I thought was, 'This knucklehead is going to celebrate in front of us?'" recalled Brian Cardinal. "It is amazing to think back on it. Because, from that point on, for the rest of the game we were so dialed in. We made them shoot jumpers and took them out of their game. It was awesome.

"Everybody saw it. And people could say they weren't trying to show us up, but look at the tape. That was real. And we knew how important that turnaround was. Because if we went down 0-2, it was going to be a monster to beat those guys."

It took some time for the angry Mavericks to collect themselves and start to pull the game back into range. They missed their first two shots coming out of the timeout, but their faith didn't waver. They had come back from steeper climbs in this postseason.

"We just said at that time, 'Let's just play and see what happens,'" Kidd recalled later. "'Let's just see if we can get it to 10. And then, once we get into single digits with five minutes left, let's see if we can put them in a situation where they haven't been, and where we can put a little pressure on them.'"

Terry got things rolling, hitting a 16-footer from the wing, followed by a layup the next time down. Miami called timeout, still leading by 11 (88-77) with 5:45 to go.

Just over a minute later, it was 88-81, as Terry hit two free throws, Marion drove for a layup, and both James and Bosh missed shots. The comeback was on.

Some would say this rally revealed more about the Heat than the Mavs, specifically that Miami plays an extremely arrogant brand of basketball. With so much ego-driven star power, the Heat can delude themselves into believing they are invincible.

Isn't it arrogance that causes a team to stop running its previously successful offense in the game's most crucial moments? With his team's lead cut to two points at 90-88 with 1:31 left, James wasted a possession by dribbling the ball 21 times outside the 3-point arc before launching a 25-foot heave as the shot clock expired. The shot missed, Haslem rebounded but had his pass stolen by Terry, and Nowitzki converted a game-tying layup at the other end with 57 seconds left.

And despite having 36 points, Wade stood idly by, watching James for many of the final possessions. The Heat's leading scorer took only three shots in the final 6:30. Each was a 3-point try that missed, including two in the final 36 seconds.

Nowitzki, on the other hand, rose to the occasion yet again. After going 6 for 18 over the first 45 minutes, Dirk was 4 for 4 in the final 2:44. His 20-footer from the left wing cut Miami's lead to two. Then, after that long James dribble-and-miss possession, Nowitzki went to his injured left hand to make a layup that tied the game, 90-90, with 57 seconds remaining.

The Mavericks buckled down again and cleared a Wade miss with a Nowitzki rebound. Dallas had the ball and a chance to take its first lead since late in the second quarter. Chandler, with the most important play that went unmentioned in the box score, set a series of screens on the left wing against Chalmers, James and Haslem. The second and third screens walled off defenders to free Nowitzki for a monster 3-point bomb that put Dallas ahead, 93-90, with 26 seconds left. Fans groaned as he rose up, and the ball splashed through in the most clutch of moments.

The possessed look on Dirk's face was priceless as the Heat took a 20-second timeout. There was no scowl this time. He simply held up three fingers to the Miami crowd and walked back to the Dallas bench as teammates ran to him.

"For Dirk to have the nuts to take that shot and to knock it down was just remarkable," Cardinal said. "The whole bench was holding each other back, and when he knocks it down there is just pandemonium on our bench as the arena is motionless. The whole range of emotions was just unreal."

Donnie Nelson couldn't have been prouder.

"Dirk's reaction there, and in the entire playoffs, was that of a guy who had one thing on his mind," Nelson said. "I think those moments show how locked in and focused he truly was."

The Heat still had some fight left. They designed a play that had James swing the ball to Chalmers deep in the far corner — the same corner where Wade had nailed his shot that riled up the Mavs' bench. To his teammates' dismay, Terry had cheated toward Wade, a decision that left Chalmers with time to set and shoot. The young guard, who had developed a knack for big shots in college when he hit "Mario's Miracle" for the Kansas Jayhawks in the 2008 NCAA championship game, buried the 3-pointer to make it 93-93 with 24 seconds left. The game was approaching classic levels.

The Mavericks could hold the ball for the final shot. Injured or not, Carlisle would run the possession for Nowitzki. Perhaps it was arrogance again that prevented Miami from double-teaming Dallas' best player or using the one foul still left to give. Nowitzki held the ball aloft at the high post as the seconds ticked off, expecting the inevitable foul or double-team. Neither came. Bosh was guarding Nowitzki this time but got no help until it was too late.

In what would become a drive for the ages, the big German went again to his injured hand. He spun by Bosh with eight seconds left, drove hard past James and flipped the shot off the glass around a flying Haslem. So clutch. So sure. He made Miami pay for the disrespect of treating one of the league's premier scorers as if he was just another player on the final possession.

"They had a foul to give, so I actually drove a little earlier than I would have," Nowitzki explained. "But the foul never came, so I was able to get to the basket and lay it in."

"And to think he finished that game-winner with his mangled finger was so awesome," Cardinal said. "He just had to show them."

Chandler played an unsung but invaluable role on the play. As Nowitzki drove, Haslem was on course to meet him in the air. Chandler gave Haslem a subtle shove in the back that probably gets whistled earlier in the game. But no referee is likely to make that call in the waning seconds of an NBA Finals game. It was a true veteran move, going unnoticed by many, but possibly crucial to the outcome.

It seemed a true Tortoise and Hare-style comeback, a bold smash-and-grab heist from right underneath Miami noses, that had evened the series at 1-1. The Mavericks had proven, to others and to themselves, they could play with the Heat. And now with three consecutive home games ahead, their spirits were rising.

"We lost a great opportunity in Game 1, and I said we had to leave with a split, no matter how it comes about," Kidd recalled later. "Then we are down 15 and it looks like we are dead in the water.

"And it all just started snowballing slowly. Once we got the lead, we knew we were going to be able to steal this one. We just got to a point of being embarrassed, and then had enough. I know people will ask why we can't just start a game off that way. When it's 0-0, we aren't in a hole. But anytime we dug ourselves a hole, we always seemed to be able to find a way out."

Miami certainly left the door cracked, but Dallas still had to make some spectacular plays. And perhaps in doing so, they kept alive their chances to realize their dream. Miami had just completed a phenomenal dunking exhibition. But, in the end, Dallas left with the "W."

Even weeks later, Cardinal still marveled at Nowitzki's gritty performance.

"He has been doing this for years. It is amazing that, only now, he gets that recognition," Cardinal said. "After playing against him for 10 years, and now to play with him and see how hard he works ... to see the complexity of the guy and for him to finish plays like this. And then you realize it is not just about Dirk or the Mavs. It is about Germany and half the world. That is why it is so emotional for him. There is so much that goes into his performances."

It wasn't the prettiest of efforts, but it kept Dallas in the series as it headed to Texas. On the back of one Dirk finger-roll, it was only just beginning.

22

MIAMI GAME 3

(June 5, 2011)

On the flight back to Dallas after the comeback that might have saved the NBA Finals, some Mavericks operatives were feeling great about the win, but not so great about the series.

Said one, "As high as I was after the comeback win, when we got back to Dallas, I remember telling my wife, 'It was great to win, but I just don't think we can do it. ... I just don't think we can beat them four times.'"

Because of that very demanding requirement, the best team almost always prevails in an NBA best-of-seven series. The Mavericks had played well at times during the first two games. But they had to admit that, if the games had been scored like a prizefight, the Heat would have won both on the judges' scorecards. Of the 24 fourth-quarter minutes that had been played in Miami, the Mavericks had held a lead for just five seconds. But since they included the final three seconds of Game 2, thanks to that improbable 22-5 run, the series was all square at one win apiece.

Now the series moved to Texas for the next three games in the 2-3-2 NBA Finals schedule format.

The American Airlines Center had not been vacant for the first two games played 1,100 miles away in South Florida. Dallas' arena had been opened to capacity crowds for watching parties, and the crowd scenes shown on ABC and internet sites amazed team personnel in Miami. These Mavericks fans could have watched the first games from the comfort of their own homes. But they had felt the need to congregate, 18,000 strong, to share the ride together. The pandemonium in reaction to Game 2's final minutes was enough to induce shivers. It was amazing to behold a building without its own game rocking with that much emotion.

Of course, now the arena clientele would change a bit. Ticket brokers were getting an average of $1,000 for a Game 3 ticket, with floor seats going for $5,000 and up. The prestige of the NBA Finals would attract the upper crust of well-heeled Dallas society, whether they had been to a game all season or not.

Meanwhile, Rick Carlisle was dealing with more troubling injury news. Backup center Brendan Haywood had left early in the fourth quarter of Game 2 with a strained right hip flexor, and now appeared doubtful to play again in the series. That left the seldom-used Ian Mahinmi as the Mavs' only cover at center, should Chandler find his way into foul trouble.

"And then there's a possibility we could look at some other lineups that would obviously be smaller," Carlisle said.

Carlisle also was facing the reality that Peja Stojakovic was simply not going to be a workable option this round, given his inability to cope with the extreme athleticism he was facing from the Heat at both ends of the floor. So far, Stojakovic had played a total of 20 scoreless minutes in the Finals, with the Mavs a net minus-10 points during his time on the floor. He had gotten off just three shots, missed them all, and was clearly a target for Miami's dynamic scorers to attack.

Carlisle's bench and player rotation were shrinking. Nine players had seen steady action since the start of the postseason. There were the five starters (Nowitzki, Marion, Chandler, Kidd and Stevenson), and usually just four players off the bench (Stojakovic for the forwards, Haywood for Chandler, Terry for Stevenson and Barea for Kidd). Now, the Dallas coach was having to hope that Mahinmi and Cardinal had followed the season-long directive to stay ready. They had played a combined 13 minutes and produced two points through the first 17 playoff games.

Heat players, meanwhile, were feeling the first stings of criticism from Miami and national media demanding answers for their collapse in Game 2. James, in particular, seemed to be getting annoyed by the lines of questioning. Why hadn't he gotten the ball to Wade late? Why had he only gone to the free-throw line six times in the first two games? And why had he incited Dallas by celebrating that 3-pointer with Wade in front of the Mavericks' bench?

"I've seen Dallas go on plenty of runs before," James said. " If (Terry) hits a three and they make a big run, he runs down the court doing the whole 'wings expanded' (bit). Do we count that as a celebration as well?

"I just think everything gets blown out of proportion when the Miami Heat does things."

James probably had a point. But, by showing his irritation, he had left blood in the water for the hungry media. King James had opened a new battle front against the press, a war that players seldom win.

========

Sunday, June 5
Game 3, NBA Finals
Dallas, Texas

Nothing can sap a team's hope faster than finding its tried-and-true methods of success no longer apply. And with their tantalizingly close 88-86 Game 3 victory, the Miami Heat were pushing the Mavericks toward that dark corner of self-doubt.

Throughout their wildly successful playoff run, the Mavericks rarely had trouble finding open shots. They never had trouble making open shots. They had not had difficulty slowing down big scorers in the closing minutes. And they had not found an opponent capable of playing two-way basketball with them at what Magic Johnson used to call "Winning Time."

Clearly, all that had changed in this final round.

Overcoming the Heat would be the Mavs' toughest accomplishment, if still even possible. The Game 3 winner of a tied Finals had won the championship all 11 times since the 2-3-2 format was adopted in 1985. And Dallas had just dropped Game 3 in agonizing fashion.

Nowitzki had been brilliant again, pouring in 15 of his 34 points in the final period. The rest of his team had managed just seven points on 3-of-11 shooting in the fourth quarter. But after Chris Bosh broke an 86-86 tie with a 16-foot jumper from the left baseline with 39 seconds left, the Mavs went to the Dirk well two more times. Somehow, they came up empty.

In truth, it was the suffocating Miami defense that deserved credit. With 30 seconds left, Nowitzki tried to pass his way out of a Udonis Haslem-led triple team a few feet inside of midcourt, and wound up throwing the ball into the stands when Marion unexpectedly cut from the corner toward the basket. That turnover seemed to have been forgiven when James missed a 3-point attempt with four seconds left. Nowitzki snatched his 11th rebound and called timeout.

Despite the criticism heaped on Eric Spoelstra after Game 2 for not double-teaming Nowitzki on the final possession, the Heat did nearly the same thing in the same spot in Game 3. Except this time it was Haslem instead of Bosh on the big German. Carlisle anticipated a double-team in his huddle and dispatched Stojakovic into the game to join Terry and Kidd around the 3-point line. When the double team went to Dirk, someone should get an open look for the win if behind the arc.

But the double-team never came, leaving Dirk to take the big shot. He spun just above the free-throw line and fired a tightly contested 16-foot jumper over the outstretched hand of Haslem, a game-tying attempt just before the buzzer. It bounced high off the back of the rim and fell harmlessly to the floor as time expired.

The look on Nowitzki's face told the story. He couldn't believe it didn't fall.

"He makes that nine out of 10 (times)," Terry said of the shot. "This was the one that he missed."

It was no complaint, just reality. Terry had scored 15 points and Marion 10, but both were shut out in the fourth quarter. So was the 38-year-old point guard, who was 0 for 2 in the final period.

"We have to have somebody step up besides Dirk," Kidd said. "We have to figure out how to get up front and play up front."

Miami's defense can make any offense look out of sync, and the Mavericks were no exception. After shooting 47.5 percent from the floor during the 82-game season, Dallas was hitting only 42 percent of its shots in the Finals. After averaging 100.2 points per game during the season, they were scoring only 88.3 in the Finals. That was a steep decline from their earlier playoff scoring averages against Portland (93.3 ppg), Los Angeles (102.3) and Oklahoma City (105.2).

Was it the pressure of The Finals' big stage or the desperation to avenge 2006 that was getting to the Mavericks? Or was it the Miami defense, which had adversely affected the shooting percentages of Philadelphia (41 percent), Boston (45 percent) and Chicago (39 percent) in the Heat's march through the Eastern Conference playoffs?

The Heat's superstar talent could stress opponents on both ends of the court. Most teams cannot claim that their best offensive players are also their best defensive players, but Miami can. They presented some near-impossible matchups on offense, but were almost equally gifted playing defense. Carlisle's challenging task was to find the right mix to cope with Miami on both sides of the ball, without exposing a liability for the Heat to exploit.

With the Mavericks in possession, the Heat challenge every pass. They push Nowitzki just a bit further out than he would like to receive the ball. They make lob passes a thing of the past by being physically able to cheat off Chandler, but not so far off him that Kidd can find him for an easy deuce. They jump passing lanes. James and Wade get their hands on more passes than any duo since Michael Jordan and Scottie Pippen played defense like this back in the 1990s. And, like those tireless Bulls champions, they were capable of playing as many minutes as needed. There seemed never to be a time when at least one of them wasn't on the court.

If the Heat forced a turnover, they were off to the races. If the Mavericks could eliminate the several unchallenged fast-break dunks they were allowing each game, they would be winning the series with ease. But it seemed every turnover resulted in fast-break points for Miami. The Mavericks' coaching staff stressed the importance of "good turnovers." This simply meant that if you were to throw the ball away, do it so that the ball went out of bounds, allowing the defense time to reset. Otherwise, Heat opponents that couldn't match their transition tempo would find themselves playing catch-up all night.

So far, the Heat were making the Mavericks play from behind constantly, adding to the stress and exhaustion of the game. And late in the fourth quarter, tired reactions could prove the difference in a tight game.

The final period of Game 3 had the often unguardable Nowitzki and Wade locked in a magnificent see-saw battle. Despite so many new characters joining them onstage, the two leads from the 2006 Finals were dueling again five years later. There were times when both players' teammates seemed to stop and join the fans in watching the show. Wade, a 6-4 shooting guard, matched 7-footers Nowitzki and Chandler with 11 rebounds, and scored seven of his team-high 29 points in the final period.

It looked as if the game would be decided by who got the final shot. The chance fell to Nowitzki, as he and most inside the arena had hoped. But the man who had made nearly every clutch shot for six weeks finally missed. And one miss exceeded the Mavs' margin for error against Miami.

Yikes.

"You want to win the game on the defensive end of the floor," Wade said, "and we got a stop."

The Heat were now in position to repeat what they'd done five years earlier — win The Finals on the Mavericks' floor. They would have to take the next two games on Tuesday and Thursday, but the ghosts of 2006 were starting to swirl. The Mavericks were feeling like the second-best animal in a two-horse race.

What the Heat can do on defense makes everything else possible, for their half-court offense isn't elaborate. They have some special players, capable of slashing into the lane or pulling up from distance. When nothing else is working, there is Wade, waiting to bail out the possession with another strike from behind the arc or a slice into the paint.

But for Miami, it all starts with defense. The Heat's quick defenders cheat away from those who do not require their full attention to help out on those who do. They fly around in passing lanes and sneak up from behind to steal the ball. They behave like a pack of hungry Dobermans on the prowl. And, when they get the ball, James and Wade can attack on the other end in the blink of an eye. They are All-NBA on both ends of the court.

The Mavericks had a nearly unstoppable offensive option and strong defenders, too. But they didn't come in the same bodies.

Nowitzki was arguably the best offensive player of the entire postseason, but he wasn't an All-NBA caliber defender. Terry, Stojakovic and Barea also had offensive skills that far exceeded their defensive capabilities.

Dallas' strongest defenders were Marion, Chandler, Kidd and Stevenson. But as good as they were at getting stops or changing an opponent's offensive approach, none were causing many matchup headaches as part of the team's set offense. They mostly scored off rebounds, in transition, or on broken plays where Nowitzki had garnered most of the attention.

Carlisle had found the right formula, a mix of each player's unique skill set, carefully measured into a concoction that had caused 48 minutes of trouble for opponents almost every night of the regular season and playoffs. The Mavericks would let Nowitzki keep pace or exceed the output of the opposition's top scorer, keep rolling out the fresh legs, and expose the enemy's inferior depth when it became a battle of the benches.

But that formula wasn't working against the Heat. There was little chance to assert a bench advantage because James and Wade hardly left the court. When Wade did rest, it fell to James, one of the best scorers in league history, to start taking more of the shots. And instead of Barea driving against some backup guard when he saw action, it was still James running the Miami defense. When the Mavs needed Terry's shooting touch to take some of the late burden off Nowitzki, James so far was snuffing him out. Terry was 0 for 5 in the series when shooting in the fourth period while guarded by James. The concerns were plenty.

What the Heat perhaps couldn't match was the Mavericks' resilience and warrior spirit, embodied most often by Chandler and Marion on defense and Nowitzki on offense. Chandler was under immense pressure to stay out of foul trouble because of Haywood's injury, yet still be an effective rebounder and inside deterrent. He did both very well.

Game 3 was not decided solely by Nowitzki's missed shot just before the buzzer, but it was a one-possession game that could have gone either way. The series had been so close, the Mavericks could just as easily have been up 2-1, or even down 0-3. This had marked the first time since 1998 that back-to-back Finals games had been decided by two points or fewer. Given all that, Dallas could live with being down 2-1, not that they had any choice.

"Look, it's seven games," Carlisle said. "Any notion that it was going to be easy would have been foolhardy, by us or anybody else."

"This definitely was a very big game and a very tough loss," added Nowitzki. "But they need two more."

Disappointment and anger hung thickly inside the Mavericks' locker room after the loss. The Heat had reclaimed homecourt advantage, and any Mavs series victory would now have to be won on the road. Perhaps no one was considering that at the moment, at least not before Brian Cardinal stood and spoke.

"I can think of worse things than going back and celebrating this thing on South Beach," Cardinal told his teammates. "Hoisting that trophy in front of their fans? If that is the worst thing that happens, we are pretty lucky, boys."

23

MIAMI GAME 4

(June 7, 2011)

"For some reason, me getting sick won us the championship."
— *Dirk Nowitzki*

Game 4 was going to be vital for Dallas if the Mavericks were to keep alive their dreams of a fairy tale ending. After stealing Game 2, they immediately gave back the homecourt edge by losing Game 3. The consensus media opinion that the Heat were the better team was difficult to argue. Of the first 144 minutes played in the NBA Finals, the Mavericks had held a lead for just 35:10 (approximately 24 percent of the series). Miami had led for 97:43 (68 percent), and had won two of the three games. Doubt may not have fully crept in, but it was certainly knocking on the door.

Even though the playoffs were entering their eighth grueling week, Dirk Nowitzki was not about to give in to the fatigue and change his routine. It was Monday, June 6, an off-night on the eve of Game 4, and Nowitzki would spend it the usual way — working on his shooting in the gym with Holger Geschwindner.

"Every night, I went to the gym with Holger during the playoffs. I'm talking about *every* night," Nowitzki said. "So, I go the gym, regular night, and I come back at 9 or 9:30 (p.m.) and eat my meal.

"For some reason, I didn't feel great. A little groggy. But, I thought, 'I'll just go to bed, get nine or 10 hours of sleep, and I will feel amazing tomorrow.'"

That wasn't what happened.

"I woke up about 2 or 3 (a.m.), just sweating," Nowitzki recalled. "I tried to sleep a couple more hours, but it just wasn't happening. I had a fever and felt groggy and couldn't sleep. And that's when I got really worried.

"I wasn't sick one time all year. But now? Before the biggest game where we could go down 3-1 in The Finals? I was devastated, laying in my bed thinking, 'Are you kidding me? This is happening to me right now?'"

Just after 7 a.m., Mavericks trainer Casey Smith received a text from Nowitzki, who said he was running a high fever and wanted to know what to do. Smith called back immediately with instructions.

"He said to just come on in (to the arena's training room), and don't let the media know," Nowitzki recalled. "That's why I came in the morning, because I just wanted to stay in bed."

Nowitzki's teammates began trickling in for the morning shootaround. But when Dirk arrived, he spoke only to Smith. It was too unusual not to notice.

"Usually, I come in and kill somebody's outfit or shoes or something," Nowitzki admitted. "So when I came in and didn't say a word in the morning, they sensed something was wrong."

Keeping Nowitzki's condition secret would not be easy. There would be a large media presence at the shootaround, traditionally a time when reporters get a few minutes of interview access to players. Nowitzki's absence would have aroused suspicions and created a bigger mystery, so he put on a brave front and spent a few minutes casually answering media questions out on the court. Moments later, he made a secret getaway.

Nowitzki and Smith slipped out a back exit, and drove to an ear, nose and throat specialist. The physician confirmed Nowitzki had a sinus infection. He was given medicine, advised to rest as much as possible and told to ingest plenty of fluids, as dehydration would be a major concern for that night's game.

"I went home and the medicine got the fever down. I was able to take a little nap," Nowitzki said. "Before the game, I always try to warm up. But I told Holger, 'We are doing exactly 20 minutes. We are keeping it short.' I just wanted to get a little sweat, to get the body used to sweating."

If this was an ordinary game in November, Nowitzki would have missed the contest, as he had several times in his career. Kidd and Barea were known to tease Nowitzki about his threshold for playing with injury versus illness. If injured, Nowitzki could still be counted on to play, usually still quite well. But when sick? Teammates would joke that Dirk needed sympathy, a hug, and whatever was the German equivalent of Mom's chicken soup.

This time, as tipoff approached, only a small circle of people inside the Mavericks' locker room knew Nowitzki's true condition. And nobody found it a laughing matter. Nowitzki wasn't in the mood for sympathy, hugs or anything else. All that mattered was winning this game. And if he wasn't dying, Dirk would be playing.

=========

Even before he learned of his star player's illness, the tumblers inside the mind of Mavericks coach Rick Carlisle had been turning. It was like trying to solve a Rubik's Cube, but there had to be a combination of Dallas players that could pose maximum difficulty for the Heat. He just had to figure it out.

Dallas had won both regular-season meetings with Miami. But in those games, the Mavericks had Caron Butler, their own athletic scorer and defender in the mold of some of the Heat's better players. Butler wasn't available for The Finals, however, still recovering from his knee surgery. So another solution had to be found, and quickly.

Where the Mavs seemed to be falling short, compared to their production earlier in the playoffs, was in scoring off the bench. The harsh reality was that Terry and Barea just were not pulling their expected weight. James was shutting Terry down late in games, holding him to 38 percent shooting overall and a 4-for-12 performance from 3-point range.

Barea, it seemed, was having trouble against Heat backup guard Mario Chalmers, who usually rotated in about the same time. Barea's ill-timed stretch of poor shooting saw him go 5 for 23 (22 percent) from the floor and 1 for 8 (12 percent) from 3-point range through the first three games. From Jan. 1 through the end of the regular season, Barea had led the league in 3-point shooting percentage. But he seemingly had lost his stroke at a most inopportune time.

Barea had no bigger supporter in the league than his own coach. Needing some kind of spark for Game 4, Carlisle made the bold decision to put Barea into the starting lineup in place of DeShawn Stevenson. The Mavs' starting lineup had been untouched for 19 playoff games until now. But with a shortened rotation, injuries, illnesses and with the Mavs' proverbial backs to the wall, Carlisle would roll the dice. Stevenson would provide his defense and toughness off the bench. Barea would get a chance to take on the Heat's starting point guard, Mike Bibby, whose footwork wasn't as quick as Chalmers'.

How would Carlisle light a fire under Terry? Turns out, Jet would do it himself.

Terry thrives off personal challenges, adrenaline and, frankly, attention. So with reporters gathered around to see what might come out of his unpredictable mouth, Terry decided to poke LeBron with a sharp verbal stick.

"I'm welcoming the challenge (of being guarded again late by James)," Terry said. "We're going to see if he can do it for seven games. That's going to be the challenge.

"Right now, it's Game 4. Can he do it again in Game 4? He wasn't able to do it in Game 2. He did it in Games 1 and 3, so Game 4 is another opportunity."

Terry was openly challenging the manhood of the player many considered the best one-on-one defender in the sport. His statements proliferated over network airwaves, newspaper web sites and the sports-geek blogosphere within minutes. Many in the Mavericks' organization wondered just what Terry had been thinking, if he had been at all.

But compared to tattooing on your arm a championship trophy you've never even touched, incendiary verbal dares are child's play. Terry was crazy all right. But he just might be crazy like a fox.

=========

Thursday, June 7
Game 4, NBA Finals
Dallas, Texas

There had been quite a few memorable nights in the 31 years of the Dallas Mavericks' basketball franchise. This one might have been the best yet.

Game 4 offered up one of the grittiest and gutsiest performances the NBA Finals had seen. Both teams engaged in a street fight of sheer will and determination, one that would leave a survivor as much as a winner. Dallas prevailed, 86-83, to even the series at 2-2.

Nowitzki was weakened considerably from his daylong bout with illness, lack of sleep and fever spikes up to 102 degrees. There still was the torn finger tendon on his left hand to consider as well. His shot never looked quite right, wasn't falling as usual, and he coughed and wheezed uncontrollably during timeouts as the training staff tried to keep him warm. He never looked himself.

But once again, when the Mavericks needed their leader most, Nowitzki rose up with a titanic fourth-quarter effort to bring the game home. He powered the Mavericks to a decisive 21-9 run over the final 10:12, scoring 10 of his 21 points in the final period. Dirk grabbed five of his 11 rebounds, made all six of his free throws and did the best he could from the floor (2 of 6 shooting) in the fourth quarter. But one of his field goals was a critical right-handed drive for a layup with 14.4 seconds left.

As vital and imperative as his final left-handed drive turned out to be in Game 2, the same could be said for Nowitzki's right-handed drive that sealed Game 4. He had stood tall once again in the clutch, despite having next to nothing in his tank.

"This is The Finals," Nowitzki explained, sniffling and coughing his way through a postgame media session in a warm-up jacked zipped to his chin. "You have to go out there and compete and try your best for your team. So that's what I did."

Nowitzki's grateful teammates could only marvel at their leader's fortitude.

"The average person has sick days (to take off)," Chandler said. "And battling a 100-something fever, it's just tough to get out of bed. This guy is playing against the best athletes in the world."

Which is what made the comparatively meek effort by a healthy LeBron James look even weaker.

James finished with eight points, his career low for a playoff contest. It was the first time in his last 434 regular-season or postseason games he hadn't scored in double figures. James made only 3 of 11 shots, and one of those was a dunk. He played all 12 minutes of the fourth quarter, took only one shot, and did not score in the period.

"I've got to do a better job of being more assertive offensively," James actually said. It hadn't taken calculations by Dr. Stephen Hawking or IBM's Watson computer to figure that out.

Had James been unnerved by the brash challenge of Terry? If so, James lost that battle, too. Terry hit 6 of 15 shots for 17 points, his high for the series thus far. Marion (16 points) and Chandler (13 points, 16 rebounds) also raised their games a notch in support of their ailing team leader.

Nowitzki nailed his first three shots of the game before the exertion started taking its toll on his already weakened condition. He missed 10 of his next 11 shots and it was obvious even to the Heat that something was wrong. Television cameras started zooming in on Nowitzki coughing and guzzling water in timeouts, draped in towels and jackets to stave off chills. It was so bad, Nowitzki even missed a free throw for the first time since Game 4 of the Western Conference finals.

"Everyone could tell, looking at him, that he labored," Carlisle said.

Critics' mantra after Game 3 had been "Dirk needs help," and everyone knew it needed to be Terry stepping up his game to lend it. Inspired by his own pregame taunting, Terry took the ball right at James, running him off screens and exploding past him to the basket. But through three quarters, Nowitzki and Terry had combined to score just 20 of Dallas' 65 points and the Mavs trailed by four.

But in the fourth quarter, the booster rockets kicked in. Nowitzki and Terry scored 18 of the Mavs' 21 points, made all of their clutch free throws, and joined their teammates in another outstanding display of late-game, lock-down defense. With every shot tightly contested, the Heat actually missed their final nine attempts of the game from within 15 feet of the rim. They were 1 for 9 from the floor overall in the final 7:23. Remarkable.

Terry poured in eight points without a turnover in the fourth quarter, nearly outperforming Miami's Big Three all by himself. Wade, James and Bosh combined for nine points with five turnovers in the final period.

In a postseason replete with gutty wins, this looked to be the Mavericks' gut-check masterpiece. There was every reason to go quietly into the night, but this team didn't ever go quietly. Their roster was packed with hungry, veteran warriors who intended to win or die trying. You had to admire these characteristics and the transformation that had taken place, given the franchise's previous reputation for soft, spiritually-weak playoff teams.

With about 10 minutes left, Miami held its biggest lead of the night at 74-65. Then the Mavericks' defense simply turned the faucet off and flipped the game with that 21-9 run. Nowitzki's performance was being compared to one of Michael Jordan's finest (38 points in Game 5 of the 1997 Finals against Utah, despite a 103-degree fever). James' performance was being compared to something else entirely.

Wade, continuing to earn respect, valiantly scored 32 to lead his team. But even he missed a critical free throw with 30 seconds left, and then fumbled an inbounds pass with 6.7 seconds remaining. He managed to tip that loose ball back to Mike Miller for a potential tying 3-pointer, but the shot wasn't close, missing the rim entirely.

Nowitzki had earned his heroic headlines, and Terry had talked and played his way back to the cockiness frequency at which he operates best. But there were so many other key contributions in this most important of team victories.

Marion, for instance, didn't play heavy minutes in the fourth, but had provided outstanding defense again as he alternated guarding Wade and James. He also scored half of the Mavs' 20 points in the third period to keep Dallas close when no one else seemed able to find the basket.

Chandler's numbers, especially the 16 rebounds, were stout, and he continued to provide the intangible leadership and intimidation factor defending the rim. And he did so smartly, steering clear of foul trouble with his backup Brendan Haywood sidelined by his hip injury. Chandler had managed to stay both available and aggressive. He had kept himself on the court for 83 minutes in the past two games, and his team was immeasurably better for it.

"I told Coach, 'You have to get me back out there. I will play 48 if I need to,'" Chandler said.

The Dallas center's determination and fighting spirit was contagious. Predecessor Erick Dampier, who it turns out would watch every minute of this series planted firmly on the Miami bench, never displayed an inner competitive fire anything close to Chandler's.

Carlisle's lineup change had paid dividends, too.

If Stevenson was bothered by losing his starting role, he showed it the best way possible: He kept his mouth shut and scored his playoff-high 11 points. That he played 26 minutes, his most in the series, assured him that his role had merely changed, not diminished. It was Stevenson, in fact, assigned to shut down James for most of the fourth quarter. He delighted in the task, performed it well, and then even outscored King James, too?

Barea, now facing Bibby for most of his 22 minutes, contributed eight points, three rebounds and four assists while causing his usual brand of penetrating havoc. Kidd had the most impactful scoreless game any player could have. His only shots were a trio of 3-pointers that missed, but he had three rebounds, three assists, three steals, directed traffic at both ends in the Mavs' favor and finished a net +12 points (best on the team) for his time on the court without even scoring. That's ridiculously hard to do, unless you're just being Jason Kidd and making everyone around you better however you can.

The series was now a best-of-three, with the potential of two final games in Miami. The Heat should have felt good about that, but didn't. They were confused, and more than a bit surprised.

Everything said and written about them since their splashy summer signings party hinted toward a rather easy championship finish. This was destined to be their year, supposedly the first of many. The national media was again accusing Miami of losing a game rather than crediting Dallas with winning one.

Why weren't these Mavericks just caving in and conceding to the greatness before them?

The prevailing question moving forward was whether Dallas could be the first team in the series to win consecutive games. Each time a team had tasted defeat, it had responded with an immediate victory. But this time, Dallas knew that Game 5 was mandatory.

It would be the Mavs' last home game of the year and without it, they would be put in the horrible position of needing to win the two remaining games in Miami. But if they could get Game 5, the pressure building on the Heat could start busting pipes internally. The series was even, but Dallas felt momentum. And, for the first time, Miami appeared vulnerable.

========

After Nowitzki finished coughing his way through his abbreviated postgame visit to the press room, his car was pulled up and he went straight home to bed. Equipment manager Al Whitley shook his head later and said, "What he did in that game should go down in history. That was simply amazing."

Weeks later, Nowitzki would recall this night that saved the season with greater clarity.

"Once the game started, I was not myself," he said. "But it was a lot better than I thought it would be. Because that morning, I just felt terrible."

But after making those first three shots, he simply couldn't keep doing the heavy lifting. He missed 10 of his next 11 shots over three periods, but his teammates rose to the occasion and picked him up until he could help in the fourth.

"That was the turning point," Nowitzki said. "The boys saw I wasn't doing well. And from that point on, everyone played amazing.

"I was worried when we lost Game 3, (even though) I don't think I ever let it show on my face or my attitude. I didn't know how we were going to respond. And then I get sick in the biggest game. ... If we lose

Game 4, the series is over. I don't think we would have won the series. To me, that was the turning point."

Nowitzki explained he saw two Dallas teams during the course of The Finals, and he didn't mean because of fever-induced double vision. The team from Games 1-3 was too tentative and passive to win The Finals. The players on that team deferred to Nowitzki and were content letting the game come to them.

But Nowitzki believes his illness, problematic as it seemed at the time, helped forge a second Dallas team for the remainder of The Finals. These players knew they had to be aggressive, they had to contribute, they had to help carry the team forward together.

"The team just started to play better," Nowitzki said. "They saw me down and — this seems silly to say — but me getting sick might have won us the championship.

"Everyone started playing out of their minds. All of a sudden, J.J. started playing out of his mind, Jet started playing out of his mind. For some reason, me getting sick won us the championship."

24

MIAMI GAME 5

(June 9, 2011)

In 1948, the Baltimore Bullets and Philadelphia Warriors tangled for the championship of the Basketball Association of America (BAA). This was the precursor league rechristened as the National Basketball Association (NBA) in 1949, after a merger with the rival National Basketball League.

In that 1948 final series, three consecutive games were decided by three points or fewer. And in the 63 years of deciding professional basketball championships that followed, that didn't happen again until Games 2, 3 and 4 of the 2011 NBA Finals between Dallas and Miami.

These teams weren't similar in their construct, but the margin between them was razor thin, according to the final scoreboards. The series was tied 2-2. And while Miami played significantly more minutes with the lead, the final quarters of the last three games had belonged mostly to Dallas.

One result of this was that people were noticing Rick Carlisle could coach.

Critics had labeled Carlisle's decision to bench DeShawn Stevenson in favor of J.J. Barea in Game 4 as a move of desperation. Who tinkers with their starting lineup midway through a championship series? It wasn't until seeing that Stevenson actually played more minutes and was more impactful in his new role coming off the bench that those critics began to grasp that Carlisle views "starting" roles in a decidedly non-traditional way.

Stevenson's 26 minutes as a Game 4 "reserve" marked only the second time he'd played that much since the Feb. 4 victory in Boston. Carlisle didn't associate "starting" with the same prestige as do media or fans. Stevenson's role had not been diminished, it had actually increased. To Carlisle, it was all about timing the right players to the right matchups as he worked his rotation like a chess grandmaster.

When Stevenson played the entire fourth quarter, not only hounding LeBron James but outscoring him as well, the player who actually "lost" minutes was Shawn Marion. It was nothing against Marion, but Carlisle decided in this instance he wanted a fourth shooter on the floor to help spread the offense and ease the pressure on Nowitzki. Stevenson was his best shooter-defender combo, since the Heat had proven early on they would exploit Stojakovic defensively, and they didn't feel compelled to guard Marion closely if he drifted toward the corners.

Of course, a bigger role for Stevenson meant more microphones at his locker. The Mavericks' Media Relations department knew this likely meant Stevenson would say something to attract headlines, and he didn't disappoint after the Wednesday afternoon workout. Stevenson told a fair portion of the national basketball media that he thought James had "checked out" during Game 4.

"I don't know if it was because Dwyane Wade was playing well, but that helped us out," Stevenson continued. "Our defense was good. But, at the same time, (James) wasn't in 'attack mode.'"

Stevenson and James had feuded for years, so it should have surprised no one that the Mavericks' swingman would poke the bear at his first opportunity. It sure didn't surprise James.

"He's been talking a long time, since our Washington-Cleveland days," James later told reporters seeking a response. "I don't let that get to us. ... Talk is cheap."

It wasn't the first time a player — and for the Mavs it usually was Terry or Stevenson — had said something controversial. One would think a coach as tightly wound as Carlisle sometimes appeared would have been angry that they had verbally antagonized one of the best players on the planet twice in three days. But, surprisingly, Carlisle seemed willing to await the results for both sides.

"Jet says what he says, and he has his reasons. I don't necessarily need to know what they are," Carlisle explained. "But I think he knew that once he says some things, he's going to have to back it up. So I give him a lot of credit. It's a lot easier to stay low-key and sort of go with the flow and then think, 'I'm going to go out there and be more aggressive.' It's another thing to say, 'I'm putting it on myself and let's see if he can.'

"At this time of year, if you're going to win and win big, you better have guys that want the responsibility and ain't afraid to talk about it. ... Look, I've got some crazy guys and I love 'em. You *want* to have that kind of crazy on your team at this time of year."

Weeks later, Carlisle further explained his tolerance of his players' verbal challenges of James.

"Earlier in my head coaching career, I would have tended to gotten more bent out of shape about these sorts of things," he said. "But here is what you learn: I played with Larry Bird and coached Reggie Miller, and (Miller) would wear a Superman shirt before games. Now, he was doing a number of different things by wearing that. He was trying to get into his opponents' heads, and he was trying to get into his own head, knowing he was going to have to back it up.

"The only message I had for my guys on all of this talking stuff was this: If we are going to talk, let's not be subtle. Let's say some real s- - -. At this level, you are not going to win The Finals by tap-dancing. If you have got something to say, say it. But be ready to back it up when you cross those lines. Don't tiptoe and say it. And then, when the ball goes up, go kick somebody's ass."

Truth was, these were the NBA Finals, the games any basketball player with an inkling of special talent has dreamed of participating in since they first learned to dribble. Verbal slings and arrows should have little motivational effect at this level.

"At this point, it doesn't matter what you say about anybody," Tyson Chandler told the Dallas Morning News. "I mean, we've got three games left in the season and we're playing for an NBA championship. I don't need anybody over there to rattle me up. They can talk about my mom. It's not going to make me more angry coming into the game than I already am. We all should be at maximum anyway."

The Mavericks got one more huge boost at Thursday's morning shootaround. Nowitzki was back on the court, smiling, practicing and feeling much healthier. Game 5 was a few hours away, and their leader would be ready.

The mathematics of the remaining series were simple and clear. This would be the Mavericks' final home game of the year, win or lose.

But if they lost, they would then have to win Games 6 and 7 on the road, nearly an impossible task.

"Game 5 is Game 7 for us," Terry said. "There's no other way. This is the last game in front of our fans at home this season, and we want to go out with a bang."

=========

Thursday, June 9
Game 5, NBA Finals
Dallas, Texas

Miami's Dwyane Wade had spent part of Thursday morning getting caught on tape with teammate LeBron James. The duo left the arena after the Heat's shootaround clowning in front of television cameras. They were faux-coughing, laughing and generally mocking the media's heroic portrayal of Dirk Nowitzki's fever-stricken performance of Game 4.

Yet, here in the critical Game 5, there was Nowitzki again, staying on the floor for 40 hard-fought minutes and leading all scorers with 29 points. And there was Wade, missing 14 minutes of action to attend to a bruised hip. And there was James, playing 46 minutes to get a triple-double, but combining with Wade to shoot just 2 for 12 (16.7 percent) on their attempts from beyond 15 feet.

Guess who got the last laugh?

Mavericks fans might have assumed that their heroes were so incensed over Wade and James' dismissive imitations of Nowitzki that they took to the court with increased fire in their eyes. The video had first appeared locally on CBS affiliate KTTV-11's Thursday evening newscast, and was seen by thousands via the internet during the game. But the players knew nothing of this, nor did ABC's national television audience.

The truth was that many of the Mavericks' players hadn't seen the video clip until they were settling on their plane, about to take off for Miami, the morning *after* their 112-103 victory that gave them a 3-2 series lead. More on that shortly.

Game 5 had been a nearly three-hour slugfest, neither side willing to concede an inch, both clubs clawing desperately and burning whatever still remained in their tanks. The Mavericks shot a scorching 60 percent through the first three quarters. The Heat briefly seized the lead in the fourth. And then, once again, Dallas dominated the crucial final minutes, outscoring the Heat 17-4 over the last 4:22 to claim their first lead of The Finals.

Win No. 15 in the Mavs' race to 16 would not soon be forgotten. The atmosphere within the American Airlines Center was electric from start to finish, and those in the crowd of 20,443 likely left having seen the single greatest sporting event they had ever attended.

Rife with noteworthy moments and compelling plot lines, one of the biggest came with 4:01 left in the first quarter.

Wade took the ball behind the 3-point stripe, shed Terry by running him into a screen by Chris Bosh, then attempted to drive the left side of the lane. Brian Cardinal met him halfway down the paint and the collision sent both players falling backward to the floor. Wade got the call — a blocking foul on Cardinal — but came up grimacing and holding his left hip (not the one that collided with Cardinal, incidentally, but rather the hip that hit the floor). Wade made his two free throws but then exited the game and went to the locker room for treatment when a timeout was called with 2:58 left in the first.

Wade didn't return to the game until subbing in for James with 8:52 left in the first half. He scored three points in the remainder of the period and went to the locker room with 11 at halftime, his team trailing Dallas, 60-57.

When his team returned to start the second half, Wade again remained in the locker room. He finally returned to the floor with 4:33 left in the third, just in time to get a good view of a ferocious Chandler dunk less than a minute later that gave the Mavs an 80-71 lead, matching their largest at any point of the series.

"I don't talk about injuries," Wade said later. "It was unfortunate I had to leave the game, but I came back and finished it."

Wade's absence seemed to bring something out of James at long last. Long the alpha male in Cleveland, he seemed comfortable dominating the ball again with Wade out. James finished with 17 points, 10 rebounds and 10 assists, a far better performance than he'd mustered in Game 4. But James again struggled to shoot from distance. His 0-for-4 night from behind the arc meant he was 3 for 23 from 3-point range since making 4 of 5 in Game 1.

Nothing in this series would be easy, however. Chandler's big dunk for the nine-point lead had the crowd in a frenzy as the Heat called timeout. Then Miami responded with a transition basketball clinic over the next 11 minutes that nearly stole the game back.

The 28-15 run for the Heat started with a James jumper and ended with a Wade 3-pointer. In between, no basket was scored outside of five feet. James had four assists early in the fourth quarter and Wade three, as Miami drove, dished and dunked with aplomb. With 4:37 left to play, the Heat were now leading, 99-95.

Neither team had managed 100 points against the other's defense thus far in The Finals, but Miami got there on a Bosh free throw with 3:38 to play. The Mavs got there 15 seconds later when a 3-pointer by Terry tied the game, 100-100. Crunch time at its finest had arrived. Each team would have five possessions before the game would be decided, with the winner just one win from a world championship.

Miami had possession first. James received the ball down in the block against Kidd, but eventually turned and retreated from the goal. He finally put up a 17-footer that glanced off the front of the rim and was rebounded by Chandler. Dallas countered before Miami's defense could get set, with Terry finding Nowitzki for a baseline drive past Bosh. Dirk's dunk put the Mavs up, 102-100.

On Miami's second possession, Wade shook off Marion with a crossover dribble and momentarily had the lane. Kidd cut him off, but Wade spotted James along the left baseline, heading for the rim. Chandler saw him too and shuffled into position for a collision. On a call that easily could have gone against Dallas, Joey Crawford whistled James for the charging foul, a gigantic turnover and defensive stand with 2:27 to go.

The Mavericks worked it around to Marion, but he missed an 8-footer at the other end. Wade grabbed the rebound and, with 2:05 on the clock, Miami had another chance to tie or take the lead. James took the ball out high and Kidd practically dared him to try for the go-ahead 3-pointer. James couldn't resist, but also couldn't make the shot. His miss was rebounded by Marion and the Heat's third consecutive possession came up empty out of LeBron's hands.

Dallas wanted to run clock and get a good shot, but Miami clogged the desired passing lane to Nowitzki in the corner. With the shot clock down to :08, Terry ran to take the ball from Kidd at the left wing, James in pursuit. Terry crossed over James and headed for the paint. The entire Heat defense collapsed and Terry kicked it back out to Kidd, waiting with his feet millimeters behind the 3-point arc at the right wing. The shot clock was down to :03 as Kidd let it fly. As the ball hung in the air, Kidd contorted his body, willing his shot through the rim. It ripped through, and Dallas led 105-100 with 1:25 to play. Timeout Heat.

Miami still had time, but a mix of carelessness and championship-caliber Dallas defense would drain some more of it away. Marion stole a ball from Wade and took it the length of the court, only to miss his driving layup attempt under pressure. Miller rebounded and hustled the ball back downcourt to Wade, but this time Chandler leaped to block Wade's 7-foot jumper. Bosh recovered the blocked shot, drew a foul from Chandler (his fourth), and made only the first of two free throws. The Heat trailed 105-101 with 55 seconds left.

Nowitzki rebounded Bosh's missed foul shot and the Mavs set up another possession. Dirk wasn't the only one who wanted the next shot. The clock ticked down and the ball moved around to the guy with the trophy tattooed on his arm. The guy whose self-confidence seemed to border sometimes on the irrational. The guy who days ago had publicly challenged one of the best defenders of all time to stop him.

And with 33 seconds on the clock, Jason Terry buried a dagger 3-pointer from 26 feet away, right in LeBron James' face. He extended his Jet arms in celebration as the Heat took a 20-second timeout, trailing 108-101 and officially out of answers.

Game Over.

Each team had enjoyed five possessions in that span of 170 seconds since the game was tied at 100. Dallas had scored eight points on Nowitzki's dunk and the 3-pointers from Kidd and Terry. Miami had managed one point on the Bosh free throw, with two missed shots and a charging-foul turnover by James, and with Wade having a shot blocked and a ball stolen. Winning Time had again been won by the Mavericks.

Kidd and Terry would each make two more free throws and James was conceded an uncontested layup over the final 29 seconds, making the final score 112-103. Dallas had finished on a 17-4 scoring run, with superior late execution the difference once again.

With Nowitzki ailing in Game 4, it had been primarily Marion, Chandler and Stevenson who stepped up to carry the load. It was a true testament to the depth and versatility of this team that in Game 5 it was guards Terry, Kidd and Barea who most supported Dirk.

Barea no longer was an opponent's afterthought, not after inflicting the damage he had against the Lakers. But Carlisle had stuck with him and tried to find more favorable matchups through which he might ignite the team. In this game, Barea provided 17 points in 26 minutes, including an integral 14-point performance in the second half. He had regained his shooting eye, too, nailing 4 of 5 3-point attempts.

Kidd, meanwhile, had to spend his 100th game of the season chasing Wade, James and Mario Chalmers around the floor. The 38-year-old had not scored in Game 4, and hadn't scored in double figures since Game 4 against Oklahoma City. It was natural to wonder if he'd hit the wall and would not be able to muster the two more big efforts it would take to get the Mavs atop the mountain. But with 13 points, 6 assists, 3 steals, a blocked shot and that instantly legendary 3-pointer with 1:25 to play, Kidd showed his tank was not empty.

And Terry? All he did was score two giant 3-pointers and assist on both of the other late baskets (Nowitzki's dunk and Kidd's trey) to save the day.

Interviewed on national television immediately after the final buzzer, Terry spoke with purpose, not pompousness.

"We are a very resilient team, you know that," he said. "We've been in tough battles all playoffs long. It's gonna get even harder, but we are determined. This is our time."

Dallas had moved to the brink of a championship. The franchise that limped to 13 wins in the entire 1993-94 regular season now had 15 in these playoffs. The 13-win season put them in position to draft Jason Kidd. Now, in the twilight of his career, the oldest member of the cast could see his dream one win away.

Annual postseason appearances during the Mark Cuban era had been exciting at first, but had proven treacherous and demoralizing as well. The Mavericks' past was littered with heartbreak.

In 2001, Dirk lost a tooth and the team lost to San Antonio. In 2002, the Mavericks bowed out to the Kings. In 2003, it was all the way to the Western Conference finals before Dirk's health and the shooting of the Spurs' Steve Kerr took them down. In 2004, it was the Kings again.

In 2005, the beloved Steve Nash and the Phoenix Suns punched Dallas in the stomach. In 2006, Miami delivered the most gutting finish of them all. In 2007, there was the humiliation of losing to Don Nelson and eighth-seeded Golden State. In 2008, Chris Paul threw lobs to Tyson Chandler to help New Orleans celebrate. In 2009, it was Denver. In 2010, it was back to a defeat to San Antonio.

If the bitter must be tasted in order to appreciate the sweet, then surely no superstar, owner and fan base had ever been more prepared than the Mavericks'. And now they stood, just 48 minutes from the end of the rainbow.

========

Nowitzki, as usual, was one of the last players or staff members to climb the stairs, duck his head and board the Mavericks' jet bound for South Florida the next morning. "Hey, what's up? How we doing?" he hollered, expecting to see teammates looking jubilant, determined or both.

He was surprised to see angry faces instead.

"Have you seen this?" Brendan Haywood asked, handing Nowitzki his iPad.

This, Nowitzki said, was the first he had heard of the now-viral video shot the previous afternoon. The one showing Wade and James mocking his Game 4 illness.

"I had no idea what he was talking about," Nowitzki said. "Everyone starts telling me that they were making fun of me coughing. I said, 'You've got to be kidding me.'"

Nowitzki pressed play and watched. Miami's two biggest stars were taped walking though a tunnel on their way out of the arena following their morning shootaround, covering their mouths with their shirt collars as they coughed, laughed and joked that they might soon be playing sick, too.

It appeared Wade was leading the routine, coughing and turning to tell James and the cameramen, "Oh, did y'all hear me cough? Think I'm sick." James was an eager comic sidekick, also coughing, gesturing toward his throat and complaining, "This weather, man. It's hard to go from 85 degree weather to 90." They clearly had little regard for what they considered the overblown story of Nowitzki's heroism in Game 4.

"I watched it and thought, 'They can't be serious,'" Nowitzki said. "I felt a little disrespected, and I just didn't think it was the right thing to do. In a Finals series where it was 2-2 (at the time)? I just didn't think it was the right thing to do."

Nowitzki walked back to his seat without saying a word. If he had thoughts on the matter, he was going to keep them to himself on the plane.

"The team saw that, and sensed that I wasn't happy with it," Nowitzki said weeks later. "And that's why, actually, the team played great in Game 6 and really took it to heart for me, too, and wanted to win it."

Game 6 would not be until Sunday, which meant the video and the Mavericks' reaction to it would be the story of the day for NBA media on Friday. Broadcasters and columnists already were taking the Heat players to task for yet another mind-boggling display of arrogance.

"This is potent stuff. This is going to have huge legs through the next couple of days," predicted commentator Skip Bayless on ESPN's morning talk show *First and 10*. "I think (the Heat) thought they should have swept, won all four of the first games. This (video) came out of that attitude. But, trust me, this will raise the Heat-hate about tenfold. If you didn't hate them already, or at least dislike them, you're going to be seething now. They're making fun of the other team's superstar, who has been killing them, game after game. They are suggesting, to me, that Dirk was faking or at least exaggerating his sinus infection.

"This wasn't some private, inside joke between them that was caught by some fan's secret camera-phone video that they weren't seeing. They're walking in front of a Dallas TV camera! This is blatant! This is childish arrogance! This, I thought, would have been beneath Dwyane Wade's dignity — not LeBron's, but Dwayne Wade's — but (Wade) is the perpetrator."

With such indignation building fast, the Mavericks called a team meeting before their players were to face the media in Florida. Nowitzki and Carlisle wanted the public pressure to mount only on Miami's increasingly unpopular players.

"In the playoffs, you never want to make something a huge deal and give the other team bulletin-board material," Nowitzki said. "You don't want to fire back, so we talked about it as a team. Carlisle said, 'We are going to leave this alone. And if anybody is going to comment about it, it is going to be Dirk.'

"And that's what I did. I said it's a little childish and left it at that. I didn't want to get into specifics or go back at them. I just wanted to leave it at that and concentrate on Game 6. There was really nothing to say for rest of the guys. I just felt like it was better that way."

Facing a packed room of reporters, Nowitzki kept his cool while delivering his pointed, public response.

"I just thought it was a little childish, a little ignorant," Nowitzki said. "I've been in this league for 13 years. I've never faked an injury or an illness before.

"But, it happened. It's over, to me. It's not going to add anything extra to me. This is the NBA Finals. If you need extra motivation, you have a problem. So, we're one win away from my dream, what I've worked on for half of my life. This is really all I'm worried about."

Later, Wade made a much less comfortable appearance before the media, and foolishly tried to deflect blame.

"First of all, it wasn't fake-coughing," Wade said. "I actually did cough. And with the cameras being right there, we made a joke out of it, because we knew you guys (in the media) were going to blow it up. You did exactly what we knew.

"We never said Dirk's name. I think he's not the only one in the world who can get sick or have a cough. We just had fun with the cameras being right in our face about the blow-up of the incident, and it held to be true. You blew it up."

It never ceases to amaze how many athletes, coaches, team executives and owners resort to the "blame the media" card as their default response to public difficulties. Surely those who do this have not paid much attention to the success rate of the tactic. The best and fastest way to quell a controversy is to publicly take responsibility, apologize, show humility and beg forgiveness. That leaves the moral compasses within the media with nowhere else to take the story. Conversely, blaming the media for doing their jobs (reporting the subject's own actions or words) only serves to irritate reporters, prolongs a controversy, creates new enemies and sets the follow-up columnists and commentators loose on the story the next day with freshly sharpened knives.

The bad blood between Nowitzki and Wade had resurfaced, with the big German taking the high road publicly, while privately finding a little more oomph for his finishing kick. Wade, meanwhile, got to spend two more days as a public pariah, reading once again about his own questionable toughness and penchant for drama over the years. The media he tried to fault happily recounted how Wade required a wheelchair to leave the court after separating his shoulder — his *shoulder* — during a 2007 game in Houston.

Former NBA coach and ABC's Finals commentator Jeff Van Gundy even hinted at reverse discrimination or jingoism. Wade and James, Van Gundy asserted, never would have mocked Kobe Bryant, Dwight Howard, Paul Pierce or other African-American players like that. He suggested this was direct disrespect of Nowitzki in particular. No matter how well Dirk performed, he just wasn't in the same club as most other NBA superstars.

=========

When Sunday arrived, the Mavericks' players continued what had become a playoff ritual. They dressed in all-black clothing to travel to the American Airlines Arena for Game 6.

The attire had been the same before every game in which a Dallas victory would end the series. The Mavs expected to be heading to their opponents' funeral, and wanted to dress for the occasion. In all three previous rounds, when it was time to take the "kill shot," Dallas' aim had been true. And no one on the Mavs' bus wanted to ponder winning a Game 7 on the road.

Their charge was simple: Get this one. Don't let momentum swing again. Don't allow Miami to regain belief. This was the night. Finish the job.

And that is what they planned to do.

25

MIAMI GAME 6

(June 12, 2011)

The Mavericks had reason for optimism heading into Game 6, and not just because their superstar was inspired to beat the insufferable Heat.

The fifth game had proven a deeply held belief: This was simply too good of a shooting team to be held to 41 percent indefinitely. The Mavs were going to start draining shots — ask the Lakers — and when they did, success would follow. Well, Dallas had broken out to shoot nearly 57 percent from the floor in Game 5, including 13 of 19 3-pointers (68.4 percent). In a close and dramatic game, the Mavs' shooting efficiency (especially late) had made the difference against a Miami team stung by too many scoreless possessions.

Dallas also believed its superior bench depth was again starting to pay dividends in a series. In each round of the playoffs, the Mavericks seemed to gain steam during the course of a series while their opponents would weaken and fade. The Mavericks had ended each series on a winning streak of at least two games, and now had won two in a row against Miami, forcing the Heat to ponder their first losing streak of the postseason. Whether through better endurance, depth or tactical adjustments, the Mavericks just seemed to get stronger as each series progressed.

Finally, the Mavs also felt as if they had cracked the code to break down Miami's troublesome defense. They had scored with relative ease against the Lakers and Thunder, and finally started to show the same ability against the Heat in Game 5. They learned that against Miami, the deeper they took each possession into the 24-second shot clock, the more success they had. Miami attempted to bait opponents into a lazy pass and then pounce for a fast-break opportunity. Dallas learned that the longer the possession lasted, the more frustrated and risky Miami would play.

Kidd then explained the key strategic adjustment that seemed to work:

"We talked about (how) the more we made them work, it would wear on them and they would start to chase," he said. "We would put Dirk on a pick-and-roll, we saw how they were blitzing the ball, and we had to make shots to make them pay for it. We ran the pick-and-roll with Jason Terry and wanted to put another shooter in the corner. We wanted to use their aggressiveness against them.

"Dirk became a wide receiver on the pick-and-roll. We told him not to even set the pick if they were blitzing the ball. So, he would slip out and catch the ball because they were over-pursuing, and then it was a 2-on-1 with Jet in the corner. He either had an easy hoop, or they would then rotate to Dirk and he became a playmaker to set up another easy three."

=========

Sunday, June 12
Game 6, NBA Finals
Miami, Florida

The Mavericks started Game 6 prepared to weather a storm. The Heat were trying to save their season, and would throw everything they had left at Dallas to stave off elimination. The Heat rightfully believed if they could get Game 6, then all the pressure would land back on the Mavericks for Game 7.

But Dallas had become used to finishing off series like a champion. In the 2011 playoffs, the Mavericks were 7-1 in Games 4-6 of their series, the lone loss being Portland's near-miraculous comeback in the fourth game of their first-round series. Dallas also had won six of seven road playoff games since that stumble 50 days ago in Oregon. The Mavericks had learned how to weather storms.

LeBron James had been under intense scrutiny throughout The Finals, and he started the game red-hot. He drilled his first four shots and scored nine points in the first 4:12, helping Miami to an early 14-

10 lead. This was a good sign for the Heat, who had seen James' scoring average plummet from 26.7 points per game in the regular season to 17.8 ppg in The Finals. According to the Elias Sports Bureau, that was the largest such discrepancy in NBA history. To finally see James start fast gave Heat fans hope that he might turn it on now and save the title. There was still time.

A few minutes later, with Dallas trailing 20-15, Nowitzki was charged with his second foul after getting pump-faked into the air by Chris Bosh. Nowitzki headed to the bench, replaced by Brian Cardinal, who had barely played in the postseason until Haywood injured his hip in Game 2. Haywood was still on the active roster for Game 6, but barely. He had missed Game 3, tried to play Game 4 (dropping out after three minutes), then missed Game 5. He was in uniform, but it would have to be quite an emergency to actually see him try returning to the floor.

Adding to Carlisle's problems, Chandler picked up a second foul with 1:29 left in the first. By then, the Mavs had fought back to take a 27-24 lead, but now they would have to put the very inexperienced Ian Mahinmi on the floor alongside Cardinal, Marion, Terry and Kidd. It was hardly Dallas' dream lineup, but the Mavericks shifted back to their zone defense and finished the opening period with a 32-27 lead.

When Nowitzki had to be replaced by Cardinal with 5:11 left in the first quarter, Carlisle also pulled Barea and unleashed Terry for the first time. No one was more fired up than Jet to rip out hearts in Miami and avenge the 2006 collapse. He had waited five long years for this chance and was not about to let the opportunity be squandered. Terry playing like a man possessed is a great thing when his shot is falling, and in the final 4:52 of the first period he racked up nine quick points on 4-of-6 shooting, one of the misses a desperate buzzer-beating heave.

Carlisle got Nowitzki back in the game starting the second quarter, surely thrilled that his team had managed to swing from five points down to five ahead in the star player's absence. Nowitzki had kept his cool during the two days of "Coughgate," had kept his temper in check despite the early foul trouble, and now would have another chance to start impacting the biggest game of his career. Tonight, Dirk wanted his game to speak for him. Unfortunately, he wanted this so badly his shooting touch deserted him.

It seemed unfathomable, but after making 1 of 3 shots in his abbreviated first quarter, Nowitzki missed everything in the second quarter. As in every shot, all nine of them. Nowitzki would finish the first half with three points on 1-of-12 shooting from the field. His only point in the second quarter came when he converted a technical foul shot midway through the period. In the biggest playoff game of his life, Dirk was having the worst postseason performance of his career.

But if there was any doubt this Dallas squad was a true team, it would soon be erased. Nowitzki couldn't score, but others could. DeShawn Stevenson, for instance, got off the bench for the first time with less than a minute to play in the first. Thirty seconds later, he buried a 3-pointer for a 32-24 lead. The Mavs' first basket of the second quarter was a stunning 12-foot jumper by Mahinmi. And Dallas' next two strikes were 3-pointers by Stevenson off feeds from Barea, prompting DeShawn to break out his 3-monocle once again as he retreated down the floor. Stevenson had given the Mavs a 40-28 lead with 9:41 left in the half, and as the Heat called timeout and began to huddle, several players took note of his extensive celebration that saw him circumnavigate most of the court on his way back to the bench.

Miami coach Eric Spoelstra had attempted to counter Barea's move to the starting lineup by giving Chalmers a starting role for Game 6. And rather than let Barea find the matchup he liked later against Mike Bibby, Spoelstra this time left the veteran Bibby languishing on the bench and gave 21 minutes to journeyman guard Eddie House.

In the Heat's previous 20 games of these playoffs, House had played all of 14 minutes and contributed two points. The cobwebs were thick, but somehow House brushed them aside to bookend a 14-0 Miami run with a pair of 3-pointers. The one that ended the spurt gave the Heat a 42-40 lead with 6:24 left in the half. Interestingly, the entire 14-0 run took place with James watching from the bench.

After hitting his second 3-pointer, House celebrated in the manner Stevenson had, reacting to the opponent's timeout by running toward the opposite end of the floor in prolonged play to the crowd. And now tempers would flare as the teams moved toward their benches. Udonis Haslem defiantly walked right across Stevenson's path, and received a shove from the Mavericks swingman. The two squared off, exchanging heated words, and teammates and coaches swarmed around them. The teams were on the brink of a melee but cooler heads intervened just in time.

Chandler and Chalmers were first responders, but a large crowd of players from both teams had gathered near midcourt. The NBA has a strict policy against players leaving the bench area, and commentators were immediately wondering whether the game and series could be marred by ejections and possible suspensions. That would have been a nightmare scenario for the league. It was a difficult interpretation for the game officials; since a timeout had been granted, shouldn't players be permitted to leave their benches?

The referees watched replays of the exchange (and undoubtedly heard from league officials). Ultimately, technical fouls were levied against Stevenson, Haslem and Chalmers, with Nowitzki making his free throw for a one-point net gain for Dallas over the exchange.

What might have helped more were the several minutes of delay while officials sorted their decisions out. From a Dallas standpoint, that might have served as the momentum-killer needed to stop the Miami run and quiet the Heat fans a bit.

But there would be more good news soon for the Heat. Less than two minutes after the near-skirmish, Wade slashed toward the hoop. Chandler, who had just re-entered the game four minutes earlier, defended the shot but was whistled for his third foul. Wade made 1 of 2 free throws to give the heat a 45-43 lead with 4:16 left in half.

Chandler's foul trouble opened the paint for Miami. Dallas tried to survive with a three-guard array backed by Nowitzki in the post and Marion at power forward, but James and Wade each tallied easy driving layups within the next minute. Nowitzki, meanwhile, continued to miss shots from all ranges and the confusion and frustration was showing on his face.

And this was where the Mavericks turned again to the red-hot Terry. Jet was still haunted by his Game 6 in the 2006 Finals (16 points, but on 7 of 25 shooting, including 2 of 11 on 3-point tries). On this long-awaited chance for redemption, he responded the way he dreamt he might. In the final 3:43 of the second quarter, Terry scored 10 straight points for the Mavericks to keep hope alive. He buried a 3-pointer off a Kidd assist. He hit a short 9-foot jumper in transition. He snatched a rebound after Chalmers missed a three, then fired home his own 3-pointer 30 seconds later. Finally, another of his patented pull-up jumpers on a break was true from 15 feet.

Terry reached halftime with 19 points on 8-of-10 shooting, and already had more points than he'd managed in any of the series' first four games (he had 21 in Game 5). He had given Dallas a 53-51 halftime lead.

Incredibly, halfway through the biggest game of his life, Nowitzki was 1 for 12 from the field and had three points, but his teammates had scored 50 and shot 65 percent. Dallas already was 7 of 14 from 3-point range, with three of those misses by Nowitzki.

The Dallas locker room was mostly quiet at halftime, most of the players relaxing, recovering, some getting treatment for minor knocks and bruises. Mostly, they were alone with their thoughts about what awaited in what they hoped would be the final 24 minutes of the season.

Terry approached Nowitzki, who was sitting at his locker stall trying to comprehend what had just happened.

"Big fella, you are not going to miss those shots all night," Terry said. "Keep shooting."

Terry leaned closer to say one more thing: "05-06."

By all accounts, Dirk didn't say a thing. But the fact that the only other human on the planet who knew exactly what that message truly meant had pulled that card on him certainly hit home. His job was clear: Forget about the first half and take us home.

It took Nowitzki only 12 seconds to score the first points of the second half, nailing a 16-foot jumper off a pass from Kidd. Dallas opened up a seven-point lead in the opening minutes of the third period, but it was cut to 63-58 with 7:56 remaining when more trouble reared its head. Chandler got caught pushing Bosh under the basket. It was his fourth foul and he would be forced to sit for the rest of the quarter.

Carlisle summoned Mahinmi, who took and missed a 13-foot jumper about a minute later. At the next whistle 14 seconds later, Carlisle yanked Mahinmi out in favor of Brian Cardinal.

The Custodian (or, as Mark Cuban preferred to call him, "Dad") likely wouldn't have had a chance to play in this series had Haywood been healthy or Stojakovic effective. But Cardinal wound up having a solid influence on the game and the series. He already had nailed a 3-pointer in the first quarter (his only shot of the night). Now he would dish out a couple of hard fouls, assist on a Nowitzki 3-pointer, and then draw a big charging foul from Wade that so infuriated the Miami star he also was hit with a technical foul, giving Dallas another precious point for a 71-65 lead with 3:55 left in the third.

In just 12 minutes of playing time, Cardinal wound up a plus-18, tying for the best plus-minus rating on the team for Game 6.

"I was able to take hard fouls and make them earn it from the line," Cardinal said. "They had been fouling us hard, so why the heck shouldn't they have to take a few, too? That is what I have always been about — to play hard and play tough. I loved it."

Carlisle still needed to get Nowitzki a short rest before the fourth-quarter push. So, after Dirk made the technical shot, the Mavs had Cardinal and Mahinmi together again. Dallas again found success switching to zone defense, and Miami could only close within three at 72-69 and 74-71.

Dallas picked up momentum in the final minute of the third. With the shot clock winding down, Kidd stepped up to hit a big 3-pointer that opened the lead to 79-71 with 47 seconds left in the quarter. On their next possession, Mahinmi rebounded a Marion miss and got the ball to Terry. Mahinmi moved outside to set a screen against James. The Mavs were running their favored pick-and-roll and, just like Dallas' coaching staff had expected, the Heat defenders blitzed the ball.

Haslem darted away from Mahinmi to help James seal off Terry. Terry jumped above the double-team and dumped the ball back to a wide-open Mahinmi, who seemed surprised by the pass. But he caught it and threw up an awkward, 16-foot shot at the buzzer that went through. The Mavericks' lead was 81-72 at the end of three, their bench was celebrating wildly and tonight, truly, everyone seemed to be contributing.

Twelve more minutes of poise and execution were all that stood between the Mavericks and their first championship in franchise history. A nine-point lead was nice, but hardly safe. As if to illustrate that point, Wade faked out Barea to open up a baseline drive, took it hard to the rim and scored despite a foul by Nowitzki. Finishing the three-point play with a free throw would have cut the Dallas lead back to five, but Wade missed the freebie. On a night when the Heat missed 13 of their 33 free throws, the costly toll was starting to add up.

Ten minutes remained, with the Dallas lead at 81-77 and Miami defending hard. Once again, the Mavs were pushed to the brink of an expiring shot clock, and once again came through with a clutch shot. This time it was Barea, nailing a 3-pointer in the face of Eddie House to push the lead back to seven.

Then Terry got going again. He stole a ball from Wade, made a free throw and hit a 19-foot jumper within the next 74 seconds to open a 10-point lead (87-77) with 8:56 to play. To this point, Terry had 24 points in 25 minutes on 10-for-13 shooting.

Miami's next two possessions came up empty, as Wade dribbled a ball off his foot and out of bounds, and James flung up an airball from about 8 feet. When Barea slipped through two defenders to score a short layup with 8:11 left, the Heat called timeout facing their biggest deficit of the game, 89-77.

Courtside cameras found Spoelstra offering plenty of encouragement (but few tactical plans) to a group of players who now seemed only half-listening. Some looked around their arena, distracted by hearing a few hundred blue-shirted Dallas fans who had traveled to Miami overpowering their home crowd with their chant: "Let's Go Mavs!"

ABC cut to live shots of the pandemonium inside the Dallas arena, then in a tavern in Wurzburg, Germany, where the local time was approaching 5 a.m. Everyone sensed the finish line was nearly in sight, including both cities' favorite 7-foot German.

It was time for Nowitzki to take charge. He was not about to let a slow start keep him from the ring. The Heat were still coming, but each time they scored, Dirk would answer. One response was a cool 16-foot jumper, all net. Another was a post move, twisting past Haslem and scoring with his injured left hand. The lead was 94-84 with six minutes left.

An inside move by Bosh scored and drew the fifth foul against Chandler. Bosh made the free throw to get Miami within 94-87. The Dallas native was keeping the Heat alive, with 19 points on 7-of-9 shooting, but he needed help.

Possessions were traded, the clock continued ticking, the night was starting to feel surreal.

Nowitzki, covered by Bosh, had the ball at the top of the key. Dirk went to his left, pulled up and nailed a 16-footer that pushed the lead back to 10, 97-87, with 3:39 left. The emotion began spilling from Nowitzki with each shot. This time, he pumped his fist demonstrably as he retreated to play defense.

Wade wasn't ready to concede, hitting a tricky fall-away shot to pull Miami back within eight. Nowitzki missed at the other end, but after a scramble Chandler helped tip the ball to Terry. Jet went for the dagger 3-pointer but missed. Marion yanked down the rebound, giving Dallas another fresh 24 on the shot clock.

Kidd and Nowitzki set up the pick-and-roll again. Nowitzki took Bosh baseline, faked to draw contact, then hit another of those unblockable fadeaway 18-footers honed by the countless extra hours in the gym. No foul was called, even though Nowitzki fell sprawling near the Miami bench. No matter. Miami called another timeout and Dirk stared far, far away as he walked back pumping his fist. It was 99-89 with 2:27 left, and Dirk could taste it now. Behind the Mavericks' bench, Cuban also thrust his fist into the air.

Miami's Big Three, for whom this title was supposedly destined, led the Heat back onto the floor. But it was Eddie House who would take their next shot, a 3-point try that missed. Nowitzki rebounded, hit Terry streaking downcourt, and the Jet's pull-up jumper pushed the lead back to 12, 101-89, with the longest 1:54 of the Mavericks' lives still to endure.

James and Chalmers would hit 3-pointers as the Heat scored twice in their final five possessions. Nowitzki drove the lane for another left-handed layup and Kidd made two free throws as Dallas scored twice in the last 29 seconds. Nowitzki had overcome that abominable first half to score 21 points, 10 in the fourth quarter.

In perfect symmetry, Nowitzki's final layup gave him a total of 62 points scored in the fourth quarters of the six-game series. James and Wade? They *combined* for 62 points in the fourth quarters.

Nowitzki's layup, stretching the lead to 11 with 29 seconds left, literally triggered celebrations around the world. Haywood was hugging Stevenson to his left and Cuban to his right on the Dallas bench. ABC's remote cameras showed bedlam erupting inside the Dallas arena, and crazed singing, crying and hugging in Wurzburg.

As Kidd made his two free throws with 18 seconds left, Terry and Nowitzki shared one of history's most meaningful man-hugs at the other free-throw line. They had finally won it all. The fact that it was back in Miami made it even sweeter, but they would have happily won it anywhere on the planet. Their redemption was complete.

As the buzzer sounded for the 105-95 final score, Dallas radio play-by-play man Chuck Cooperstein delighted fans with his call: "The Mavericks have scaled the NBA playoff mountain and they have planted their flag! They are the NBA champions for 2010-2011!"

Cuban found and hugged Carlisle. Terry embraced Kidd. Chandler was yelling into the air for all to hear. Players who, seconds before, could not count a championship anywhere amongst their number, were now immortalized, having reached the pinnacle of their profession. The surge of emotion was overwhelming.

"It was just an incredible rush," Cardinal recalled. "Seeing the clock count down and the excitement on everyone's faces — and the dejection on LeBron and Dwyane's faces, too. They were supposed to win this thing. To be able to beat those guys, and to see how excited Carlisle and Cuban were, was the best.

"To be able to hug all of those guys; to hug Rick, who called me before camp started and invited me … it all was so great. And to see Kidd, to think what must have been going through his mind after all of those years. And Peja, after all of his years. And to see everyone's faces and the grind that went into it to get to this point, it was something I will never forget."

They were all there, sharing the moment together. All except the one man for whom the cameras were searching.

Dirk Nowitzki had climbed over the scorer's table and retreated to the locker room as the final seconds expired. He needed to compose himself. He had no idea what to expect if he made it atop this mountain. And now that he was there, the overpowering rush of emotions and tears was too much to contain.

A few weeks later, Dirk returned to that moment in time. He said the only thing that partially compared to winning the NBA title was leading Germany to its first Olympics tournament berth since 1992. He did that by defeating J.J. Barea's Puerto Rico squad in the 2008 FIBA qualifying tournament in Greece, then was selected as his nation's flag bearer for the 2008 Beijing Summer Games.

"I had two huge dreams in my basketball career," Nowitzki said. "One was making it to the Olympics with Germany, and the other was to win a championship here. When I made it to the Olympics, I just broke down for like 30 minutes afterwards. I felt it as soon as the game was over. I couldn't control it. I left the court pretty quick in Athens, because I felt it.

"And then (Game 6) in Miami, it wasn't really quite a close game down the stretch. I was able to make that layup and then there were some free throws. So, this feeling that I felt in Athens was coming back. I feel it coming. I felt a couple tears coming in my eyes. And so I was like, 'Shoot, if I have a 30-minute breakdown again like I had in Athens, I have to get out of here. I'm not going to lay on the stage.' So, I just had to get out of there quick and have a moment for myself."

He knew the emotions were overwhelming him, and wasn't comfortable with the whole world watching.

"It was just that feeling that I had when we made the Olympics, and I just wanted to be by myself — real quick," he said. "I went back, had a towel over my face and laid on a wooden bench in the shower, just crying."

Tim Frank, the NBA's Senior Vice President of Basketball Communications, literally chased Nowitzki into the locker room, begging him to come back to the floor. Not only was the team's championship trophy waiting, but so was Hall of Famer Bill Russell, to present Nowitzki with the NBA Finals MVP award.

"Tim Frank, who I love, said, 'Come on, get out. I know this is your moment, but come on. The presentation is about to start,'" Nowitzki recalled. "I was like, 'I don't want it. Give the trophy to somebody else.'

"He said, 'We're coming back — the commercial is almost over. We need you!' And I'm still crying, and I said, 'Whatever.'

"And then Scooter (Mavericks communications manager Scott Tomlin) came in. He said, 'Hey buddy, I'm so happy for you,' and he gave me a hug. 'But we need you out there. This is what you worked so hard for. And, trust me, in a couple years, you are going to want to see that picture where you are holding that trophy.'

"He was right. So, I wiped my tears away, and I tried to go out there and enjoy the time with my team. But, at first, when I was laying there, I didn't feel like going out there.

"But (Tomlin) was so right. This picture of me first hoisting the trophy, with the whole team around me going nuts, is the best picture there is. And I already have it hanging here in the house."

=========

As NBA commissioner David Stern brought the league's Larry O'Brien championship trophy to the team waiting on the podium, the German 7-footer tried to sneak up the stairs and join his team.

But Nowitzki was in no position to sneak anywhere on this night, because the whole world was looking for him. And when he lifted that trophy he had chased for 13 years high over his head, an idea for a billboard was inspired.

"ALLE TRAUME KLINGEN VERRUCKT. BIS SIE WAHR WERDEN."

"All dreams sound crazy. Until they become true."

This year was truly different.

EPILOGUE

Achieving a lifelong dream can leave one with a peculiar sensation.

Years were spent trying to formulate a battle plan through which aspirations could be attained. You work diligently on that plan, never shirking from the work it requires. You focus all of your being on attaining a single goal.

And then, with what seems like amazing suddenness, you reach it. You are asked a thousand different ways by a hundred different people how you did it and how you feel about it.

They are seeking some profound answer, a foolproof means by which others might realize their own goals. But despite the cliche or trite answers you may be offering, deep down inside you are asking yourself the same question: How *did* you do it? Why did it work this time? What was the right formula? What was different?

Before long, maybe you realize that sometimes it just all falls into place.

The 2011 Dallas Mavericks did not follow a previously successful formula. In fact, had they adhered to the teachings of history or the prevailing notions of common sense, they might have disbanded their squad after the 2010 loss in San Antonio and rebuilt with a younger team that might grow into something special someday. They did not have a multitude of superstars, something most consider essential in today's NBA. Duncan, Ginobili and Parker. Garnett, Pierce, and Allen. Bryant, Gasol and Odom.

And, as the preseason scriptures decreed, James, Wade and Bosh.

Dallas couldn't find that superstar in his prime to come join Dirk Nowitzki. People called the team assembled around him a group of castoffs and journeymen. New Jersey couldn't wait to trade Jason Kidd. Charlotte had little regard for Tyson Chandler. Toronto was more than happy to give up Shawn Marion. J.J. Barea was undrafted.

Jason Terry was considered aging and with a contract that made him untradeable. There were players of some renown, but the more sarcastic talking heads joked that the Mavericks were trying to win in 2011 with the 2004 NBA All-Star team. Fat chance, they said dismissively.

Instead, Dirk and the Boys had brought home a trophy, setting off proud celebrations in Dallas that lasted for weeks. Talk of the impending lockout that would threaten the next season didn't even seem so dire, if only because it allowed more time for Mavericks fans to celebrate their championship.

Titles had been won by teams in this city. But with the possible exception of the 1971 Dallas Cowboys, none followed such agonizing buildup and fear there might never be a payoff. The Mavericks and their fans had been teased with this dream in the late 1980s and then, legitimately, since 2003. For it not to be delivered until eight seasons later made the destination all the more magical once it was reached.

After Game 6, the Mavericks were afforded about 10 minutes of private time inside the cramped visitors locker room in Miami. The customary champagne was sprayed and the players embraced and screamed. Chandler donned a professional wrestling-style championship belt, an idea inspired by Green Bay Packers quarterback Aaron Rodgers' celebration after the Super Bowl won at Cowboys Stadium.

Carlisle gave Stojakovic a kiss on the cheek. Caron Butler, an emotional leader on the sideline during the postseason, shared hugs and congratulations. He had worked so hard to make it back to the court from his New Year's Day injury, but knew he needed a few more weeks to return.

The group's joy was immeasurable. There had been so much invested in this dream, and such reluctance to look ahead during the journey, that this glorious end of the road almost seemed to sneak up on them. Now they were there, and none of them knew whether this would be their last chance at glory. Either way, they would treasure this time, because they knew for certain this title would always be their first.

When one considers the unlikelihood of this championship, the odds of a team with so many older players coming together to form the right formula at the right time, it really does seem remarkable. Since 1960, there never had been an NBA title-winning team comprised of so many veterans without a single championship ring amongst them.

It was accepted wisdom in the NBA that at least some championship-winning experience had to be on your roster to put a team over the top. Otherwise, a young and inexperienced but physically superior team like the Oklahoma City Thunder would be winning the title every year. You had to acquire a piece that had been there and won that title, that is just what the league believed.

And yet, here were the 2011 Dallas Mavericks, a team with 109 years of service time, all of it ring-less: Kidd (16 seasons prior to his title season), Nowitzki (12), Stojakovic (12), Terry (11), Marion (11), Cardinal (10), Stevenson (10), Chandler (9), Haywood (9), Barea (4), Brewer (3), and Mahinmi (2). Combined, the 12 players that made up the NBA Finals roster had accumulated 109 previous seasons of experience (not to mention 362 years of age) that had ended without a championship.

No other NBA championship winner of the past 50 years comes remotely close to that statistic. The runner-up was the 1989 Detroit Pistons, whose cast had combined for 67 seasons of title-less basketball before winning the first rings. The 1991 Chicago Bulls could claim 52 seasons and the 1983 Philadelphia 76ers 45 seasons before their titles. The Mavs' aggregate 109 ringless seasons is just off the charts.

"We had no champions on this team," Chandler said. "And we walked away with a team full of champions."

And consider Nowitzki's personal burden as one of the league greatest players to have never won a title. Dirk entered the postseason having scored 22,792 career points in the regular season. According to the Elias Sports Bureau, the only players who had scored more points before winning their first NBA title were Oscar Robertson (23,578), Wilt Chamberlain (23,442) and Jerry West (22,988).

And yet, Dallas defied the odds. What had this amazing journey taught Mark Cuban?

"What I learned is that chemistry matters," Cuban said. "That it's a team game. That you have to have players that believe in each other and trust their coach. And that is a process. It doesn't happen overnight, and there are no quick solutions. There is not a single template for winning a championship. If there was, then everyone would do it.

"You just have to ignore people from the outside and really stick to what you know and try to get smarter. And be opportunistic in building a team, and that is what we tried to be."

And as far as sticking with his German superstar for 13 years, when many thought Dallas might never win a title with Nowitzki?

"I've never questioned Dirk. Never even a little bit," Cuban said. "I remember one time, years ago, when Kobe was available. And there were discussions, and (Dirk) came to me and said, 'I understand if this is a deal you need to pull (trading Nowitzki in a package for Bryant).' And I was like, 'It ain't gonna happen.' Because chemistry is important — no disrespect to Kobe.

"Kobe is obviously a great player with lots of rings. But Dirk sets the culture of the team. And culture is critically important for an organization and a successful team. You hope you get a little lucky and things break your way, and you go out there and do it. And Dirk has always been the cornerstone for that."

========

Every time a title is won, because of the special and personal attachment to the characters involved, local fans feel this title is somehow more important than others. Often, the win doesn't stand the test of time, historically speaking. But there was something about this particular title that struck basketball people in many cities as being especially meaningful.

The Mavericks' victory was seen as a testament to the old-school values of teamwork, team chemistry, and playing a style that emphasizes the contributions of the group over those of a few stars surrounded by spare parts. Every player served a purpose, some at surprisingly critical times of the season and postseason. Personal agendas were never permitted to supersede the team's goals. And there were many personal agendas to consider, as six Mavericks would become free agents after the NBA Finals: Chandler, Barea, Stevenson, Cardinal, Stojakovic and Butler.

"We were always together, one through 12 on the roster," explained Jason Kidd. "I think the other thing about this team that really hasn't been talked about was all of the (pending) free agents.

"When you have a ton of free agents, everyone can start thinking about themselves. And (it can be hard) to not think about 'I,' but to think about the team and if the team does well, then you will do well financially individually. I think it is remarkable to have six free agents and not have people thinking about numbers, but thinking about wins. That is the example of a team. There were guys who could have broke it off and started thinking about themselves. That happens a lot in this league."

But not on this team. Shawn Marion took a spot on the bench. Brendan Haywood accepted his role. Jason Terry knew the team would be better if he didn't start. Nearly everyone saw their individual numbers settle well below their career bests. But individual numbers do not get a player remembered. Being part of a champion will never be forgotten.

"This is a win for team basketball," Nowitzki said after Game 6. "This is win for playing as a team on both ends of the floor. For sharing the ball and for passing the ball. ... We never looked at ourselves as soft, not for one minute. We just kept fighting."

========

The five Mavericks on the court in virtually all the key scenarios each had an amazing story. That closing-time crew managed to win at the end over and over again for nearly 60 days, finishing 16-5 in the postseason, including 7-3 on the road. They wanted their rings and fought valiantly together to get them:

Shawn Marion — Almost always asked to guard the most dangerous scorer the opposition could provide. Kobe Bryant. Kevin Durant. LeBron James. These living, breathing nightmares undoubtedly pushed Marion's body to the limit. But his energy never wavered, and he always seemed to grab a demoralizing offensive rebound at just the right moment to help stick a dagger in the opponent. However unorthodox his offensive game appears, he was able to supplement the scoring in a big-time fashion. In the victorious locker room, there was little doubt the level of pride and accomplishment that he enjoyed from scaling this mountain. He had waited a long time to get this title.

Tyson Chandler — The big man who was considered table scraps by some a year earlier. In him, the Mavericks found an emotional heart and soul who could push them just a little further whenever adversity was staring them down. His fearless attitude, and a defensive game that could back it up, inspired his mates all season long. He was the perfect complement to Nowitzki as a big man who didn't need the ball, but could handle it and would never leave the paint unattended. Leadership was his biggest attribute, and for it to come from the center position made him the perfect fit next to Dirk. There is no question history will consider him the key to the entire accomplishment.

Jason Kidd — The oldest starting player in NBA history ever to win his first ring. The 38-year old point guard brought the perfect composure and calm to a team that perhaps lost the 2006 Finals because they had lacked both. There was nothing Kidd had not seen in his long NBA career, except the inside of a locker room where championship champagne was being sprayed. Kidd was always there to make shots, make stops, and lead the team to the right move at the right time. His defense, thought by some to be his biggest weakness in his advancing age, was gigantic. Ask Kobe Bryant, Russell Westbrook or Dwyane Wade. Though it was not universally hailed at the time, Donnie Nelson said the acquisition of Kidd was one of the most important to the title. "To have a true point guard that settles us down when we need to be settled down, through the whole playoffs, was huge," Nelson said. "I can't tell you how important that is. Because last time we were here (in The Finals), with Devin Harris and Jet (playing point), it didn't work out as well. And at the age of 38? He can play till he is 48."

Jason Terry — **The** man who was never going to stop believing, in himself or his team. Terry spoke with unrivaled confidence no matter the situation. He was not going to be disrespected, and he had no plans to back down or be pushed aside. He always was willing to take the big shot at the biggest moments. That was never more evident than in The Finals, when Miami tried taking him off the board by putting LeBron James on him in crunch time. Through three games, it was working pretty well. Then, when the talking stepped up (from James, Terry, even from Dirk), Terry found his scoring touch at just the right time. You cannot measure the enormity of some of his clutch shots, many coming from spots or angles with high degrees of difficulty. Yet he knocks them down. And don't discount that his reputation as a scorer in this league is largely based on his effectiveness in road games. In Game 6 of The Finals in Miami, he went 11 for 16 and scored 27 points. When Dirk couldn't buy a shot, Terry carried them through. Terry worked as hard for this ring as anyone.

Dirk Nowitzki — Does anyone really understand how hard Nowitzki has worked for this franchise and its only championship, over so many years? His greatness and physical gifts had been apparent for more than a decade. Yet, for all the countless battles he had won, his legacy threatened to be that he had never won the big one. Many suggested his window had closed, that he might have to take a supporting role elsewhere to ever lift the trophy. But his determination and work ethic never wavered. He continued to develop his game, and became even more driven. He learned to constantly challenge himself and his team to do more. He was never backing down from a challenge, and there was but one goal on his mind. So much so that he disappeared from the Western Conference trophy presentation, reminding everyone on his team there were still four more wins to find. With his exceptional play and utter domination of the fourth quarters, his place among the NBA's legends is now secured. He dedicated everything to win this title. "It feels amazing to know that nobody can ever take this away from us again," Nowitzki said. "And, for one year, we were the best team out there. That feels amazing."

Those five did yeoman work throughout this 16-win journey. But this most solid team effort owed an enormous debt to the remarkable contributors up and down the bench, too. In the Heat series, where was this team without DeShawn Stevenson? Do the Mavs beat Portland without Peja Stojakovic's efforts? Do they frustrate and ultimately dominate the Lakers if J.J. Barea doesn't carve them up?

The backup bigs — Brendan Haywood, Brian Cardinal, and Ian Mahinmi — each had games or moments of great significance and contribution. Corey Brewer helped the Mavericks rally against the Lakers in Game 1. Even Caron Butler and Rodrigue Beaubois had important stage time during the long but necessary prelude of the regular season. This team had a bench full of hard-nosed veterans who suppressed their egos and stayed ready to make plays when called upon, just as their coach demanded.

The way this champion was built restores faith in the team dynamic. Sure, NBA teams need their stars. But championship teams require a resolve shared by every guy who wears the jersey.

"This is a true team," Carlisle said. "This is an old bunch. We don't run fast or jump high. But these guys had each other's backs. We played the right way: Trusting the pass, playing collectively, believing in each other.

"They have made a colossal statement. Not just about our team, but about the game in general. ... Our team is not about individual ability. It is about collective will, collective grit and collective guts. And, you know, we are skilled and talented, too."

His first title would not give Carlisle the high-profile cachet of a multi-winner such as Pat Riley or Phil Jackson. And, seeing all the experience on the Dallas roster, it might be easy for some to marginalize the coach's role if they hadn't paid close attention. But those who did lauded Carlisle for his tactics and his man-management.

His ability to convince players to accept new roles and always stay ready had proven essential to the Mavericks' success.

There were no "marginal" or "fringe" players to Carlisle. This coach knew that a team needed all hands on deck, prepared and ready to take on whatever duties fell to them, even suddenly. When they did, Carlisle always sought to recognize them. Consider what he came up with after Game 6, when asked to cite favorite moments of the final series:

"I guess if I was really going to look fondly on a few moments, it would be guys like Brian Cardinal being ready to step forward and play significant roles in a championship series," Carlisle said. "A guy like Ian Mahinmi, coming in to a very challenging situation in Game 6 and getting a couple of big buckets, making a couple of loose-ball plays and having a positive impact when Tyson is in foul trouble. I mean, that's huge. DeShawn, and just what he stood for all year. His toughness and grit was a big part of our team and who we were."

The coach knew Dirk, Terry and Kidd would get enough plaudits elsewhere. He was going to make sure Cardinal, Mahinmi and Stevenson were mentioned. Classic Carlisle, the kind of coach for whom an *entire* roster loved to play.

========

For Cuban, Donnie Nelson, Nowitzki and Terry, no question was asked more often after Game 6 than to revisit 2006 and elicit what it had meant facing Miami again. Would defeating the team that had ripped their hearts out somehow add even greater meaning to their crowning achievement?

"I could care less about the Heat," said Cuban, who swore it didn't matter to him who the Mavs played.

Terry, as he was prone to do, gave contradictory responses depending when he was asked. But immediately after Game 6, he admitted it was a driving force for him.

"Just seeing the faces of the Miami Heat when we won. Not only the players, but the fans," Terry said. "Going through that arena, and remembering what they did to us. To do it on their court ... It would've been special doing it in front of our fans, but on *their* court ... I didn't want to use that as a motivating factor going in. But, walking out of that same locker room, those same ballboys — all that played a factor."

Nowitzki also admitted changing his answer a time or two along the way.

Speaking with The Hardline, on Dallas' Sports Radio 1310-The Ticket, he said, "I always said it really doesn't matter who you play, because the energy you spend to get back takes so much. It took us five years to get here, so I would have played the Clippers. But to beat them at their place, like they did to us in 2006, made it that much sweeter."

Nowitzki said Terry constantly invoked Miami to inspire him. "At one timeout, he said to me, 'Keep pushing! Remember '06!'" Nowitzki said. "If I would have won early in my career, maybe I wouldn't have put all the work and time in that I have."

Then Nowitzki confessed to just how deeply he and Terry had been wounded by the heartbreak of 2006. The pair was so devastated, they went on a responsibly planned three-week drinking binge.

"Jet would pick me up with a party bus almost every day," he said, "and we went somewhere to forget and have a good time."

The image of those two hugging on the court as the final free throws of Game 6 were made, just before Nowitzki had to run off the court into hiding, remains indelible.

And finally, there was Donnie Nelson, the guy who has been here the longest among the quartet of '06 survivors. Nelson tends to watch games from the shadows, where prying camera lenses won't find him. But to underrate the role of the man who assembled this talent would be naive. He, too, had survived some rocky times with this franchise. And, like the other three, would not settle, give in or compromise.

After the trophy presentation following Game 6, Nelson appeared on Dallas' WFAA-Channel 8 and was asked whether the demons of 2006 had been laid to rest.

"They are officially exorcised," Nelson proclaimed. "For us, for the guys inside our locker room, and for all of our fans out there."

Nothing could make Mavericks lovers happier. No more nightmares starring Dwyane Wade, Gary Payton and referee Bennett Salvatore. In an odd way, 2006 had evolved from an unbearable heartbreak into the precursor conflict needed for 2011's happy ending to fully bloom.

But what of Wade? What did the star of Coughgate and the guy bad-mouthing Nowitzki since 2006 think of Dirk's accomplishment?

"I think he's played awesome, man," Wade told reporters. "Obviously, Dirk, five years ago, it burned in him. He learned from that experience. There's no question he's been a great individual player. And now that he's a champion, it goes without saying what it does for his career. So congratulations to him.

"We give credit to the Dallas Mavericks. They're a helluva team. We ran into a team that, at this time, is obviously better than us."

And James? Humble to the end, LeBron tweeted on his @KingJames feed: "The Greater Man upstairs know when it's my time. Right now isn't the time."

========

The victors celebrated late into the warm Miami night, taking the Larry O'Brien Trophy with them on an impromptu tour of some of South Beach's most exclusive nightclubs. The music was thumping, the boys were smiling, and hazy stories would soon emerge about a $90,000 bottle of champagne finally meeting a buyer visiting from Texas. To the winners go the spoils, and sleep could certainly wait.

The team's plane landed around midday Monday at Dallas' Love Field, where a huge crowd had gathered around the surrounding fences. Cuban carried the O'Brien trophy down the steps (he first had tweeted from the plane a picture of it sitting comfortably in the first-class seat next to him). Nowitzki held his Finals MVP trophy aloft. The team and the trophies circled around the fences, greeting and posing for their adoring fans. The elation of an entire city continued to build until the long-awaited event scheduled for Thursday.

"Parade" was a word that had been practically forbidden inside the Dallas city limits for five long years. It had become synonymous with choking, jinxing or somehow missing out on the opportunity of a lifetime. But no longer. This parade would prove this dream was real. It *had* actually happened. The Mavericks had won it all.

Fans, players, coaches, staff, media — everyone, it seemed was looking forward to celebrating wildly on what clearly was an unofficial but fully observed new holiday in North Texas. It seemed so perfect in so many ways. So perfect, in fact, some wondered whether the elder statesman of the team might decide to walk away at age 38 on this greatest of days.

"It was a thought," Jason Kidd admitted.

"I always said if I made a hole-in-one, I would quit golf. And if I ever won a championship, I would move on. But it was only a thought. Because I want to defend and see if we can do it again. It would be a lot of fun to do it again.

"It's funny, when you start in October and don't end until June. I was telling Dirk and some of the guys, you just have to respect those who do win two or three in a row. And I would love to see if we can do it again."

And there it was. The first acknowledgment that there would be a title to defend soon enough.

========

The third work stoppage in NBA history commenced on July 1, 2011, just 18 days after the Mavericks brought their championship trophy home to Dallas.

For business reason few fans cared to hear, the owners locked out the players the first minute after the league's collective bargaining agreement expired.

"We had a great year, in terms of the appreciation of our fans for our game," NBA commissioner David Stern explained. "It just wasn't a profitable one for the owners, and it wasn't one that many of the smaller-market teams particularly enjoyed or felt included in. The goal here has been to make the league profitable and to have a league where all 30 teams can compete."

Stern claimed 22 of the league's 30 teams were losing money, and that the previous agreement granting players 57 percent of the league's basketball-related revenue was flawed. Both sides took their positions, digging in for what looked to be a long, contentious battle that threatened the scheduled start — and perhaps entire existence — of the 2011-12 season.

"The problem is that there's such a gap in terms of the numbers — where they are and where we are — and we just can't find any way to bridge that gap," said Billy Hunter, head of the NBA players' union.

No team in the NBA enjoyed a closer owner-players relationship than the Mavericks with Cuban. But as soon as the lockout began, nobody working for the Mavs' organization (including their owner) was allowed to have contact with players.

A small exception was granted for July 13, when ESPN's annual televised sports awards show — The ESPYs — would be held in Los Angeles. The Mavericks were to rake in a host of awards (Best Team, Best Male Athlete and Best NBA Player-Nowitzki, Best Coach/Manager-Carlisle), and NBA officials agreed that Cuban and Carlisle should be able to talk casually and enjoy the night with their players without facing the threat of fines.

Their reunion was filled with laughs, especially when host Seth Myers addressed The Finals during his monologue:

- "LeBron James, Dwyane Wade and Chris Bosh refer to themselves as the Big Three, in honor of how many quarters they play."
- "Congratulations to Mavs owner Mark Cuban. Yeah, I think we can all agree it's nice when good things happen to loud billionaires."
- "Due to terms of the NBA lockout, Mark Cuban is here but he can't talk to his players. The Mavericks are calling this arrangement 'better than a championship.'"
- "My favorite Maverick is Brian Cardinal, The Custodian. I love Brian Cardinal because anytime he goes into the game, it just looks like a crazed fan ran on the floor. I just keep waiting for security to taser him. This show just started and Brian Cardinal already has three fouls."

But Cuban also got a chance to speak, and his immense pride in his club showed through as he accepted the ESPY for Best Team.

"Every guy on this team, every year (the media) told me we should trade them, get rid of them, they're too old, they're always hurt, and they can't get the job done. Who let the Dad (Cardinal) on the court? Who let the baby (Barea) on the court?

"You learn over time it is a very humbling game. But, you also learn to trust, to believe and to care. And if this Dallas Mavericks team proves anything, it's that good guys do win and can win and will win."

=========

Rick Carlisle was gracious enough to grant a lengthy interview for this book, which ended with a final question: What was the ultimate lesson of this magical season for the veteran coach and his players?

Carlisle took a long pause, and finally said, "Let me get back to you on that one."

A few days later, this deeply thoughtful response from Carlisle arrived via e-mail:

"In an NBA season where there were no fewer than eight or nine teams that could have emerged as champions, the Dallas Mavericks were more opportunistic, resourceful, persistent and tougher than the other contenders. And they won with character and class.

"From a basketball standpoint, our guys had to play an inventive, instinctive and unselfish game to have ultimate success, and they had to do it together. On the coaching side, the challenge was to focus on the essential concepts for success and to stay out of the way enough to allow the players to make it happen.

"From an ownership perspective, Mark Cuban's decision to remain silent during our entire playoff run, and let the team take center stage and perform without distraction was key. Our guys were able to maintain a laser-like focus and function at the highest possible level.

"Championships are not won without great players. Jason Terry played a tremendous all-around game for us throughout the playoffs. There is no doubt that Jet has now established himself as an all-time great Maverick. Shawn Marion became nothing less than the ultimate X factor for us at both ends of the floor in every playoff series.

"Jason Kidd is one of the greatest ever at his position, and constantly engaged the guys around him to achieve at, and oftentimes beyond, their abilities.

"Tyson Chandler brought energy and toughness, solidifying our culture as a legitimate lock-down defensive team. Caron Butler played great early in the season, then became a daily source of inspiration with the heart and effort he put into his rehab from major knee surgery.

"J.J. Barea was, perhaps, the best metaphor for what our entire team came to stand for – the guy who shouldn't be able to do what he does on paper, but just keeps attacking you until he beats you.

"Brendan Haywood, DeShawn Stevenson, Peja Stojakovic, Brian Cardinal, Ian Mahinmi and Corey Brewer all filled their roles brilliantly, and were consummate professionals.

"We all know the greatness of Dirk Nowitzki's game, but what's most unique is what defines his character. He got far greater satisfaction and fulfillment from delivering a championship to the great fans and city of Dallas than he did from silencing any and all critics. Once and for all, he proved that he is one of the very best to EVER play this game.

"As the months and years go on, the accomplishment of winning an NBA championship will continue to sink in for all of us. There is one thing that is certain. Winning it in the city of Dallas is big — and it is important. During my three years in Dallas, I've been fortunate to meet and spend time with Roger Staubach, Troy Aikman, Emmitt Smith, Mike Modano, Brett Hull and several other Dallas championship legends.

"These men are held in such high regard because the city of Dallas is uncompromising and thinks only one way – about being the BEST. I am very proud that our guys now enter this pantheon of great achievement. They have all earned it and, most importantly, they earned it with true class – and they earned it together."

THIS YEAR IS DIFFERENT

(to the tune of Radiohead's *Creep*)

When we were here before
You hit us right between the eyes
You took away our trophy
And made us sports cry

For five years we've waited
To get you back in the ring
But this time is different
It's so very different

'Cause we got Dirk,
We got Tyson
What's Miami gonna do now?
'Cause we brought Barea

Sure, Norm, it hurts
A place we didn't want to go
But Dirk got with Holger
And learned to play in the post

He wants to beat Bron Bron
Like he took Kobe down
And this year is different
It's so very different

'Cause we got Dirk
We got Tyson
What's Miami gonna do now?
'Cause we brought The Matrix

He's locking down LeBron
He's locking down LeBron
Bron, Bron, Bron, Broooooooooon

We want our freakin' trophy
We want it right now

257

'Cause this year is different
It's so very different

'Cause we got Dirk,
We got Tyson
What's Miami gonna do now?
'Cause we brought Barea
We brought Barea

— Lyrics by Robert Sturm

Performed with the Timewasters at The Ticket's Summerbash, June 10, 2011.

Performance video at http://www.youtube.com/watch?v=ntR08tKK398

Printed in the USA
CPSIA information can be obtained
at www.ICGtesting.com
JSHW031704140824
68134JS00036B/3506

9 781626 811416